Right-Brained Children in a Left-Brained World

Unlocking
the Potential
of Your ADD Child

Jeffrey Freed, M.A.T., and Laurie Parsons

SIMON & SCHUSTER PAPERBACKS
New York   London   Toronto   Sydney

SIMON & SCHUSTER PAPERBACKS
Rockefeller Center
1230 Avenue of the Americas
New York, NY 10020

Copyright © 1997 by Jeffrey Freed and Laurie Parsons
All rights reserved,
including the right of reproduction
in whole or in part in any form.

SIMON & SCHUSTER PAPERBACKS and colophon are registered
trademarks of Simon & Schuster, Inc.

For information about special discounts for bulk purchases,
please contact Simon & Schuster Special Sales:
1-800-456-6798 or business@simonandschuster.com.

Designed by Irving Perkins Associates, Inc.

Manufactured in the United States of America

17   19   20   18   16

The Library of Congress has cataloged the hardcover edition as follows:
Freed, Jeffrey.
Right-brained children in a left-brained world : unlocking the potential
of your ADD child / Jeffrey Freed and Laurie Parsons.
p.   cm.
Includes bibliographical references (p.) and index.
  1. Attention-deficit-disordered children—Education—
United States.   2. Education—Parent participation—United States.
3. Brain—Localization of functions.   I. Parsons, Laurie.   II. Title.
LC4713.4.F74   1997
371.93—dc21   97-39515

ISBN-13: 978-0-684-84271-4
ISBN-10:   0-684-84271-8
ISBN-13: 978-0-684-84793-1 (Pbk)
ISBN-10:   0-684-84793-0 (Pbk)

Acknowledgments

Loving thanks to Laurie's children, Zach, Sarah, Taylor, and David, for being the unique and special kids that you are. Some say it's impossible to work outside the home *and* raise four children as a single parent. Yet somehow the Parsons and Cantillos (plus neurotic dog and Garfield-like cat) make it work.

To Jeffrey's son, Jeremy, who gave Jeff a chance to practice what he preaches: Jeff couldn't be more proud of you! Jeremy's mature and easygoing nature gave Jeff the time he needed to work with other children. To Beth, for your consistent help to me on a daily basis with my work. Our deepest gratitude to our agent, Faith Hamlin, who was inspired by the premise of this book and helped us take it to a level we never dreamed possible. Thanks to Drs. Daniel Feiten and Marianne Neifert for providing us with a sounding board on Attention Deficit Disorder from the pediatrician's perspective. Our heartfelt thanks to Dr. George Dorry for offering his invaluable insights on ADD and visual-spatial thinkers.

Jeff extends his deepest gratitude to Anne Kloth and Julie Billett for their tireless efforts in founding the Jeffrey Freed Institute. We are grateful to Sharon Saulsberry for entrusting Jeff to work with her three children for the last ten years. Jeff thanks the Sweeneys for being "absolutely the best clients of all time." And he extends his sincere appreciation to the Laytons for their enthusiastic support of him and his work.

To our editors, Becky Saletan and Denise Roy, for being always on target with your guidance and for appreciating the timeless nature of our message. To Jess Hamilton for your wisdom, encouragement, and loving support. To B. J. Johnson, Leslie Fox, and Patty Kincaid for your unconditional friendship. To John Gehron and our friends at Harpo for changing the world through empowering, inspirational radio and television. Keep walking the walk.

Finally, we'd like to thank you, the reader, for spreading the good word about our work. The word of mouth about our approach and teaching methods has been staggering. Your enthusiastic, unflagging support of your children and challenges to the status quo in education are making a difference. We receive emails every day—from every continent except Antarctica—saying this book is changing lives and removing the veil of shame from bright, creative children who are in danger of falling through the cracks. Even though it was written a decade ago, *Right-Brained Children in a Left-Brained World* is timelier than ever, as our society continues to produce a new wave of visual learners. Will we medicate and mislabel these children? Or will we honor their souls, treasuring and nurturing their uniqueness? The future is in our hands . . . and theirs.

To Al Tanner

You helped me survive the school system so I could change it. You're the kind of individual who *should* be teaching and coaching our youth. J.F.

For Zach
Love, Mom

CONTENTS

Preface

by Laurie Parsons

▣ It's one thing to read that more than 2.5 million children nationwide have Attention Deficit Disorder, and quite another to learn that your child is among them. Several years ago I was told that I should have my preschool son evaluated for ADD. Zachary, at age four, was fidgety and moody, and had trouble finishing things. Minor things would set him off; he was touchy, and angry outbursts were followed by hours of sullen silence. People would often tell me, "Your son is *so* sensitive." He hated being held or cuddled. Everything seemed to irritate him. Zach wore a ball cap to cut down on glare; he would cover his ears in pain when exposed to loud noises; and he insisted that every label be cut out of his clothes. His typical reaction to a new situation was to crawl under a table. I remember lying awake at night wondering how I'd failed as a parent.

Yet in spite of all this, I saw a child blessed with many gifts. Zach had an exceptional vocabulary for his age, was intensely curious, and could easily assemble Legos and Tinker Toys into complicated structures. But the trait that amazed me the most was his ability to memorize a book, word for word, after it had been read out loud to him just once or twice. In subsequent readings Zach would effortlessly fill in the blanks, page after page. His memory was unparalleled.

The diagnosis of ADD was bittersweet. On the one hand, it was a relief to know what was causing his worrisome behavior. And yet it was like hearing that Zach had cancer. Like many parents, I anguished over his condition, alternating between crying and denial. As a broadcast medical reporter, I decided to educate myself about ADD, becoming almost obsessed with it.

I took Zachary to several psychologists, who interviewed him, watched him play, and ran him through a battery of tests (Zach refused to cooperate with most of them). One psychiatrist pronounced that Zach had not only ADD but ODD (Oppositional Defiant Disorder). Shaking his head and speaking in the grave, soothing tones of a mortician, he suggested I brace myself for the likelihood that Zach would someday be a "juvenile delinquent," since so many of these kids turn out that way. I was aghast. This arrogant and judgmental labeling of a four-year-old gave me a taste of maternal fury I hadn't known I possessed. With the added incentive of proving this man wrong, I redoubled my efforts to help Zach. All the while I wondered about the parents who accept such diagnoses and see them become self-fulfilling prophecies.

My crusade took me to the pediatrician's office, where we discussed changing my son's diet, eliminating sugar and additives. I investigated support groups for parents of children with ADD. The school pressured us to try Ritalin, which for Zachary produced no change except for an alarming weight loss. I spent a fortune at the bookstore, buying everything that was ever written on parenting and ADD. While it was comforting to learn that there are many other distraught parents out there, I didn't find any advice or explanations that made a difference. I knew Zach needed me, but I felt powerless to help him.

About this same time I attended a radio programming retreat and learned something very startling about *myself*. Through a brain dominance test to determine management styles, I discovered that although I had always considered myself whole-brained, I was "off the chart" on the right-brained side. This means I'm a creative, intuitive, holistic problem solver but not strong on details and organization. This revelation about myself planted a seed in my mind: Could Zach also be extremely right-brained? Could that have something to do with ADD?

It turns out someone else made this connection years ago. Jeffrey Freed, M.A.T., a private educational consultant, had been quietly working with more than one thousand gifted and ADD children in the Denver metropolitan area, helping to turn their lives around. His name kept cropping up at ADD support groups, from parents who described him as a "miracle worker with kids." One evening, under pressure from Zach's teacher, I attended (with a bag over my head) a local ADD support group meeting at which Jeffrey Freed was the featured speaker. I was riveted by what he had to say.

As Freed spoke of the characteristics of his ADD-labeled students, I found that with each trait he was describing my son. Freed related that all children who are labeled as ADD are right-brained and have a *visual learning style*. Instead of focusing on the deficits of these kids, which our schools and doctors are all too quick to do, Freed emphasizes their many strengths. These children are creative, can do difficult math problems in their heads, and are excellent speed readers. They tend to do poorly in school because educators tend to be left-brained: detail-oriented, auditory processors who view visual learners as "flawed." Freed says that what these children need isn't a prescription for pills but a prescription for a *different teaching method*. For the first time I was hearing something about this mysterious thing called ADD that made sense.

Jeff had more than a two-year waiting list for new clients, but I made a pest of myself and finally persuaded him to work with my son. At the first tutoring session I watched, with tears in my eyes, as Jeff coaxed Zach out of his shell, making him feel confident and smart. When Zach made a spelling mistake and crawled under the table, berating himself, Jeff used humor and face-saving techniques to get him back in the game. I gaped as my son, too surly and insecure to even pick up a pencil, used his incredible memory to spell words forward and backward.

After several months of working with Jeff in weekly forty-five-minute sessions, Zach was writing his name, learning words by sight, and doing long series of math equations in his head. Today Zach is a happy, well-adjusted teenager who routinely gets straight A's in a challenging double honors program. His test scores are in the ninety-ninth percentile and he is setting his sights on an Ivy League school, where he plans to major in engineering. Zach is accomplished at rowing, tennis, snowboarding, and kayaking. He is a curious, adventurous soul who likes travel and new experiences. Far from the blond preschooler who cowered under the table at social gatherings, Zach is now full of self-confidence and has many friends.

I've often wondered what it would be like to reunite Zach with the judgmental psychologist who pronounced him a juvenile-delinquent-in-training. Would I feel smug, or would I feel a profound sadness? Zach is one of the most decent, principled human beings I've ever known. I'll never forget the day that I came home early from work just in time to find him helping an elderly woman who had fallen on a sidewalk. I smile every day as I watch Zach playing patiently and lovingly with his six-year-old freckled brother, who worships him. I shudder to think of the damage that's been done to similarly gifted children who are mislabeled and shamed into thinking they're broken.

Thank you, Jeff, for showing me Zach's many gifts and for encouraging me not to give up. And thank you, Zach, for sharing your story so that other parents can know the joy of bettering their children's lives.

Introduction

So many colors in a flower,
And I see every one.

—from "Flowers Are Red"
by HARRY CHAPIN

Jason is a six-year-old bundle of energy. The oldest child of wealthy, overachieving parents, he is bright and precocious, yet he is struggling in kindergarten. Always into everything, Jason bounces from one activity to the next, frequently disrupting other children. His parents get the news at a parent-teacher conference: While he's excellent at puzzles, mazes, and computers, Jason is unruly and uncooperative, draws a blank when it comes to phonics, and refuses to even pick up a pencil. Once a happy youngster, Jason is becoming surly and defensive, acting out his frustrations by bullying other children on the playground.

Jason is diagnosed with Attention Deficit/Hyperactivity Disorder (ADHD) and takes Ritalin. His parents crack down on Jason's misbehavior, sending him to his room for hours at a time. Jason, now believing he is "bad," basks in all the attention he receives for his misdeeds, and the disruptive behavior snowballs. He figures if he can't be the best at being good, he'll be the best at being the worst.

Jana, nine years old, is a pale, slender girl with thick glasses. By the third grade she is still not reading. Learning specialists have worked one-on-one with her for months, to no avail. The only subject that seems to hold her attention is art, in which she excels. Jana is easily frustrated, picky about food, and often wakes up in the morning with a sore throat, stomachache, or cold that keeps her out of school on a regular basis. Her pediatrician can't find anything wrong with her.

Josh, age fourteen, was a teacher's pet in elementary school, yet now he's a surly middle schooler who hangs out with a bad crowd. He smokes pot, cuts school, and dabbles in the occult. Academically, Josh is hopelessly disorganized; he's notorious for either forgetting homework assignments or turning them in a day late. While he gets A's and B's on tests, he frequently gets zeros on his homework, lowering his overall grades to D's and F's. His parents take him to several psychologists in the hope of discovering why their once bright, inquisitive child now hates school, has low self-esteem, and is openly defiant.

Eddie, dark-haired and freckled, is eight years old and a second grader at a rural elementary school. The only child of middle-class parents, Eddie is small for his age and withdrawn. Eddie's father is a mechanic for a farm implements dealer, and Eddie, too, is good with his hands. Even at age four he was able to build Legos without reading the directions, and he is now taking apart radios and putting them back together.

In spite of his mechanical skills, Eddie is barely keeping afloat in school. While he can devote hours at a time to Tinker Toys, Eddie is unable to focus in the classroom. He picks up on everything: the sound of a rope clanging against the flagpole outside, the note being passed at the front of the class, the hum of the clock. While Eddie can slowly and painfully sound out words, he has virtually no comprehension. His teacher urges him to slow down and "concentrate." Spelling is a nightmare. Eddie frequently reverses letters and continues to have problems with letters such as *d* and *b*. He labors over multiplication tables. Eddie is labeled dyslexic; no one suspects ADD because he follows the rules and is not disruptive. Eddie is quietly failing second grade.

Kyle's parents call me in desperation. At eleven years old, Kyle's in fifth grade, yet he has the basic skills of a first grader. An African American at an inner-city school, Kyle can hardly read, cannot complete even the simplest math problem, and sits in the corner and stares into space for hours at a time, both at home and at school.

Kyle has other problems as well. He's obsessed with rap music, is consumed by violent video games, and is a pathological liar. Kyle doesn't play by the rules. He hangs out with a tough crowd and is suspended for several days for carrying a knife to school. His teachers are convinced that Kyle will eventually be expelled, so they're investing very little time and energy on him. What little attention Kyle gets is in the form of harsh discipline, which he now requires to stay in line.

A specialist at his school runs Kyle through a battery of tests and proclaims that he has ADD, Oppositional Defiant Disorder (ODD), and a below-average IQ of around 60. A psychologist who evaluates Kyle is disturbed by his anger and withdrawal, pronouncing him a "juvenile delinquent in training."

The IQ test and diagnosis of Kyle only reinforce his low esteem and exacerbate his violent tendencies. When his teachers learn of his supposed low IQ, they treat him as if he were dull. Kyle, extremely observant and perceptive child that he is, picks up on these doubts and fears, and they further magnify his feelings of inadequacy.

There are Jasons, Janas, Joshes, Eddies, and Kyles in classrooms all over the world, and they make it hard for me to sleep at night. First of all, I *was* one of these children. Second, I know that although they were once in the minority, they are becoming the norm in our schools; they are a harbinger of what's to come. The so-called crisis in education is simply the failure of our schools to identify these growing numbers of children and determine the best way to teach them. Instead of treating them as "defective" and "disordered," we need to recognize their innate strengths and improve their esteem and enthusiasm for learning.

Through more than a decade of working one-on-one, first with gifted and then with ADD children, I've had the framework to make a startling discovery: Most gifted and virtually all children with ADD *share the same learning style.* Simply put, they are all highly visual, nonsequential processors who learn by remembering the way things look and by taking words and turning them into mental pictures. The teaching techniques that work so well for gifted, right-brained students also work for children with ADD. This is a simple, yet revolutionary notion.

While our schools have been harping on the deficits of children with ADD, I've had the pleasure of unearthing their many gifts. These children can do difficult math problems in their head, remember long lists of words, and are excellent speed-readers. So why do they do so poorly in school? Because educators tend to be left-brained: very detail-oriented, auditory processors who view visual learners as flawed. Our educational system hammers at visual learners' weaknesses rather than utilizing their greatest strength: an uncanny visual memory. The cost of such rigidity is incalculable, and the lost potential is astronomical.

I'll give you a typical scenario: Nicholas, age twelve, is summoned to appear for a school staffing conference, which might better be termed an inquisition. The charges: Nicholas is disruptive, disorganized, and difficult to teach. Nicholas appears before a tribunal of ten stone-faced adults, including the middle school principal, his classroom teachers, and a battery of learning specialists.

The meeting begins with the special education teacher wagging a finger at Nicholas and saying, "Nothing works with you. You just don't get it. I've tried everything, including buying you a special assignment book with my own money. You won't even write in it." The proceeding continues with a roundtable recital from Nicholas's four teachers lamenting that he's unable to focus in class, writes poorly, never turns in his homework on time, and is a bad influence on his peers. Nicholas's body begins to sag.

Now it's my turn to talk. As a private tutor of ADD children, I'm well aware of Nicholas's many strengths. I've been working with him for several weeks. Once I got him to relax and trust me, I discovered that he is very bright. I explain that Nicholas has a photographic memory, can spell words forward and backward, and can do double-digit multiplication in his head. But the teachers cut me off, shaking their heads, conceding that while Nicholas may be intelligent, he's unable to apply himself. In the presence of this sensitive little boy, his special education teacher moans, "I've never been at such a loss as to how to teach a child. No one knows how to reach him."

As Nicholas's mother fights back tears, I gently persist in explaining that this child is extremely sensitive and right-brained, which means he has a learning style that is different from the norm. Nicholas, I relate, does not think the way his teachers do. He processes information in a random, nonlinear style and is quite visual in the way he learns. He has a remarkable memory, which can be harnessed to help him succeed in school. What Nicholas needs isn't kid gloves or special treatment but teachers who understand his differences and can adapt their teaching methods and expectations accordingly.

I can see that my comments are getting nowhere. The special ed teacher interrupts me again, saying, "There's no question Nicholas has ADD, and he's also stubborn and oppositional. What he needs is Ritalin and another year in sixth grade." She shifts her gaze to Nicholas. "What do *you* think is wrong with your education here, Nick? What do *you* think would make school better for you?"

There's no answer from Nicholas because, glassy-eyed, he's effectively shut down. The staffing conference may be the school's version of "tough love," with the intent of shocking Nick into flying straight, the consequence being Ritalin or repeating school. But the message Nick receives is that he's a failure, that there's something fundamentally wrong with him. Nicholas is being treated as if he's broken. In truth, what's breaking during this conference is this boy's spirit. It will be a long time before Nicholas trusts anyone, including himself and his considerable talents, again. A fragile ego that's just emerging will retreat into its cocoon for a long time.

What kids like Nick need isn't a prescription for pills but a prescription for a different teaching method. Catching these children early and intervening with proper teaching techniques has a snowball effect: It builds confidence and esteem, helps children succeed, and reduces our dependence on Ritalin. Ultimately, this will pay off in huge dividends to our society, lowering dropout and juvenile crime rates and helping a growing percentage of our citizens reach their potential.

I work with a dozen of these misunderstood right-brained kids every day. I'm about to share with you some of my secrets for tapping their true potential. Once you understand the logic behind these methods, you, too, will be able to use them to help your child learn—whether or not you can also get the school to use them. (More on that later.)

Let's look at a typical first meeting between me and a student—in this case, fourteen-year-old Michael. He was referred to me by an ADD specialist who says Michael is bright but academically lazy and has a bad attitude about school.

JEFF: What's up, my brother? I hear things aren't going too well in school, huh?

MICHAEL: School sucks, man. What can I say? I hate it. The only good thing about it is my friends.

JEFF: I hear that. But school affects your life. Maybe we can get to the bottom of what's bothering you. Unless I'm mistaken, you don't hate *learning*, do you?

MICHAEL: No. As a matter of fact, up until fourth grade I kinda liked it. It was fun . . . a lotta give and take . . . a lotta art . . . work with my hands. The teachers didn't suck the life out of every subject like they do now.

JEFF: This is the way we're gonna tackle the problem. I'm going to give you an easy test to find out what your learning style is. I suspect that because you're smart, creative, and artistic, you're a visual learner. That means you see things mostly in pictures, and you don't need a lot of repetition like homework to learn things. I'll bet you also have problems with deadlines, though you do pretty well taking tests when they're not timed. Am I right?

MICHAEL: That's pretty much it, all right. You know what? There are a lot of kids like me in school. We're not nerds, so the teachers don't like us. And I don't know what I'm gonna do. I'm really worried about it, and my parents are always on my back. I can't seem to succeed, and I'm just about ready to give up trying. Screw it!

JEFF: What if I were to tell you that not only is there nothing wrong with you, but you have a learning style that is common and in many ways superior to that of many of your classmates and even your teachers. If you stick it out and somehow survive the next few years of school, you may be a very successful person, because the way college teachers approach learning tends to be less rigid and more creative, a better fit with the way you think and learn.

I'm not saying that you don't have to learn this stuff. I'm just saying that you learn in a different way, sort of backward from how many people do. You tend to get the whole picture right away and then fill in the details later, while other kids start with a detail, add another detail, and eventually figure out the whole pattern. This isn't just how many of your classmates learn, it's the way most of your *teachers* learn. So it's no wonder you don't fit in! The deck is stacked against you. What we're going to do is level the playing field so you have a better chance.

I can teach you ways to do what your teachers want you to do quite well. I'm going to teach you how to speed-read, study more efficiently, do math in your head, and understand the intricacies of *how* you learn. So when I'm not there and you're faced with a distrusting teacher who thinks you're trying to get out of work, you can explain to her why you're having trouble with the assignment. You can advocate for yourself—tell the teacher that you've learned the material, but you're going to show her you've mastered it in a different way. I can also get the school to compromise —to understand more what's going on with you and maybe even be an ally in helping you survive or even excel in school. After all, I've been doing this for more than ten years with kids just like you, with an extremely high success rate. Are you with me?

MICHAEL: Sounds good! I sure am glad to hear I'm not some hopeless loser. I was beginning to wonder. If I knew things were gonna get better, I could probably put up with the crap they dole out.

After just eight forty-five-minute sessions with Michael, he's a different kid: His enthusiasm for learning has been rekindled. He has not only caught up with his classmates in most subject areas but he's been able to use his talents to work beyond grade-level expectations. For the first time in his life Michael thinks he's smart. Your child can, too.

Is There Any Such Thing as ADD?

Today's child is a scanner. His experience with electronic media has taught him to scan life the way his eye scans a television set or his ears scan auditory signals from a radio or stereo speaker.

—TONY SCHWARTZ, *The Responsive Chord*

Attention Deficit Disorder (ADD) is described in current medical literature as a neurological syndrome that has three primary symptoms: impulsivity, distractibility, and hyperactivity or excess energy. Nowadays it's trendy to refer to ADD as ADHD, which incorporates the hyperactivity component, although for the purposes of this book I use the two terms interchangeably. Although they're certainly preferable to their predecessor, "minimal brain dysfunction," I agree with Drs. Edward M. Hallowell and John J. Ratey, authors of *Driven to Distraction*, that the labels ADD and ADHD are misleading and shame-producing. "The syndrome is not one of attention deficit but of attention inconsistency," they write. "Most of us with ADD can in fact hyperfocus at times. Hyperactivity may or may not be present; in fact, some children and adults with ADD are quite dreamy and quiet. . . . Finally, the word 'disorder' puts the syndrome entirely in the domain of pathology, where it should not entirely be."

Once considered a condition affecting only children, ADD is now considered a disorder impacting both children and adults. Some people are said to simply "outgrow" it; some never do. ADD cuts across all socioeconomic and ethnic groups. Boys are five or six times more likely than girls to be diagnosed with ADHD because they're more apt to be hyperactive and disruptive (hence the use of the term "him" throughout this book to refer to the ADD child). Girls with

ADD are more likely to be daydreamers who have trouble finishing things.

While most experts will tell you that 5 to 10 percent of the juvenile population has ADD, it's interesting to note that within individual classrooms and schools the percentage varies wildly, from none to almost half the students. ADD is by far the most commonly diagnosed "psychiatric problem" in children; it accounts for about 50 percent of child and teen visits to mental health clinics. There is no blood test for Attention Deficit Disorder; children are labeled ADD as the result of a highly subjective evaluation process.

Kids who may have ADD in the classroom can show an uncanny ability to focus on a project that interests them at home. Very few children exhibit ADD-like behavior in the doctor's office. Some children may appear to have ADD in one class but be very attentive and focused in another. Ronald D. Davis, founder of the Davis Dyslexia Association, suggests in *The Gift of Dyslexia* that ADD is a cover for faulty teaching, that students will never be interested in a subject that is poorly taught. "It is interesting that very good teachers rarely seem to have students with ADD in their classes," he notes, "even though some of the same students are labeled as suffering from ADD in other classes."

Dr. Thomas Armstrong, in his controversial book *The Myth of the ADD Child*, reminds me of the brave soul who revealed that the emperor wasn't wearing any clothes. He makes a very persuasive case that ADD is little more than a convenient catch-all term for children who don't fit someone's definition of how children *should* behave. These are more likely than not to be nonconformist children who question rules and authority. They have probing, inquisitive minds, a strong sense of fairness and justice, and don't respond well to "You'll do it because *I said so.*" Armstrong proclaims, "The term *attention deficit disorder* gives parents and teachers a relatively simple way of explaining troublesome behaviors." Hallowell has said that while many children are being accurately diagnosed and treated for attention deficits, "the bad news is that ADHD has become a very seductive diagnosis that is unfortunately easy to confuse with the symptoms of daily life."

Many parents and teachers actually embrace the label of ADD with relief, as it offers a name—an explanation for the inexplicable. Dr.

Armstrong, who admits to being booed off stages when he suggests ADD doesn't exist, noted, "The ADD label also provides a central point around which parents, teachers, and professionals can rally for political and economic support. . . . Teachers who are disturbed by a child's behavior can now petition to have him removed to a special classroom. Parents can press to have their ADD children taught in expensive private schools at public school expense and sue if they feel their children aren't being given an appropriate education." Though schools don't like to talk about it, they get a handsome federal bonus ($420 in 1997) for each child labeled disabled, prompting the U.S. Department of Education's Jim Bradshaw to say we've gone too far: "We have a problem with overidentification."

Dr. Armstrong makes a credible case, and I admire his courage in questioning this rampant labeling of children. I believe, however, that there really *is* such a thing as ADD and that it affects perhaps 2 to 3 percent of the population. The percentage is growing because of cultural influences and the failure of our educational system to understand and adequately address it. While ADD is difficult to define, after working with thousands of children over the years, I know it when I see it.

These children are:

hyperimpulsive
hypersensory
hypersensitive
hypervisual
hyperdistractible

and in most cases,

hyperactive

The child with genuine ADD typically has just two speeds: full tilt and collapse. He consistently has a short attention span, which means he fails to hold a thought for more than a few seconds. He rarely finishes a task, bouncing like a pinball from one activity to another. He doesn't have a built-in "brake" in his brain that tells him to look before he leaps. His lightning-fast visual mind flashes from random thought to random thought; his thought patterns are like a brainstorming session run amok. He is nonlogical, nonsequential, and nonverbal (although he talks constantly), physically and socially clumsy, and hopelessly disorganized. He may or may not respond well to medication. Rather than being labeled as ADD, this child might be more accurately termed a "hyperimpulsive random visual processor." Whatever you choose to call it, it's a tremendous challenge to parent and teach this kind of child.

THE BUCKETS by Scott Stantis

THE BUCKETS reprinted by permission of United Feature Syndicate, Inc.

This form of ADD has a genetic component that is triggered by environmental stimuli. It's probably been around for generations, although children with what we now call ADD used to be given other labels: "difficult," "a handful," or "a bundle of energy." In some eras and in some cultures even today many of the traits of ADD are valued. Thom Hartmann, author of several thought-provoking books on the roots of ADD, compares people with ADD to hunters and the rest of us to farmers. Hartmann says there's a startlingly high percentage of ADD among members of hunting tribes, thereby raising the possibility that ADD was once a useful adaptation for survival.

Nowadays, it seems every child who has a high energy level, who is bored in school, or who sasses his teacher is said to have ADD. Attention Deficit Disorder is a convenient umbrella term for a myriad of other problems and conditions. Many children exhibit symptoms of ADD during stressful events, such as divorce or relocation, or when they have problems with peers. Emotional and adjustment problems can also masquerade as ADD or occur in tandem with ADD. For example, some children labeled as ADD may suffer from depression, anxiety, bipolar disorder, Tourette's syndrome, or post-traumatic stress disorder resulting from trauma or abuse.

I believe the *majority* of children who are now labeled ADD actually have what Hallowell and Ratey term *pseudo*-ADD. They weren't born this way; we *made* them the way they are. These children are a product of our fast-paced, visual, overstimulating culture. Drs. Hallowell and Ratey address this pseudo-ADD phenomenon in their followup book *Answers to Distraction:*

> ADD is like life these days. I [Hallowell] don't want to sound too high-flown in my claims, but I do believe that this medical syndrome meshes with the gears of current American culture. The fast pace of everyday life, the search for the sound bite, the love of fast food and instant gratification, the proliferation of fax machines, cellular telephones, computer networks, bulletin boards, and E-mail systems, our appetite for violence and action and adventure, our rush to get to the bottom line, our widespread impatience, the boom in gambling, our love of extremes and danger—all these very American traits are also very ADD-like.
>
> This may help explain why ADD is fascinating to so many people, and why it is a seductive diagnosis. When you hear a description of ADD, it can sound like a description of urban life in this country. Doesn't everyone in Los Angeles or Manhattan have ADD? It can seem that way. Of course, it is important to underline that they *do not.* But it would be fair, I think, to diagnose our urban culture as inducing an ADD-like syndrome, or what I call pseudo-ADD. . . . Millions of Americans have pseudo-ADD.

How does one tell the difference between *real* and *pseudo*-ADD? While this is certainly not an exact science, consider the following:

- *the degree of severity:* Is the child's behavior so extreme that it consistently gets in the way of his ability to do well in school, complete tasks, and form normal bonds with family and peers?
- *whether the behavior is pronounced both inside and outside the classroom:* This is a key point. If you're taken·aback when your child's

teacher suggests he be evaluated for ADD, it could be that ADD-like behavior is only observable in the classroom. Your child may be acting out because of boredom and faulty teaching, not because of an underlying disorder.

The popularity of managed health care may be a factor in the frequent diagnosis of ADD. As Dr. Daniel Feiten, a Denver-area pediatrician and professor at the University of Colorado Health Sciences Center, points out, "Managed care has caused many of these kids to be treated in private pediatricians' offices" instead of being referred to a specialist. "These children are often seen by doctors with very little knowledge of ADD, because Attention Deficit Disorder has only come to the forefront in the last five to ten years. You could say that *half* of primary care doctors are poorly trained in this particular area. Misdiagnosis or overdiagnosis is easy to do."

Dr. Feiten also notes that there's a tremendous amount of pressure on family doctors to "fix" these kids with a pill. Certainly, giving Johnny a pill is cheaper and easier than sending him to lengthy sessions with a psychologist or developing an elaborate behavior modification program. Of parents who come to Dr. Feiten seeking an ADD evaluation for their child, he says, "Fully 50 percent of them are demanding medication . . . not *asking* for it . . . but *demanding* medication."

It's interesting that Dr. Feiten and other pediatricians like him notice a surge in ADD referrals immediately following report card time and parent-teacher conferences. Physicians especially notice a peak at the end of the school year when, Dr. Feiten says, "people are panicking." He notes that the most intense pressure for Ritalin comes from schools. At the same time, he says, "I don't think schools understand Attention Deficit Disorder, and I don't think they understand what to do with it."

Schools demand obedience, and many teachers see the road to obedience as being paved with Ritalin. But do we want to raise children who simply follow orders unquestioningly, or do we want to rear children with an *internal* sense of fair play? Of right and wrong? It may be every teacher's fantasy to shout, "Michael, quit that!" and he does. Or to order Nicole to clean out her cubby, and she complies. It certainly makes controlling the classroom much easier.

Jane Bluestein, Ph.D., and Lynn Collins write about the difference between obedient and cooperative children in an excellent article in the *Joyful Child Journal:* "Obedient children quickly learn that they are safe, accepted, valued, and worthwhile when they are doing what other people want. Cooperative children, on the other hand, may do things that are very pleasing to the people in their lives—and may be more likely to do so in an environment of emotional safety and acceptance. But their motivation is not exclusively the other person's positive reaction. In other words, because these kids don't need to people-please to stay safe, they are therefore far less vulnerable to pressure from outside themselves—including peer pressure—than children who are raised to be obedient."

There's a high price for churning out obedient kids on Ritalin. While great at following orders, these children are less capable of making responsible decisions on their own. As teenagers they are more likely to bow to peer pressure when it comes to drugs, sex, and petty crimes. As adults they are indecisive and are constantly turning to others for validation of their judgments. They make great followers but poor leaders. This is the price of valuing compliance over cooperation. It's no wonder we face such a crisis in leadership today.

There's much more at stake in the overdiagnosis of ADD. It's a tremendous drain on our economic resources as well. About two million children and teenagers now take Ritalin, four times as many as in 1990. Ciba-Geigy and other pharmaceutical giants are raking in millions of dollars a year from sales of Ritalin and other stimulants for children with ADD. The marketing research firm IMS America reports that the number of prescriptions for the three main stimulants used to treat ADD and their generic versions (Ritalin, Dexedrine, and Cylert) *tripled* from 1990 to 1994. Demand for Ritalin reportedly led to a shortage of the drug in 1994. Possible side effects of Ritalin include insomnia, loss of appetite, rapid heartbeat, and dizziness. Perhaps the most common side effect is the emotional drop that children experience three or four hours after taking it. About 20 percent of kids taking it will become weepy as the drug wears off. It's interesting to note that while Ritalin can improve compliance in children and help them finish things, some adults who take it say it diminishes their creativity. (More on Ritalin later.)

Many psychologists and M.D.s now specialize in diagnosing ADD, recommending medications and teaching specific behavior management techniques. It can cost from $1,000 to $2,000 to get a medical diagnosis of ADD. This growth industry has also produced a plethora of conferences and workshops, as well as shelves of books with advice on coping with ADD. Few, if any, recognize it as a learning style.

This rampant ADD labeling also exacts a toll on the most vulnerable and precious members of our society: our children. The very term "disorder" is shameful. Never mind his many positive attributes; the ADD child gets a very clear message that something is very wrong with him. ADD becomes a stigma that can follow him into adulthood and affect all aspects of his life. As Denver psychologist and ADD expert Dr. George Dorry notes, "For an individual who has an extraordinary strength in visual-spatial or right-brained functioning to be called 'learning disabled' because he doesn't fit the left-brained classroom is appalling. It's a definitional issue that is locked in by the left-brainers, who say, 'If you don't have our skill, you are a learning disabled student.' "

Sadly, for many children, labels such as "disordered," "defiant," or "disabled" become a self-fulfilling prophecy. The child who believes that his parents and teachers have written him off as flawed and who therefore no longer believes in himself is much more likely to make bad choices. He is at risk of becoming a dropout, a drug abuser, or a delinquent. Almost one-third of students with ADD never finish high school. Dr. Daniel G. Amen, in his book *Windows into the ADD Mind*, reports that over 40 percent of ADD teens and adults have problems with drugs or alcohol. Dr. Amen says in one shocking study that almost *half* of untreated hyperactive boys with ADD were arrested for a felony by the time they were sixteen. ADD does not produce delinquency, but I believe the mislabeling and shaming associated with it are contributing factors. The majority of these rebellious misfits might have led happy, productive lives were it not for their "crime" of having a different learning style.

It's disheartening that so much research has been done on the deficiencies of children with ADD, but very little has been written about their remarkable strengths. Dr. Armstrong's *The Myth of the ADD Child* takes an exhaustive look at current research on ADD, noting that only a couple of studies have been done on *positive* aspects of ADD. One showed that many kids who are labeled hyperactive or ADD have huge reserves of creative energy. Another indicated that kids labeled ADD tell more novel stories than so-called normal kids. New research is also finding that children with ADD are more likely to be gifted. Dr. Armstrong laments, "Other than these studies . . . there was nothing. Yet there are thousands of studies telling us what ADD kids *can't* do. This is a tragedy, since it suggests researchers are more interested in the deficits of these children than in their potentials."

In his pioneering book *In the Mind's Eye*, computer consultant Thomas G. West surveys the learning styles of great thinkers and finds compelling evidence that many of them were visual, right-brained learners. A number of famous historical figures—including Hans Christian Andersen, Albert Einstein, Thomas Edison, Leonardo da Vinci, George S. Patton, Nelson Rockefeller, and William Butler Yeats—were identified by grade school teachers as having dyslexia or another learning disability. Today, many of them would probably be labeled ADD!

A key hypothesis of West's book is that many of these people achieve success not in spite of their perceived difficulties in school but *because of them*. Says West, "They may have been so much in touch with their visual-spatial, nonverbal, right-hemisphere modes of thought that they have difficulty in doing orderly, sequential, verbal-mathematical, left-hemisphere tasks in a culture where left-hemisphere capabilities are so highly valued." West theorizes that such right-brained geniuses succeed because they *cannot* compensate and adapt, that their strengths emerge in spite of efforts by educators to "break them" of their learning style and make them conform to a different mode of thinking.

West goes on to point out that what most perceive as a handicap can actually be thought of as a gift. "In other words, the complex of traits referred to as 'learning difficulties' or 'dyslexia' may be in part the outward manifestation of the relative strength of a different mode of thought, one that is available to everyone to one degree or another, but one that a few children (and adults) find difficult to suppress. Too often, the gift is not recognized and is regarded only as a problem."

This is particularly true of the world of education. People who go into teaching tend to have done well in school themselves. They gravitate toward the orderliness, sequentiality, and familiarity of education. Teaching is congruent with the left-brained way that they think. As Dr. John Philo Dixon, expert in gifted education, writes in *The Spatial Child*, "Elementary school teachers are often those who themselves experienced comfort and success when they were being introduced in first grade to the memorized intricacies of reading, writing, and arithmetic. . . . It is the rare teacher who has any extensive training in the nature of spatial and mechanical skills or who uses spatially dominant activities as anything but a passing fancy in the classroom." Dr. Dixon notes that there are right-hemispheric children who have "the potential for understanding the interconnected patterns in quantum theory, quasars, path analysis, thermodynamics, matrix algebra, spatial analysis, etc." Yet they go undiscovered in our left-brained educational system because "some of these same children have trouble deciphering Dick and Jane in the first grade."

How many children begin kindergarten full of exuberance and energy, eager to learn about their world, only to have their enthusiasm extinguished by teachers who perceive them as defective? Drs. Hallowell and Ratey give one such example in *Driven to Distraction:* "Follow the face of a little girl who doesn't read very well and is told to try harder; who tends to daydream and is told she better pay attention; who talks out in class when she sees something fascinating, like a butterfly on the windowpane, and is told to leave the class and report to the principal; who forgets her homework and is told she will just never learn; who writes a story rich in imagination and insight and is told her handwriting and spelling are atrocious; who asks for help and is told she should try harder herself before getting others to do her work for her; who begins to feel unhappy in school and is told that big girls try harder. This is the brutal process of breaking down the spirit of a child."

◼ Visit the front lines of education—the schools—and you'll find teachers shaking their heads and wringing their hands and wondering what's wrong with kids these days. They'll tell you they're dealing with a "new breed of child." More and more of the children in their classes are fidgety and easily frustrated, their attention spans are minimal, and they can't hold a thought. They're reading later and their standardized test scores are declining. They drop out more frequently and exhibit more behavioral problems, forcing teachers to spend less time teaching the three R's and more time on the "three D's": drugs, distractions, and discipline. More of these children have "special needs," stretching already lean school budgets to the breaking point.

From Joanne, a twenty-five-year veteran teacher: "I don't know what's wrong with these kids. I'm glad I'm getting out of teaching. Nobody can teach these children. They're too wild, undisciplined, and nothing holds their attention."

From Betsy, a private school director: "These kids are getting more difficult to teach every year. The only things that hold their attention are art projects and the computer."

From Toni, an eight-year public school teaching veteran: "Education must change. We're reaching fewer and fewer children each year."

From Andrea, a high school physics teacher: "I don't know what's happening anymore with these kids. They have no attention span; nobody can stick to anything. I'm so glad I'm retiring. God help the teachers of the next century."

Meet the twenty-first-century child: He is the product of today's short attention span culture, which demands constant stimulation and bombards us with sensory overload and rapid-fire images. From birth his environment literally wires and rewires pathways in the brain.

The human brain is as mysterious as it is awesome. This three-pound mass of gray matter not only controls the most basic functions, such as breathing, reflexes, and seeing, it's also the control center for all our thoughts and emotions. The human brain has 100 billion cells; man's closest relative, the monkey, has just 10 billion. It's this difference that gives man the capacity for self-awareness, abstract thinking, and a sense of right and wrong.

Just a decade ago we thought the human brain was hardwired at birth, that, for example, you were either born smart or you weren't. But advances in molecular biology and imaging are now giving us a very different picture: The brain now appears to be very plastic—a super sponge, if you will—constantly changing and adapting in response to outside stimuli. Every childhood experience—every smile, bedtime story, lullaby, or game of peekaboo—triggers an electrical response along an infant's neural pathways, laying the foundation for future thoughts. Pulitzer Prize–winning science writer Ronald Kotulak, author of *Inside the Brain*, describes the connection between nature and nurture this way: "Researchers believe that genes, the chemical blueprints of life, establish the framework of the brain, but then the environment takes over and provides the customized finishing touches. They work in tandem. The genes provide the building blocks, and the environment acts like an on-the-job foreman, providing instruction for final construction." So early childhood experiences not only influence development of personality and behavior, they can *actually affect intelligence*. Dr. Frederick Goodwin, past director of the National Institute of Mental Health, says, "You can't make a 70 IQ person into a 120 IQ person, but you can change their IQ measure in different ways, perhaps as much as 20 points up or down, based on their environment."

This concept is exciting and frightening at the same time. We now know that while parents cannot turn a child into a genius, they can provide an environment in which children can reach their true potential. As Jacqulyn Saunders and Pamela Espeland note in *Bringing Out the Best: A Resource Guide for Parents of Young Gifted Children*, "Regardless of the original quality of a child's brain cells, the quality of brain material he or she ultimately has can be helped or hurt by the amount of exercise it gets. As the foremost educators of our children, it is both exhilarating and awesome to realize that we have the ability to alter the structure of their brains."

A pudgy baby may appear passive in her crib, but her brain is pulsing with activity as tremendous numbers of connections between neurons called synapses are formed. During the first year of life, the number of synapses jumps *twentyfold*, from about 50 trillion to more than 1,000 trillion. These pathways between brain cells are reinforced by what the infant sees, smells, hears, and touches. Connections that are made repeatedly between brain cells are strengthened; for example, when a mother coos to her child, pathways to the circuits that regulate emotion and the auditory cortex are stimulated. When an infant focuses on her mother while nursing, synapses to the visual cortex are reinforced. How remarkable that nature has seen fit to allow a baby to focus best at the exact distance from the crook of Mother's cradling arm to her smiling face.

In the same way that we may lose a memory if we don't access it, pathways in the brain that are not reinforced during that critical first year will become dormant in a process known as pruning. A dramatic example of this "use it or lose it" philosophy comes from a Harvard study of newborn kittens. Researchers sewed one eye of a kitten shut for several weeks to test the effect of sensory deprivation on the brain. Lo and behold, when the stitches were removed, the eye was no longer able to see. But the amazing, adaptable brain compensated for the loss: The eye that stayed open during the entire experiment could actually see much better than it might have normally.

We find similar phenomena in humans. For example, as Kotulak says, "The critical period for learning a spoken language is totally lost by age ten. Children who grow up alone in the wild, never hearing another human, cannot learn to speak if they are introduced to civilization after that deadline." If you had a history of ear infections as a child, you're more likely to be a visual learner because the auditory input you received was distorted or obstructed. The amazing, adaptable brain compensated for your less-than-perfect hearing by sharpening your visual circuitry. Dr. Dorry says, "Give me a child who has at least one surgically implanted ear tube, and I'll show you somebody who's more a visual-spatial learner than he would have turned out otherwise."

While there's no question that important neural circuitry is being laid down in the first years of human life, another critical stage in brain development occurs from approximately ages four through ten, when the brain is supercharged with activity. Using positron-emission tomography (PET) scans, doctors have been able to measure energy levels in the brain from birth to old age. They've found the brains of these preschool and grade school children to be literally glowing with activity, pulsing at levels at least twice that of adults. In most people, half of the synapses established in the first few years of life will go unused by puberty, starving for stimuli. But the number of connections we ultimately retain may fluctuate as much as 25 percent, depending on whether we grow up in a rich, stimulating environment or a stark, impoverished one.

We need to lay the foundations for learning in early childhood by stimulating children's brains with a variety of activities that exercise the visual, auditory, and kinesthetic parts of the brain. This isn't to say that we should be enrolling babies in preschool prep courses but rather that we should read to our children, talk in "parentese" to them, and sing nursery rhymes. Children should be introduced to foreign languages at an early age, perhaps three or four, when the brain is most plastic. In the words of Wayne State University pediatric neurologist Harry Chugani, "Who's the idiot who decided that youngsters should learn foreign languages in high school? . . . The time to learn languages is when the brain is receptive to those kinds of things, and that's much earlier, in preschool or elementary school."

Whenever I speak about my hypothesis that virtually all children labeled ADD are right-brained, visual learners, inevitably a hand goes up and someone asks, "Is there any scientific research to support it? Can we actually *measure* differences between the brains of ADD children and so-called normal children?" There have been some preliminary studies that use brain imaging technology to focus on the defective aspects of the brains of children with ADD, but, frankly, little or no research has been done on the brain dominance and intrinsic strengths of these children.

Perhaps the most intriguing research comes from a 1990 study published in the highly respected medical journal *Lancet*, which used PET scans to measure activity in the brain. While this study involved only nine children with ADHD, the findings were significant: The distribution of regional cerebral activity was abnormally low in the frontal areas of the brain responsible for concentration, language development, attention span, impulse control and logical, sequential reasoning. On the other hand, researchers found high brain activity in the occipital or rear lobe, the primary visual area of the brain. A study published in the 1989 *Archives of Neurology* also found striking differences in blood flow in the brains of children with ADHD. Children with ADHD had lower levels of activity in the frontal and central brain structures, but higher levels in the occipital lobe, the visual part of the brain.

A more recent study published in the July 1996 *Archives of General Psychiatry* compared the brains of fifty-five so-called normal boys with those of fifty-seven boys who'd been diagnosed with ADHD, this time using magnetic resonance imaging (MRI). (The MRI is more acceptable than the PET scan as a brain research tool for children because it doesn't have any radiation associated with it.) Lead researcher Dr. F. Xavier Castellanos of the National Institute of Mental Health notes that the subjects with ADHD had 4.7 percent smaller total cerebral volume than the control group, primarily due to differences in the frontal area of the brain and in the basal ganglia, which serves as a switching mechanism to send signals to other appropriate areas of the brain. Dr. Castellanos says these areas of the brain are associated with the ability to carry out executive functions and inhibit one's actions. This is congruent with the behavior of children with ADD who, he notes, "don't inhibit sufficiently. They'll grab something, tend to blurt things out, take a toy from another child, without realizing the child is going to be resentful. This lack of inhibitions seems to be a central characteristic of the ADHD child. Certain brain circuits are very crucial to allow inhibitions to take place, and they're slightly smaller in these children."

When I asked Dr. Castellanos to react to my hypothesis that virtually all children with ADD are right-brained, visual learners, he responded, "I would agree with that. I certainly see it clinically, although not a lot of research has been done in that area." He laments that we aren't devoting more funds to this kind of research, especially since we know about the plasticity of the human brain in the earliest years of life. Does he believe ADD is the result of nature or nurture? While his studies don't answer that question, Dr. Castellanos believes the two are inseparable: "It's almost certain there are some people who have ADHD with no genetics for it—no one in the family has had it. It's likely the majority of cases are familial and do have a strong genetic loading. But even when genetic loading is there, not every case is going to have the kinds of symptoms diagnosed as having ADHD. In other words, there's a genetic vulnerability, and then the interplay of the environment helps determine whether it will manifest as a true disorder."

Dr. Castellanos underscores the difficulty of identifying who has ADD and who doesn't, pointing out that one in five children in his study who were diagnosed with ADD had clinically "normal" brains. Does he envision a day when *all* children are routinely screened for ADD and other learning disabilities using MRI or other technology? "Not in the foreseeable future. But if you had asked me, 'Is it ever possible to clone a sheep?' I would have said no, and now we're cloning sheep."

▣ If you want the short course on why children think differently today, sit down with your child and spend a few minutes watching *Sesame Street* or MTV. See how you respond to the dizzyingly rapid-fire images on Super Bowl commercials. Watch how your child sits, transfixed, processing an almost impossible amount of visual information. If that weren't enough, technology has brought us even more ADD-like options for TV viewing: picture-within-a-picture and split-frame features, and the omnipresent remote control. In the words of Drs. Hallowell and Ratey, in *Driven to Distraction*, "Remote control

Calvin and Hobbes   by Bill Watterson

CALVIN AND HOBBES © 1990 Watterson. Dist. by UNIVERSAL PRESS SYNDICATE.
Reprinted with permission. All rights reserved.

switch in hand, we switch from station to station taking in dozens of programs at once, catching a line here, an image there, getting the gist of the show in a millisecond, getting bored with it in a full second, blipping on to the next show, the next bit of stimulation, the next quick pick."

This visual chaos can't help but change the way we think. Psychiatrist Matthew Dumont says, "I would like to suggest that the constant shifting of visual frames in television shows is related to the hyperkinetic syndrome. . . . There are incessant changes of camera and focus, so that the viewer's reference point shifts every few seconds. This technique literally programs a short attention span." Movie critic Michael Medved warns that the attenuated attention spans that TV viewing produces are even more harmful than the content of television programs today. As historian Gertrude Himmelfarb observes, "The combination of sound bites and striking visual effects shapes the young mind, incapacitating it for the longer, slower, less febrile tempo of the book."

It used to be that the oral and written tradition reigned in our society. Man evolved from telling stories around the fire to reading, writing, and lecturing. But today's child now learns visually, almost from birth. We stimulate babies with black-and-white geometric designs in the crib. We entertain them with photos and videotaped images of themselves. Children sit for hours at a time watching television. Advertising is becoming increasingly visual and less verbal. People get more information from television and computers, and less from the printed page. Newspapers are becoming more visual in order to compete: *USA Today* is leading the pack with its emphasis on color graphics, pie charts, bar graphs, and easily digested "McNews."

It can be argued that this heavy visual orientation stimulates and reinforces visual pathways in a child's brain at the expense of auditory pathways. In his book *Beyond ADD*, Thom Hartmann, father of an ADD child and former director of a treatment facility for emotionally disturbed children, wonders if the brains of today's children are somehow wired differently from those of our parents. "Could it be that this difference is real," he poses, "and that what it's really about is the transition people are making from an auditory to a visual learning style?" As one who works with these children every day, I can say that based on my observations, it's happening as you read this. Dr. Dorry concurs: "Very clearly, we are moving away from the linearity of print and moving into a more intensely visual experience."

The evidence of this visual shift in our young people is all around us. Evan I. Schwartz reports in the January 1995 *Omni* magazine that the brains of today's children are different from those of their parents or grandparents. Coaches find that players can no longer follow a play explained by using a chalkboard with x's and o's; instead they show videotapes. Our parents grew up listening to radio dramas, and most of us grew up with a couple of movie theaters and four or five television channels. Our children are exposed to an overwhelming array of cable channels, computer programs, video games, and web sites. It's no wonder they think differently.

Dr. Armstrong hits the nail on the head when he says, "Our culture may be producing a whole new generation of 'short-attention-span kids.'" He continues, "Today's fast-paced media—MTV, video software, multimedia computer programs, Nintendo games, and other electronic marvels—shower children with an ever more rapid succession of images and bits of information. As a result, many kids seem to have evolved attentional strategies based on grasping information in quick and rapid chunks. . . . Many of these fast-paced, media-fed kids may be labeled as ADD by adults who live life in the slow lane." In short, these children are exposed to so much stimuli, that they're afraid if they stay focused on one thing too long, they'll miss something else. Instead of lingering over a meal, our children have fast-food brains. In *Endangered Minds*, Dr. Jane Healy sums it up this way: "The current generation of two-minute minds (don't blame them, folks, we did it to them) are unschooled in persistence or reflection; if they don't like something, they change the channel or persuade their dad to sue the school."

Dr. Healy has done exhaustive research on this new breed of child and is puzzled by this apparent contradiction: These major changes in a generation of brains have *no effect on IQ scores*. In fact, if anything, students today appear to score better than children of previous generations. While there's no simple explanation for this, Healy did pick up on one fascinating trend when comparing verbal sections of IQ tests (which measure vocabulary, verbal expression, and reasoning, all left-brained skills) with the nonverbal sections (mazes, puzzles, and block construction, all right-brained skills). Healy writes, "Studies over the last few decades did suggest that verbal abilities have recently begun to decline relative to nonverbal ones. This pattern, which has surprised researchers, is beginning to be seen in several European countries, but the United States is leading the way."

Visionary author Alvin Toffler worried about the effect of our fast-paced society on the human brain decades ago. In his 1970 blockbuster *Future Shock*, he wrote, "We are forcing people to adapt to a new life pace, to confront novel situations and master them in even shorter intervals. . . . We are forcing them to choose among fast-multiplying options. We are, in other words, forcing them to process information at a far more rapid pace than was necessary in slowly-evolving societies. There can be little doubt that we are subjecting at least some of them to cognitive overstimulation. What consequences this may have for mental health in the techno-societies has yet to be determined."

It's shocking to hear that the average child spends more time watching TV from kindergarten to twelfth grade than he spends in the classroom or interacting with family and friends. In many homes and day care centers, TV acts as an electronic baby-sitter, lulling children into a calm, almost mesmerized state. With the television on, adults don't have to spend as much time supervising, breaking up fights, and structuring active play. While parents fret about violence, language, and sex on TV and we argue about television rating systems, it seems that we're missing the big picture. The problem with TV isn't so much what children are seeing, it's what they're *not doing* when they're spending so much time glued to the tube.

Justin, now a twenty-year-old college sophomore, is a fascinating product of the "television generation." Quiet and unassuming, with red hair and freckles, he spoke softly with me one day about what it was like to grow up in front of a TV set.

Justin's parents divorced when he was three years old. His mother, a realtor, wanted the best for Justin and his younger sister, and was trying desperately to make ends meet. Seven-day work weeks were the norm. In his mother's absence, Justin discovered television. He says, "It was a baby-sitter. It helped keep me out of my mom's hair when she was trying to work." Justin sat transfixed in front of the television set from the moment he came home from school until bedtime, digesting cartoons, dramas, and sitcoms even during dinner. If he had trouble sleeping, Justin would sneak into the TV room and watch late-night movies until he fell asleep on the floor.

During the summer months when he was with his father, who is self-employed, Justin continued to feed his TV habit, spending entire days and even weeks glued to the tube. He says with a shrug, "I wasn't very social back then. I had a lot of self-image problems and was too insecure to go out. It was easier to sit around and watch TV and not have to deal with people."

Justin says there's no question that being hooked on TV affected his performance in school. Aside from art, math, and gym classes, he had little interest in schoolwork and couldn't even read until he repeated fourth grade. His teachers suspected he was dyslexic and complained about his daydreaming and limited attention span. He found the classroom a dull place that moved at a snail's pace. "I would find myself wanting things to just happen *right now* and then go on to new things. My mind would wander. . . . I would just sit there staring in class at people's heads or the floor or out the window . . . not comprehending anything that was going on."

Justin's TV addiction mushroomed still further when a VCR was introduced into the home. He recalls entire weekends as a teenager when he and his sister sat in front of the television set, watching movie after movie. He says it wasn't uncommon for him to watch television from the moment he woke up in the morning until the moment he tumbled into bed. Like so many of us, Justin found that television had a pacifying effect. "It was easy. . . . I didn't have to work hard to do it or anything . . . it was just there. It wasn't interactive at all. I didn't have to think or anything. It was just a quick, easy fix. It was a sedative . . . a kind of 'sit around and absorb everything' feeling. But I yearned to do other things as well. I wanted to do more with my life, but I always wondered how. All I knew was how to flip channels."

It wasn't until Justin found a friend to hang out with and discovered high school athletics that his interest in television waned. Justin was fortunate to be blessed with a high IQ and quickly made up for lost time, taking several honors classes and graduating with a 3.8 grade point average. He discovered the world beyond the boob tube, busily learning and exploring, so that television occupied only an hour or two a week of his time. A typical late bloomer, Justin says of high school, "I kept myself involved and really enjoyed the atmosphere. I finally was able to cut my umbilical cord to the TV, and it felt really good."

But looking back, Justin believes that thousands of hours of television not only made him lazy, it changed the way he thinks. "I am definitely a visual learner, and I think TV enhanced it. The TV screen is big and bright, with vivid colors, and you see images flash before you. You get more information via your eyes in a matter of seconds than you can get in many minutes of someone speaking to you." Even today, college lectures are tedious for Justin because he has an inherent weakness in auditory processing. "I know I have to write everything down, almost word for word, or else I don't understand what's going on." He takes copious notes but does not absorb the information until later, when he has time to reread his notes and visualize what they mean.

Justin isn't bitter that TV gave him a late start in living his life. He reasons that his parents did the best they could with him under difficult circumstances. He is more wistful than angry when he confesses, "I missed my childhood."

The influence of the Internet on the way children learn has yet to be studied, but unquestionably it is profound. As Gertrude Himmelfarb points out, channel surfing on television is child's play next to cyber surfing and the infinite amount of information it puts literally at our fingertips. She observes, "The constant exposure to a myriad of texts, sounds, and images that often are only tangentially related to each other is hardly conducive to the cultivation of logical, rational, systematic habits of thought."

These days it's also not uncommon to see children on the streets, on buses, and at shopping malls wearing personal stereo headphones, rocking out to loud pop or heavy metal music. In addition to concerns about hearing loss, one can't help but wonder what effect this musical immersion has on the developing brain. Reading specialist Priscilla Vail, author of *The World of the Gifted Child* and *Smart Kids with School Problems*, shares this concern: "I am particularly worried about the kids who conform to the listening patterns of pop music. Their brains are being trained to listen uncritically to lyrics that are limited to repetitive syllables or short phrases that hardly sound like English. The beat overrides the melody, and there is no beginning, no middle, and no end. That is a poor training ground for understanding language."

As you may have guessed by now, the parts of the brain that *do* respond to music are in the right hemisphere, so as the "Walkman kid" is starving the neural circuitry on the left side of the brain, he's reinforcing the pathways on the right.

But while television, the Internet, and rock music are easy targets, there are other societal forces that shape today's evolving brains. Most of us grew up, if not in a *Leave It to Beaver* family, then at least in a family with a working father and a stay-at-home mother. We remained in the constant care of our parents or relatives, enjoying quality personal interactions through our infancy and the critical preschool years. The term "latchkey child" hadn't been coined yet.

There's no question that children today are under more pressure than ever before. Pediatrics professor and child psychologist Dr. Antoinette Saunders and coauthor Bonnie Remsberg tell us in *The Stress-Proof Child:* "Our children experience the stress of illness, divorce, financial problems, living with single parents, death, school, remarriage, jealousy, achievement, vacations, stepbrothers and sisters, sex, drugs, sensory bombardment, violence, the threat of nuclear war—a long, long list. The effect can be overwhelming." It can be argued that many of the symptoms that appear as ADD—distractibility, impulsivity, and defiance—are simply children's reactions to the stressful world in which we live.

Our mothers most likely had healthy, relatively stress-free pregnancies. Yet many children who come into the world today are born to stressed-out single or working mothers, or mothers who drink or take drugs. We know from animal experiments that rats stressed during pregnancy give birth to offspring that are extremely emotional and reactive. It could be deduced that the same applies to humans. Paula Tallal, co-director of the Center for Molecular and Behavioral Neuroscience at Rutgers University, says language problems in children are also associated with stressful pregnancies. She's quoted by Ronald Kotulak in *Inside the Brain* as saying that "having a very stressful pregnancy is highly correlated with the failure to show the expected structural lateralization (left and right hemisphere differences) in the brain." In other words, stress hormones have a direct impact on the developing brain, especially the late-blooming left brain, if stress is high when the male sex hormone, testosterone, kicks in. These boys may be at higher risk down the road for problems such as dyslexia, stuttering, and reading delays.

Today's children are exposed to a succession of caregivers. The majority of babies born in the United States are now placed in full-time day care within one year, often at two or three months of age, so their mothers can go back to work. It's rare for children to have the same nanny or day care provider for more than a year, and quality, affordable care is hard to find. Many centers do nothing more than warehouse children, emphasizing quiet and order over creativity, communication, and language development. A 1995 study at the University of Colorado finds many day care programs are unlicensed; many are staffed with poorly trained adults. Nine out of ten don't even have basic toys, acceptable hygiene, or a healthy ratio of caregivers to children. "A full 40 percent are downright hazardous, both to a child's health and safety as well as to her social and intellectual development."

The infant who spends his day sitting in a playpen or crib with little adult interaction is missing crucial opportunities for language development. Researchers have found a strong correlation between the size of a toddler's vocabulary and how much his mother talks to him. Janellen Huttenlocher of the University of Chicago has found that at twenty months, children of talkative mothers averaged 131 more words than children who had less chatty mothers. At age two, the gap had almost doubled, to almost 300 words. One has to worry about the impact of substandard day care, particularly in the first two years of life, when vital neural connections are being formed.

Even privileged kids today have so little time to just be kids. Instead of being allowed to swing on tire swings, make mud pies, or read comic books, many of them are placed on the academic "fast track" from birth. New parents are snapping up educational toys, Mozart CDs, and flash cards, with the goal of giving Junior an edge over his less fortunate peers. Children are hustled by frazzled parents from school to soccer practice to piano lessons to computer camp. There are even tapes being marketed to give babies a head start while they are still in the womb, via Mom wearing headphones on her bulging stomach!

We may think we're stimulating our children to be geniuses, but in fact we're overstimulating them to exhibit characteristics of ADD while robbing them of their childhoods. These children of "fast-track" parents are destined for a highly structured life of rigor and competition almost from the crib as they become alter egos of their highly successful, driven parents. Andrée Aelion Brooks, a noted journalist and lecturer who specializes in family issues, writes, "With their heavy emphasis on achievement it is hardly any wonder such parents typically insist that these children receive a blue-chip education at the finest private or public schools, enriched by the best extracurricular activities money can buy—ballet, horseback riding, skating, gymnastics, music, or karate lessons. It used to be one or two of these. But more and more children are taking part in all of the above, or at least almost all. Often very little unstructured playtime is left in any day."

As parents push their children to achieve higher and higher goals, one has to wonder: Who is this really for? Certainly parents should expose children to a variety of pursuits to see if anything strikes a chord. But all too often parents are in the driver's seat, insisting that their children take piano lessons, or French lessons, or go to computer labs when the child would rather climb trees or engage in imaginary play. Dr. Benjamin Bloom, author of *Developing Talent in Young People*, has studied people who've climbed to the pinnacle of success. He finds that superachievers were all *exposed* to their fields of expertise as children and then *allowed to fall in love with them on their own*. The sheer joy of the sport or activity comes first, providing the foundation for the drive and discipline to succeed.

Children who are whisked among too many choices may find it difficult to become immersed in any of them. When faced with the pressure to choose from soccer, Little League, swimming, hockey, piano lessons, art class, and science camp, they are tempted to say "all of the above," lest they miss something; their antennae are always up. They want to keep up with their peers, and their guilty or competitive parents want to make sure *they* keep up with the Joneses. As a defense against excessive stimulation, children resist delving too deeply into any one activity. How ironic that their parents then criticize them for not being able to focus intently on a single activity in school!

We're only beginning to turn a critical research eye to the question of how our stressful culture is affecting children's minds. A major 1995 study published in the AMA's *Archives of General Psychiatry* set out to determine if family-environment risk factors are associated with ADD. A summary of the article notes, "The findings support earlier research that a positive association appears to exist between the risk for ADHD and adversity indicators such as severe marital discord, low social class, large family size, paternal criminality, maternal mental disorder, and foster care placement." An accompanying article in the same issue points out how little we really know about ADD: "There are key questions remaining that another twenty-five years of research should answer." I submit that we can't wait that long.

The Left-Right Brain Continuum

We live in a society that shows most respect for people who are "left-brain dominant." The left-brain–dominant schoolgirl who remembers names, adds numbers properly, and works with a great sense of order and tidiness is praised and gets a star beside her name. The right-brain–dominant child who daydreams and stares at distant clouds, preferring to make up stories rather than learn her lesson, is sent home with a disciplinary note.

—Marilee Zdenek, *The Right Brain Experience*

I didn't belong as a kid, and that always bothered me. If only I'd known that one day my differences would be an asset.

—Bette Midler

Through my many years of teaching gifted children and children with ADD, I've become quite proficient at placing individuals on a "left-right brain continuum," based on their learning style and personality characteristics. I can generally assess where a person falls on this continuum by asking a series of questions and by working with him or her in a single tutoring session.

While there are some fairly sophisticated tests that professionals use to measure hemisphericity (one is the Hermann Brain Dominance Test), the following "quiz" should give you a pretty good idea whether your preadolescent child (ages five through thirteen) is left-, right-, or whole-brained:

Learning Styles Inventory

1. Is your child extremely wiggly?
2. Does your child have difficulty with coloring or handwriting?
3. Was your child a late walker?
4. Is your child extremely sensitive to criticism?
5. Does your child have allergies or asthma?
6. Is your child good with building toys, such as Lincoln Logs, Legos, and Tinker Toys?
7. Is your child good at puzzles and mazes?
8. If you read a book to your child two or three times, is he or she capable of filling in missing words with almost perfect recall?
9. Is it extremely important that your child like his or her teacher in order to do well in class?
10. Is your child easily distracted, or does he daydream a lot?
11. Is your child unable to consistently finish tasks?
12. Does your child tend to act first and think later?
13. Do you have to cut labels out of your child's clothes? Does he only want to wear clothing that's especially soft and well worn?
14. Is your child overwhelmed at sporting events, loud parties, amusement parks?
15. Does your child tend to shy away from hugs?
16. Does your child need constant reminders to do certain things?
17. Is your child extremely competitive and a poor loser?
18. Does your child have a good sense of humor? Does he have a better-than-average ability to understand or create puns?
19. Is your child a perfectionist to the point that it gets in the way of trying new things?
20. Can your child recall a summer vacation or other event from one or two years ago in vivid detail?

The following quiz will help determine left- or right-brainedness for teenagers and adults:

1. Are you better at remembering faces than names?
2. When you're presented with a toy or piece of furniture to assemble, are you likely to discard the printed directions and figure out how to build it yourself?

3. Are you better at thinking of ideas if you're left alone to concentrate, rather than working with a group?
4. Do you rely mostly on pictures to remember things, as opposed to names and words?
5. Do you have especially acute hearing?
6. Do you cut the labels out of clothes? Do you favor garments that are especially soft and well worn, finding most clothing too rough or scratchy?
7. Do you tend to put yourself down a lot?
8. When you're asked to spell a word, do you "see" it in your head rather than sound it out phonetically?
9. When you're studying a subject, do you prefer to get the "big picture" as opposed to learning a lot of facts?
10. Are you good with puzzles and mazes?
11. Can you imagine things well in three dimensions? In other words, can you visualize a cube in your mind, rotate it, and view it from every angle without difficulty?
12. Were you considered a late bloomer?
13. Did you need to like your teacher to do well in his or her class?
14. Are you easily distracted to the point that you find yourself daydreaming a lot?
15. Are you a perfectionist to the point that it gets in the way of trying new things?
16. Are you ultra-competitive, hating to lose more than most people do?
17. Are you good at figuring people out? Do others tell you that you're good at "reading" people?
18. Is your handwriting below average or poor?
19. Were you a late walker, or did you have other delayed motor skills as a child?
20. When you're in a new place, do you tend to find your way around easily?

The more yes responses you have, the more to the right you or your child will be on my left-right brain continuum. In general, 0–4 yes answers indicate you're very left-brained, 5–8 somewhat left-brained, 9–12 whole-brained, 13–16 somewhat right-brained, and

17–20 very right-brained. Again, while this is not a scientific test, it will give you a general understanding of your brain dominance.

Note: If you're working with a preschooler or kindergartner who doesn't yet have full letter recognition, you can use the following exercise to give you an early indication of his brain dominance. This is a fun activity that can give you a clue as to how right-brained and visual your little one really is.

On a piece of plain white paper, draw seven circles of approximately the same size in a straight line across the page. Randomly use three or four different colored markers or crayons so that the sequence might be: *green, blue, red, red, yellow, green, yellow.* Instruct your child to study the circles for at least twenty seconds, until he feels confident he can remember them.

Remove the paper and ask your child to name the colors from left to right, and then right to left. The results may surprise you! Most children with ADD will be able to do this by hyperfocusing and using their visual memory. Notice whether your child closes his eyes or looks upward, an indication that he's getting a picture of those colored circles in his mind.

The Left-Brained Individual

If you answered yes to fewer than nine questions, you fall at the left of the continuum. People like this love to make lists, perform well in middle-management positions, are highly logical and analytical, and are usually very reliable. These individuals tend to do very well in school. In the workforce, they may fill clerical or actuarial positions, doing what's expected of them to help the system operate efficiently. They are excellent at showing up every day but are not especially imaginative. They're uncomfortable with challenges, new ideas, and shifts in routine. When they think, they have *some* ability to think in pictures but prefer to function in an auditory world.

Left-brained individuals, when asked to remember someone in their distant past, can easily recall the name but struggle with the face or any other details about the individual. They tend to store information in names and words rather than images. They may give directions to

The Left-Right Brain Continuum

left	whole	right
schizophrenia—		
"word salad"	(most teachers)	ADD dyslexia autism

<———————————————————————————————————————>

their home by reciting a list of street names and mileages or numbers of blocks rather than drawing a map or describing landmarks. Left-brained individuals also think sequentially; it's important that step A lead logically to step B, step B lead logically to step C, and so on. They prefer to be told, step by step, how to complete a task, rather than have it demonstrated to them. When learning a new skill such as a tennis serve, they start with the proper grip on the racket, then move on to the proper stance, the right way to throw the ball, and so forth, in a part-to-whole fashion. Left-brainers digest information piece by piece until there's an "aha!"; a light bulb goes off in their heads, and they suddenly get the big picture.

Left-brained people thrive in classrooms that involve a lot of listening but not much active participation. They enjoy talking and writing things down. They generally find it easier to grasp rules of spelling, grammar, and punctuation; they more easily master foreign languages. Left-brainers tend to excel in timed testing situations and at solving problems that involve sequential logic. As children they tend to prefer group projects rather than working on their own; as adults they are joiners, and they may be quick to embrace group ideology in the form of religious dogma or political movements. These individuals like making and following rules. They have a greater tendency to accept and appreciate what they hear and read rather than questioning and thinking independently. They like the familiar and the predictable; they often feel uncomfortable with new ideas, challenges, and surprises. They shine in jobs that involve a lot of routine and are at their worst when a crisis erupts that calls for creative problem solving. This is the profile of the typical schoolteacher.

The Whole-Brained Individual

In the middle of the left-right brain continuum we find the whole-brained souls, who in some respects have the best of both worlds. These lucky people can access the strengths of the left-brained population as well as the strengths of right-brained individuals. They have a wonderful ability to shift tasks to the hemisphere of the brain that's best equipped to tackle them. When it comes to reading directions or doing a logical exercise, whole-brained people are efficient and able to sequence enough to complete the project. They also enjoy creative abilities and can paint, create music, and use their intuition. The whole-brained individual makes a good CEO, because she has both the holistic ability to solve larger problems *and* the attention to detail to apply it to a solution. This individual sees *both* the forest and the trees. However, she does have some limitations: The whole-brained person probably lacks the great organizational strengths of the left-brained individual and the creative brilliance of the very right-brained subject.

The Right-Brained Individual

The further right an individual falls on the continuum, the more intuitive and random in processing he will be, and the more apt to store information primarily in pictures. When asked to recall an event or person, the right-brained individual will flash instantly on an image, remembering even the most minute detail. For example, a right-brained person would be more likely to visualize the face of his first-grade teacher, while a left-brained individual would recall the name. The right-brained person has an excellent visual memory and uses list-making as more of a "safety net" than a necessity.

As nature gives the right-brained individual a strong visual memory, it also tends to diminish the ability to perform logical, linguistic tasks. While the right-brainer has a head start in the world of pictures, he's handicapped in the world of words. Unfortunately for him, our schools are primarily worlds of words.

The right-brained, visual child may experience a delay in auditory processing as he struggles to turn the teacher's words into a mental picture. Georgetown psychiatry professor Dr. Larry Silver, who has researched ADD for twenty years, refers to this as an "auditory lag." Silver offers this illustration: "A teacher explains a math problem. A child with auditory lag hears and understands steps one, two, and three, then misses step four, picks up again with step five, and is lost and confused. To parents or teachers talking to this child, he or she appears not to be paying attention or not to understand what is being said."

If you're right-brained, you're less sequential in your processing. While the left-brained child will build a model by following the written directions step by step, the right-brained child either studies the pictures or throws out the directions, preferring to build it his own way. Right-brained people are holistic, whole-to-part learners. They pick up skills more easily by having them *demonstrated* than by having the steps *explained*. Instead of learning to ride a bike through trial and error (getting on and falling off), they'll study how others ride a bicycle, then jump on and do it when they feel confident they're ready. They tend to be late walkers for this reason. They tend to master larger concepts first, then prefer to go back and fill in the informational gaps. While they prefer to spell visually, they can still access the left hemisphere of the brain enough to also learn to sound out words phonetically.

Moderately right-brained people enjoy doing several things at once; they may check their E-mail, send faxes, and talk on their cell phones. They prefer occupations that allow them to move around, rather than forcing them to sit at a desk. They see a minimal need for rules, are impulsive, question authority, and embrace new challenges and ideas. They are highly competitive and perfectionistic.

Right-brainers can be creative geniuses. They may be naturals at art, music, or problem solving. They are spatial and three-dimensional in their thinking; they prefer drawing and creating to writing and talking. They have a natural ability to hold images in their heads for prolonged periods of time, far surpassing their left- and whole-brained counterparts in this area. For example, many architects and builders say they can "see" in their mind an image of the finished product long before it's translated into a blueprint. Artists will report they can visualize exquisite details of a painting in their mind's eye before they're transferred to canvas. It is precisely this ability to hold images that, if harnessed, can enable right-brained individuals to succeed in an academic environment.

The Right-Brained/ADD Connection

My hypothesis is that children who are labeled ADD fall on the right end of my continuum. This is the headline: *Children who are labeled with Attention Deficit Disorder are right-brained, visual, and random in their processing.* While I know of no formal research in this area, I know it anecdotally through years of working with these kids. My premise is shared by psychologist Dr. George Dorry of Denver's Attention and Behavior Center, an expert on children and adults with ADD. I asked him one day if he'd ever seen a child with ADD who was left-brained and linear in his processing. Dorry's response: "It is the very nature of ADD to be distractible and nonlinear in one's thinking. So the answer would have to be *no.*" Dorry does add this footnote with regard to ADD children who are also highly gifted: "It is certainly possible for the ADD individual, particularly one of overall high intelligence, to have left-brained as well as right-brained capabilities. Where you see more intelligence, the likelihood is greater that the individual will exhibit both left- and right-brained functioning."

The ADD individual stands out from other right-brained children because his nervous system is on overload, and he has difficulty filtering out all the stimuli. His nervous system gives him a range of hypersensitivities. Kids with ADD literally *feel* more than do other children. They lack impulse control, have poor organizational skills, and are often clumsy. It's very common for parents to report that children who are diagnosed with ADD at age seven or eight are the same kids who were late walkers and had delayed gross or fine motor skills as toddlers and preschoolers. These children may be the last in their peer group to hop on one leg, hold a pencil, or learn to Rollerblade.

Dr. Rick Fowler, who has ADD, and his wife, Jerilyn, make the connection between ADD and right-brainedness in their book *"Honey,*

Are You Listening?" How Attention Deficit Disorder Could Be Affecting Your Marriage. They observe, "In most cases, people with Attention Deficit Disorder are extremely right-brained. . . . That's one of the reasons that ADD individuals often clash with the majority of the rest of the population. Lefties fit comfortably into our modern world. They maintain schedules and order. They fit seamlessly into the educational system because over these many years the system has been fine-tuned to accommodate and encourage the kind of thinking that happens in the left hemisphere of the brain."

Hypersensitivities of ADD Children

Imagine a submarine at sea with conventional sonar. It's able to navigate and maneuver smoothly through the ocean. Then along comes the next generation of subs with a sort of "super radar" that allows the crew to hear sounds that went virtually undetected before. It could be said that ADD and very right-brained children have this "super radar." Put simply, they have heightened senses that allow them to hear, see, and feel more than the rest of us. When I speak to parents of gifted and ADD children, I always see heads nodding around the room as I describe these sensory characteristics. As I run through the list, I can count on many "light bulbs" going off in the room, as parents gasp and say, "That's exactly what my Johnny [or Jenny] is like!"

The most common and perhaps the most interesting of these sensory exaggerations is the phenomenon of accentuated hearing. One of the most startling examples I've ever encountered of this phenomenon was with a thirteen-year-old named Herb. Herb was an ADD adolescent with an IQ of more than 140, as measured on the WISC-III, the Wechsler Intelligence Scale for Children, third edition. He struggled mightily in school with the sequentiality of the teaching style and with organizational and homework issues.

One day while working with Herb, I noticed that he could identify a word I wrote *from the sound my pencil made on the paper*, even though he was sitting about fifteen feet away. Stunned, I asked him if he could do this kind of thing all the time. Herb responded, "Of course. Can't everybody?" Clearly, he didn't realize that he had an unusually developed sense of hearing. I then asked him about the fluorescent lights in school and whether or not he could tell when one was going out, because I could. He said, "Sure. Can't everyone?" He said he could always hear the crackling sound and the different tone the light made when it was losing its power.

I asked Herb if he found this noise distracting and whether it kept him from focusing in school. He replied, "It's a big problem. Many times I lose the train of thought of a lecture because of the sound." I decided to press him further. "Do you hear every whisper, rustle of paper, and pencil tapping, and do these distractions keep you from focusing in school?" As I expected, he found that school was a veritable cacophony of sounds and distractions that forever frustrated him in his attempt to get good grades.

Intrigued by these responses, I decided to try an experiment. I asked Herb to move to the opposite side of the room, some thirty feet away from me. I then proceeded to write at random some words selected from a spelling assignment. I deliberately avoided writing heavily or making loud scratching noises, and I chose fairly similar words, such as *essentially, totalitarian, repetitious, calligraphy,* and *bellicose.* I asked him which word I was writing, and he told me the correct word without hesitation twenty straight times.

Herb explained that by listening very carefully he could formulate in his mind the letters I was making. With his heightened hearing, the sounds of my strokes were distinct to him. Herb's mother recalled how, ever since he was a small child, he'd always assumed people were yelling at him when they were actually using a conversational tone of voice.

Virtually all the children I've become acquainted with who have this learning style report unusual hearing abilities. Although Herb's degree of sensitivity is unsurpassed in my experience, most right-brained children can hear whispers at distances unheard of among the left-brained population, and they continually complain about distractions such as coughing or the rustling of paper. But while most right-brained people have incredibly sensitive hearing, they can't fine-tune it enough to hear vowel sounds. Vowels are the essence of phonics, and without the ability to discriminate slight differences among them, the student has difficulty spelling auditorily, a common problem in children with ADD.

▣   Next to hearing prowess, the most prevalent sensory characteristic of extremely right-brained, ADD children is touch sensitivity. They really do seem to *feel* more than other children do.

Any parent of a child like this will tell you stories about having to cut the labels off all his clothing, washing a new shirt a half-dozen times before he will wear it, or being embarrassed when he wears the same shirt to school for days at a time. Laurie's son Zach complains that he can't wear a loose-knit shirt because he can "feel the cool air on his skin through the holes." Wool, mohair, or sometimes even 100 percent cotton can make these children itch, squirm, and break out in rashes.

Occupational therapists often see children like this and report that they suffer from a condition known as "tactile defensiveness." What they are observing is the child's extreme reaction to touch. These children literally feel the pressure of a hand or a squeeze more than others do. A handshake or a hug that may seem mild to most people feels like a bone-crushing vice grip. Such children resist being touched, stroked, and hugged for this reason. They are also hypersensitive to the emotion of the person who's touching them, which contributes to their sensation of being overwhelmed.

▣   Sense of smell is also commonly exaggerated in very right-brained children and can make their lives quite miserable. For example, Michael will not let anyone else urinate in his bathroom. He claims that he can smell the residue for "months," and it makes him physically ill to go anywhere near the bathroom. I am forbidden to eat in Michael's presence because not only can he hear me salivating but he can smell the food very strongly, which makes him sick. At school he must eat alone and avoid the sounds and smells of the cafeteria. Michael, it must be said, is brilliant and a great artist and actor. His grades are good, though not great, because his moodiness and distractibility combined with organizational difficulties make school a fatiguing ordeal for him.

Early finickiness with food is common for children with this learning style and is usually associated with their strong sense of smell. Carolyn, age seven, is a good example of this. A colicky infant, Carolyn had been a typical picky eater since toddlerhood. But when she reached grade school, any stress at home or school would exacerbate her finickiness to such an extreme that she would eat only two or three chosen foods for weeks at a time. When I began working with Carolyn, her diet consisted of carrots, celery, and crackers. At the end of second grade she weighed thirty pounds soaking wet and looked more like a four-year-old than a girl of seven. She became weak and anemic.

Her parents were in a panic, taking her from one eating disorders specialist to another. Carolyn's teachers believed she was withholding food as a passive-aggressive expression of anger. I was able to convince them that this child simply had such an acute sense of smell and taste that most foods made her physically ill.

▣ Another exaggerated sensitivity present in many right-brained and ADD children is that of heightened sensitivity to light. I've noticed that many of these students have trouble focusing in school because of the almost painful glare of the lighting. In some cases, early reading difficulties can be traced to the fact that children cannot focus well because of the harshness of classroom light and the reflection of it on the printed page. The child reports a jumbling of the words, and the resulting frustration leads to poor reading.

A very successful technique involves having the child wear glasses that are tinted a particular color. What is probably occurring here is what is known as the "sunglasses effect": The coloring is effectively dimming the light and cutting down on reflective glare. Many children have reported that the words jumble less when they wear these filters, and they like reading more as a result.

You may be able to accomplish the same thing with ordinary sunglasses or by persuading the teacher to dim the lights in the classroom. It may also be advantageous to provide highly sensitive children with incandescent rather than fluorescent lighting, since many of them can actually see the pulsing of fluorescent lights, which is an additional distraction. Research has established a link between fluorescent lighting and greater risk of headache in the "average" person; imagine the effect that this type of lighting has on a hypersensitive child!

It's often been said that ADD children have "eagle eyes." In fact, there's a popular children's book out with this title. Author Jeanne Gehret, M.A., writes about a boy named Ben who is told he has Attention Deficit Disorder. "Dad explained that I have eagle eyes; I notice everything. But eagles know when to stop looking around and zoom in on their prey. Me, I just keep noticing more things and miss my catch."

Ben doesn't necessarily have better vision than the average student. He and thousands like him literally see and process everything; nothing is filtered. While another child may be focusing on the teacher in front of the classroom, the ADD child sees the teacher, the trees outside swaying in the breeze, the trashman, the fly buzzing in the window, and the holes in the ceiling tiles. One psychologist noted that, without exception, every child visiting his office who was diagnosed with ADD would comment on the tiny piece of paper lodged in the air vent in the ceiling. Other children would fail to notice it.

Is looking out the window during math class such a bad thing? Drs. Edward M. Hallowell and John J. Ratey give us a more positive spin on ADD in *Driven to Distraction*, noting, "People with ADD do look out windows. They do not stay on track. They stray. But they also see new things or find new ways to see old things. They are not just the tuned-out of this world; they are also tuned in, often to the fresh and new. They are often the inventors and the innovators, the movers and the doers. Good Do-Bees they may not always be, but we should be wise enough not to force them into a mold they'll never fit."

These children are "watchers," observers of life. They're capable of noticing the most minute details about a person. All of this clashes with the conventional wisdom that people with ADD are incapable of reading social situations. Why the contradiction? Because of their sensitivities, people with ADD are often flooded with information, which can become tiresome, frustrating, and exceedingly difficult to filter. The more severe the ADD, the more intense the sensory bombardment will be. They solve the dilemma by shutting down. By refusing to intake any more information, they no longer have to worry about the tiresome task of filtering. The sad reality is that nature is throwing a major catch-22 at children who are visual, right-brained learners. If it is a given that these youngsters must visualize in order to learn and that they process exclusively in pictures, and it is also true that visualization takes focus and concentration, how cruel and ironic it seems that at the very time these people need to be focusing and visualizing, they are distracted by their hypersenses.

Other Traits of ADD Children

POWERFUL MEMORY

Once I identify a child as having a right-brained, visual learning style, I can be certain of one thing: This child will also have a powerful memory—whether he knows it or not. Bear in mind, there are different types of memory. As Dr. Jane Healy writes in *Endangered Minds*, "Many times when students come to me to complain about a 'memory problem,' it turns out they are really talking about *verbal memory* for things they read or hear; they may be terrific at remembering where Dad mislaid his car keys or how to put a Rubik's cube together."

We all remember the college classmate who never studied until the eve of a big exam, then crammed all night and wound up with the highest grade in the class. It's most likely that she had a right-brained, visual learning style, which allowed her not only to speed-read the material but to recall it with amazing ease and accuracy. And what of "human calculators" who go on variety shows, dazzling the audience with their ability to multiply four-digit numbers in their heads? These individuals are also very right-brained, with the ability to visualize and hold numbers in their minds.

PERFECTIONISM/COMPETITIVENESS

Right-brained children are born perfectionists. They have such a driving desire to succeed—to be the absolute best at everything—that it can lead to paralysis. Zach may refuse to write his name because he knows he won't do it perfectly. The feeling of trying his hardest and still making a tiny mistake hurts too much. As psychologist Dr. George Dorry writes in *ADD and Adolescence*, "The marked contrast between high expectations and the reality of consistently inconsistent performance can leave the child's self-esteem looking like a car after a demolition derby, and may, over time, discourage the child from attempting to try to do his or her best." To learn many new skills, such as handwriting, requires a certain amount of trial and error, a concept that's totally foreign to the right-brained perfectionist. He'd rather sit on the sidelines until he's certain he can master a skill than risk the horror of failing.

Many psychologists mistakenly assume that these perfectionistic children have been pushed too hard by demanding parents. You can relax. While parents can certainly make perfectionism worse, this is a trait that simply goes hand in hand with being bright, right-brained, and extremely sensitive.

It may help you to cope with this child to know that, first, it's not your fault. Second, perfectionism is as much a part of your child as his fingerprint. It can only be tempered; it will never be completely erased, nor should it be. Work with your child's perfectionism; don't try to break him of it. If you confront it directly, he's likely to shut down and refuse to try. Know that as your child's self-confidence improves, you can gradually chip away at this obsessive drive to be the best. It's through higher self-esteem that these children feel more comfortable taking risks, because then failure is not so devastating. (We'll discuss specific techniques for coping with perfectionism later.)

Perfectionism is not necessarily bad; in fact, it can be a marvelous asset if harnessed correctly. The key is to allow the student to get past his fear of failure and learn to build on his successes.

Self-Deprecation

If your child is perfectionistic and competitive, he's most likely hard—even brutal—on himself. He may get nineteen out of twenty problems correct on a math test, but because he missed one, he belittles himself with comments like "I'm such a loser," "Only a moron would miss that," and "I can't do anything right." If he's trying to write a spelling word and his handwriting doesn't measure up to his standard of perfectionism, he may angrily wad up the paper and throw his pencil across the room, all the while berating himself for his "stupidity." This performance will continue in spite of the interventions of a well-intentioned parent or teacher, who may try to soothe the child with comments like "Oh, honey, don't worry about missing one problem; look how many you got *right*!" or "That's okay . . . just try harder next time." Some parents may get angry and try to argue with the child about his feelings: "Don't you ever call yourself a loser. You're *not* a loser!"

As hard as it may be, try not to take this behavior personally. Self-deprecation is very common in children who are right-brained, intelligent, and doing poorly in school. It is directly proportionate to how well the child feels he's doing in school and in life. Frustration and low self-esteem exacerbate it; it diminishes markedly when these children feel good about themselves and their performance. Self-deprecation could be considered a preemptive strike: If the child degrades himself, no one can knock him down any further. I've found that while I can't erase it, I can minimize it by doing my best to ignore it and by taking other opportunities to sincerely compliment the child on his strengths.

IMPULSIVITY

If you have a child who continually acts first and thinks later, you very likely have a right-brained child with ADD. Impulsivity is one of the most easily identifiable characteristics of the ADD child. As Hallowell and Ratey write in *Driven to Distraction*, "The hallmark symptoms of ADD are easy distractibility, impulsivity, and sometimes, but not always, hyperactivity or excess energy." As discussed earlier, these children apparently have deficits in the area of the brain that controls executive functions. The impulsive child is more likely to hit when angry, blurt out the wrong thing without thinking, or chase a ball into the street without considering the consequences. Hallowell and Ratey tell of twin boys who were described by their adoptive parents as "wild, out-of-control kids." Their mother said, "If they wanted something, they just went after it. If they were outside and felt like climbing up six feet on a pole and jumping off, at the age of four, they would do it! They had no control over their behavior at all."

One offshoot of the ADD child's impulsivity is his demand for instant gratification. This child does not pay attention to admonishments to "be patient." If a playmate has a toy he wants, he'll grab it without bothering to ask. If he wants that G.I. Joe advertised on TV, he wants it *now*; the notion of saving up his allowance or waiting until his birthday is foreign to him.

DELAYED MOTOR SKILLS

Children with ADD are notoriously clumsy. They bump into things, trip over their own feet, and rush headlong into doors, lamps, or other children. They're the kids who have omnipresent scabs on the knees, who never lose a tooth in the natural course of things, and who always seem to have a patchwork of bumps and bruises on their bodies. While certainly not all right-brained children are clumsy, children with ADD tend to have problems with how they perceive their bodies in relation to space. So if in addition to being impulsive, your child rivals former President Gerald Ford for the "klutz award," you might begin to suspect ADD.

The general awkwardness of these children, in fact, is a by-product of their impulsivity. In other words, the random-thinking child with ADD gets an idea and acts on it without thinking about what might happen. He lives "in the moment" or "in his own head," without regard for the feelings or even the existence of people and objects around him. He's far more consumed by his own thoughts and perceptions than with how he's perceived by others. By contrast, the non-ADD child is more in tune with his environment and has a better "road map" for his travels through life. He's more likely to plan his actions and anticipate likely consequences (for example, "If I jump off the roof, I might break my neck").

Signs of clumsiness or delayed motor skills in children with ADD can show up as early as infancy. These children may be late walkers, perhaps skipping the crawling phase altogether. They may have difficulty standing on one foot, hopping, or acquiring the balancing skills needed to ride a bike. Their fine motor skills are often delayed as well, to the extent that writing is a chore.

Programs such as sensory integration and occupational therapy, which are designed to get the body to function in sync, can help the ADD child come out of his own head and stop, look, and listen before he acts and reacts. While not a panacea, they can reduce his physical and social awkwardness. Many parents find that activities such as gymnastics and tae kwon do also help a child develop greater focus and mental discipline.

INTUITIVENESS

Children with ADD and a right-brained learning style are so powerfully intuitive, one might wonder whether they have a hypersensitive "sixth sense" as well. If you live with a child like this, you no doubt know how hard it is to keep a secret from him. He is extremely sensitive to your moods and expressions, reading your body language, tone of voice, and look in your eyes far better than do most people. He can tell the moment you walk in the door if you had a good or a bad day at the office. If you're happy, he'll pick up on your giddiness; if you're on edge, he's apt to act out and show anger as well.

Drs. Dana Scott Spears and Ron L. Braund, authors of *Strong-Willed Child or Dreamer?*, use the term "dreamer" to describe the very perceptive, sensitive, right-brained child we're discussing in this book. They note, "We might be tempted to think of dreamers as lacking attention to detail. But dreamers are very detailed about some things. Sensitive to every nuance of human interaction, dreamers notice abstract details such as implied meaning in a comment or facial expression. In some ways, we could say that dreamers are overly attuned to abstract detail. Their intuition makes them sensitive, but also makes them too preoccupied to notice 'less meaningful' details of life, such as clutter and dirty dishes." I believe that an integral part of having a right-brained, visual learning style is having the ability to jump from one's own head into the heads of others. Renowned autistic Temple Grandin even speaks of the ability to crawl into the heads of animals.

This gift of perceptiveness is a mixed blessing because it produces added distractions in school. For example, Tyler is more apt to notice the edginess of his math teacher when she's had a fight with her husband than the division problem on the blackboard.

Some extremely right-brained children seem to be almost psychic in their ability to follow hunches and make predictions. Zach, at age eight, is exceptionally good at guessing book and movie endings. He shrugs, "I can see things in fast-forward. It's like a video. I see things before they happen." Sometimes to reward children during an intense work session I'll play a "guessing game" with them. I'll tell them I'm writing a number from zero to ten. They get three guesses at the number. I have encountered numerous children who can guess the number I write down on the first or second try, twenty or thirty times in a row. This is so commonplace, it no longer astonishes me.

Being a visual-spatial thinker goes hand in hand with keen intuition because intuitiveness, or "filling in the gaps," is what the visual thinker does by nature. Ronald D. Davis, a dyslexic who founded the Davis Dyslexia Foundation, makes an excellent case for this in *The Gift of Dyslexia* when he notes that picture thinking occurs at the dizzyingly rapid speed of thirty-two images per second. "This is somewhat faster than the incidence of awareness at 1/25 of a second, but slower than the subliminal limit of 1/36 of a second. So picture thinking falls within the subliminal band." He concludes that the right-brained, visual thinker will often have a thought but not be consciously aware of it. "As a result, we can begin to understand *intuition*, because picture thinking is the same as intuitive thinking. The person becomes aware of the product of the thought process as soon as it occurs, but is not aware of the process as it is happening. The person knows the answer without knowing why it is the answer."

I suspect that just as very right-brained individuals have heightened senses of touch, taste, smell, hearing, and sight (autistic Donna Williams sees dust particles in the air as "stars"), their sense of intuition, of being able to "read" people, is heightened as well. Don't ever play poker with these kids!

ADD and Related Conditions

DYSLEXIA

This novel framework from which we view Attention Deficit Disorder also gives us a new perspective on dyslexia. Dyslexia, like ADD, affects a large and seemingly growing percentage of the population. When dyslexia was first recognized a half-century ago, the definition was narrower, referring to an individual who was prone to reversals in reading, writing, and the composition of letters and numbers. Estimates at that time placed the population of dyslexics at 2 to 5 percent. Today, estimates range from 5 to 30 percent, with most experts agreeing it's close to 20 percent, a significant percentage of the population.

In recent years, dyslexia has been redefined to refer to a significant delay in processing, manifesting as problems with reading, writing, and spelling. Yale pediatrician and neuroscientist Sally E. Shaywitz refers to it as a difficulty with phonemes, the building blocks of language, the smallest units of sound. (For example, there are three phonemes in the word *cat:* "kuh," "aah," and "tuh.") According to Dr. Shaywitz, there are just forty-four phonemes that produce every word in the English language. Before words can be correctly identified, understood, or pulled from one's memory banks, they must be broken down into these phonetic units. Dyslexics struggle with learning these basic phonemes and piecing them together.

For the average child who is not dyslexic, learning these sounds comes naturally. These children are able to put phonemes together in a sequential manner to form words. But when a child is dyslexic, there is apparently a deficit in the part of the brain that handles the succession of sounds.

We're now beginning to realize that people with dyslexia are also very right-brained and spatial. These individuals have the ability to see things from many perspectives, which can be a blessing if you're an architect but a curse if you're trying to read, write, or spell. Ronald Davis writes in *The Gift of Dyslexia* that human beings think in two different ways, what he calls "verbal conceptualization" and "nonverbal conceptualization." He states that "during the period when the learning disability aspect of dyslexia is formed, between the ages of three and thirteen, the potential dyslexic must be primarily a nonverbal thinker—a person who thinks in pictures." For the dyslexic, who makes mental images as he reads, words that have no picture (such as *the* and *for*) can be a nightmare. Davis gives an example of the dyslexic child who is reading the sentence, "The brown horse jumped over the stone fence and ran through the pasture." Davis points out that while words such as *brown, horse, jumped,* and *fence* produce a picture, the dyslexic becomes disoriented and loses concentration when he stumbles across *the, and,* and again *the* in the same sentence. His mental blackboard is wiped clean by the little words, and the letters begin to swim on the page.

Dyslexics have a delay in translating words into pictures; conversely, they stumble when making the leap from these sometimes rich, three-dimensional images to symbols on a page. At the same time, as Thomas G. West writes in his wonderful book *In the Mind's Eye*, dyslexics have extraordinary spatial abilities that allow them to see things from many angles. For every strength in the brain, however, there's a corresponding weakness. In this case, it's the ability to read phonologically. Left-brained children who think primarily in words and love to go from part to whole have a tremendous advantage over right-brained students in reading. The left-brained child has only two choices when it comes to mentally processing words, left or right. The right-brained child deals with a dizzying array of choices—up, down, sideways, at a 45-degree angle, in a mirror image, and so on.

Dr. John Philo Dixon has an interesting take on dyslexia in *The Spatial Child*, in which he discusses the dyslexic's difficulty in recognizing the difference between a *b* and a *d*. Dixon says this left-to-right confusion is, in a sense, a "natural, adaptive phenomenon." He reminds us that "during the course of evolution, it was crucial that any animal learn to recognize that the lion who walks toward the left is the same lion who previously walked toward the right. Otherwise, our animal ancestors would have always seen the same lion as being two different things, and not applied lessons learned from the left-facing lion to the right-facing lion. And there is evidence that as a result of this evolutionary necessity, our brains encode spatial information both as we see it and also in its left-right reversal. This is a valuable adaptation in the world of objects. In nature, a lion is a lion is a lion, whichever way he is facing. In reading, however, a *b* is not a *d*. To the extent that a child tends to treat letters as spatial objects rather than symbols, left-right confusions will be natural."

Dixon says many reading difficulties are the result of poor lateralization of the brain. For example, a poor reader may be actively using both the left and right hemispheres rather than relying mostly on the left verbal hemisphere. This child may be more likely to throw with the right hand but hop on the left foot. A high percentage of dyslexic children exhibit this crossed dominance, or ambidexterity. Many experts agree this poor lateralization and left-right confusion are closely connected.

Dyslexics, especially those who are very right-brained, share many of the characteristics of ADD children: They're intelligent and they have exaggerated senses. One of these sensitivities is unquestionably hypersensitivity to light. For dyslexics, the glare on a page can make words appear fuzzy or appear to move, which can make reading a hopeless task. The child may have difficulty identifying letters and words, may skip words or entire lines, and will likely tire easily while reading.

But dyslexia and ADD do not always overlap, say Hallowell and Ratey in *Driven to Distraction:* "In terms of overlap, ADD occurs more frequently among dyslexics than in the population at large. However, there is not an increased incidence of dyslexia among the ADD population. Put differently, you are more likely than the average person to have ADD if you have dyslexia; but you are no more likely than the average person to have dyslexia if you have ADD."

AUTISM

Tessa was a mystery child. At nine years old, an only child, Tessa certainly appeared "normal." She was a beautiful smiling blond, always well groomed, who looked about three years older than she was. But Tessa exhibited some perplexing traits and behaviors. When speaking, her voice was eerily monotone, deep, and devoid of expression. She appeared to be extremely developmentally delayed, scoring only 80 on an IQ test. When I asked her mother what Tessa did for fun, she said her little girl lived in a fantasy world. She would play games with her dolls or with imaginary playmates; these fantasy games were incredibly intricate and highly orchestrated, and would feature unbelievably sophisticated dialogue for a child so young. Tessa would also spend a great deal of time engrossed in ritualistic activities, such as reciting rhymes, rocking, pacing around her room in circles, or spinning her hands through the air.

Tessa had a visual memory that was second to none. Her mother would shake her head at how Tessa could speak of places the family had visited when she was three years old, describing them in perfect detail, right down to the colors of the rugs or the smell of the flowers in the room. Tessa was also an extremely sensitive child. Her mother said that whenever a thunderstorm was approaching, Tessa would feel it even before the clouds had formed into a thunderhead. She said she could sense the electricity in the air. When the storm started, Tessa would retreat to her room and hide under the pillows, because the clap of the thunder was too painful for her.

Working with Tessa was an experience unlike any other. I noticed right away that she was watching me with probing eyes, scrutinizing me in a way I'd never been scrutinized before. It made me very uncomfortable; I had the strong feeling that she was dissecting me, trying to determine whether or not I could be trusted. Evidently, what she saw satisfied her because she allowed me to work with her. I noticed that when I read to her, her comprehension was superior. Yet her own reading was stilted and slow. She seemed to be trying to remember by sight what the words were, and she struggled to sound them out. Her mother told me that the school's educational consultant had tried without much success to get Tessa to read using a phonetic approach. I found that while Tessa was totally unable to visualize spelling words in order, she could remember all the letters and colors nonsequentially. So the word *lighthouse* might come back *tighlthoues*.

After just one session with Tessa, I had more than a strong hunch about her. Tessa was not only a right-brained, visual learner but she was, I told her mother, most likely autistic. Even though I'm not an expert on autism, the signs were obvious. Tessa is now getting the special help that she needs. Her mother assures me that she'll do whatever it takes to help her daughter achieve her potential. This woman's perseverance probably saved her child's life.

Autism is found at the extreme right end of my continuum; it's the most pronounced form of hypersensitivity and right-brainedness. Ronald Davis starts from the same premise, saying, "As a child, I had a problem called autism. It is like super-dyslexia, only with more severe disorientations triggered by auditory stimuli." As Davis suggests, the senses of these individuals are so heightened and overwhelmed, they simply shut down to survive. The antennae of autistics pick up so much that they lack the ability to screen the often overwhelming stimuli from the environment. When autistics obsessively pace or rock, it may be their way of attempting to make order out of the chaos they perceive.

Perhaps the nation's best-known autistic is Temple Grandin, who has a Ph.D. in animal science and is the author of several fascinating books on autism. She writes eloquently of these hypersensitivities, magnified many times over, in her latest work, *Thinking in Pictures*. Grandin recalls that as a child she hated being hugged, calling it a "great, all-engulfing wave of stimulation, and I reacted like a wild animal." Grandin also reports that loud noises actually caused her pain; the sound of a hair dryer was like that of a jet taking off.

Autistics almost exclusively view the world in pictures. Grandin writes of her processing style: "Words are like a second language to me. I translate both spoken and written words into full-color movies, complete with sound, which run like a VCR tape in my head. When somebody speaks to me, his words are instantly translated into pictures. Language-based thinkers often find this phenomenon difficult to understand." In fact, much as left-brained people have difficulty comprehending anyone's thinking in pictures, Grandin always assumed that her visual style of processing was the norm. She didn't realize that she was "different" until she reached adulthood.

Now she writes extensively about the strengths of autistics, lamenting that "there is too much emphasis on deficits and not enough emphasis on developing abilities. For example, ability in art often shows up at an early age. At meetings, parents, teachers, and people with autism have given me astonishing drawings by very young children. Autistic children as young as seven will sometimes draw in three-dimensional perspective. . . . Teenagers and adults with autism need to build on their strengths and use their interests. They should be encouraged to develop abilities in fields such as computer programming, engine repair, and graphic arts." Grandin herself used her three-dimensional abilities to design one-third of all the livestock-holding facilities in the United States.

As other autistics emerge from their self-imposed exile, they reveal right-brained genius by demonstrating other forms of spatial ability, a wonderful visual memory, or artistic talents. Do you remember the odd character played by Dustin Hoffman in the movie *Rain Man* who is obsessive and ritualistic, yet can memorize an entire phone book? Boston College psychology professor Dr. Ellen Winner discusses autism and savants in *Gifted Children*, noting that "people with autism have excellent visual-spatial abilities, as shown by their skill in recognizing hidden figures in pictures and by their high scores on two parts of the IQ test—block design and object assembly. They also often excel at assembling jigsaw puzzles, which they can solve just by fitting local shapes together, without using the overall picture as a guide."

Winner describes savants as extreme versions of gifted children with well-defined patterns of strengths and weaknesses. Like autistics, "savants tend to have highly developed right-hemisphere, visual-spatial abilities and severe deficits in the left-hemisphere function of language." She notes that their extraordinary abilities tend to fall in four general categories: music (most are pianists), visual arts (typically realistic drawing), calendrical calculation, and "human calculators" who can do rapid-fire mental math. Yet for every remarkable strength there's a corresponding weakness. In the case of autistics and savants, it's typically language difficulty and profound social problems.

BIPOLAR DISORDER

Individuals who are manic-depressive (or bipolar, as it's now called) also exhibit right-brained charactertistics. Some doctors who are not acquainted with the finer points of each disorder may confuse bipolar disorder with ADD. While the person with ADD may have mood swings, his ups and downs are not nearly as pronounced—or debilitating—as those associated with manic-depression. Dr. John J. Ratey and Catherine Johnson, Ph.D., refer to the bipolar personality in *Shadow Syndromes* as one "who delights in the tumult and glory of life." These individuals manifest extreme mood swings characterized by deep, powerful feelings of depression followed by periods of euphoria.

I've worked with about a dozen students over the years who've been diagnosed as bipolar and have discovered that while their moods swings are extreme, many are brilliant writers and artists. On their "good" days they function beautifully and can create great sculptures or extraordinary poems. At other times they are haunted by deep depression—even suicidal thoughts—and nonproductivity. Their blessing is also their curse.

SCHIZOPHRENIA

We can also find fascinating extremes on the left side of the left-right brain continuum. Psychologist George Dorry points to the example of the schizophrenic who is so far left, he speaks in what is called "word salad." The schizophrenic does not always have control over his cognitive function and sometimes wanders over the double-yellow line between reality and nonreality. While the schizophrenic can often function adequately in the world, when his neurochemistry is over-stimulated or chemically imbalanced, Dorry says he may "randomly throw out words in conversation, speaking faster than any New York cabdriver."

THE GIFTED/ADD CONNECTION

All children are gifted in one way or another, although the standard definition of a gifted child is an individual who has an IQ, or intelligence quotient, higher than 136, as measured on the Stanford-Binet test from the American Psychological Association. About 1 percent of the population fits this definition.

We're just beginning to catch glimpses of a notable overlap between the universe of students who've been identified as gifted and the population of children who've been diagnosed with ADD. During my early years as a tutor, I worked almost exclusively with gifted children who were not living up to their giftedness; this was before most of us had ever heard of Attention Deficit Disorder. Mostly through trial and error I discovered that visual teaching methods worked extremely well with most gifted children.

In 1990 I started getting referrals of a very different nature. Clients and pediatricians began giving my name to concerned parents of children with this new thing called ADD. I wasn't familiar with Attention Deficit Disorder, but I was curious about this new breed of child. It didn't take long for me to figure out that my teaching methods worked every bit as effectively with ADD students as with gifted kids. ADD children, I discovered, have the same innate perfectionism and exaggerated sensory characteristics as right-brained, gifted students. I hypothesized that children are more likely to be labeled as having ADD if they are gifted and that, conversely, children who are diagnosed with ADD are more likely to be gifted. This is not to imply that all gifted children have ADD or that all ADD children are gifted but to point out that there is a *significant overlap* between the two groups.

It's satisfying to learn that recent research validates my hypothesis. A recent study reports that highly gifted children are more likely to be misdiagnosed with ADD. In other words, while many gifted children tend to be mentally and physically active, they are not *hyper*active even though they may be mislabeled as such. Dr. Dorry has clinically observed a gifted/ADD connection as well, noting that "Children with ADHD tend to be of higher intelligence than the average. While firm research findings are not yet available, it may be that highly gifted children have a higher incidence of ADHD-like symptoms, if not diagnosable ADHD."

My program works extremely well with gifted students—with this caveat: They must be at least *somewhat* right-brained. One way to determine if your gifted child has a good chance of success with this program is to ask yourself: Is he already doing well in school? If he is, he's probably left- or whole-brained, and you're probably not reading this book. If your gifted child is failing to live up to his or her potential, there's a strong chance he's right-brained and visual, and is not being served by the system.

You will get good results in a short period of time with right-brained children with an IQ over 125 who are frustrated and doing poorly in school. These are my favorite children to work with because the results are so dramatic and come so rapidly and easily. The most difficult child to work with using this program is the one with an IQ of 120 or higher who is extremely left-brained. It's rare to find one of these kids who needs special tutoring, or, if he does, the reasons often have more to do with underlying family or psychological problems. I can only offer minimal assistance to these children and instead will refer them to a tutor who specializes in drill and repetition.

I recently had the wonderful experience of visiting a classroom designed for the gifted in which the teacher was a brilliant, right-brained educator. This is precisely the type of classroom that we need to encourage, in geometric proportions, as we enter the twenty-first century. We must find a vehicle to harness the strengths of these children, instead of labeling them learning disabled and harping on their weaknesses. These are the children who, because of their innovativeness, creativity, and holistic thinking skills, will lead us into the new millennium.

The Collision Between Left-Brained Schools and Right-Brained Kids

The problem [ADD] has been around ever since teachers have attempted to teach students subjects that didn't interest them. In most cases, it should be described not as a learning disability but as a teaching disability.

—RONALD D. DAVIS, *The Gift of Dyslexia*

Both our society and the world in general are becoming more visual. But many of our institutions, particularly our schools, have not kept up.

—THOM HARTMANN, *Beyond ADD*

The misery the child may suffer while trying to conform to verbosely dominated schools can only be imagined by those who have themselves suffered the "Alice in Wonderland" experience, the experience of being in a place where nothing can quite be put together to make sense.

—DR. JOHN PHILO DIXON, *The Spatial Child*

Why are we facing such a crisis in education? I would argue that our left-brained American schools have rarely placed an emphasis on creative, critical thinking. Our schools have historically churned out graduates who—while strong on regurgitating information—lack problem-solving skills. American children are taught to conform rather than challenge authority; the result is they often lack the ability to make connections and think in fresh, inventive ways. The traditional American school, with its emphasis on order, drill, and repetition, probably did a respectable job educating children at a time when kids were also left-brained, less hyperactive, and not so overstimulated. The problem is that students today are *fundamentally different:* Our classrooms are being flooded by a new generation of right-brained, visual kids. While our school system plods along using the same teaching methods that were in vogue decades ago, students are finding it more and more difficult to learn that way. As our culture becomes more visual and brain dominance shifts to the right, the chasm widens between teacher and pupil. Our schools are no longer congruent with the way many children think.

Calvin and Hobbes
by Bill Watterson

CALVIN AND HOBBES © 1988 Watterson. Dist. by UNIVERSAL PRESS SYNDICATE.
Reprinted with permission. All rights reserved.

When you take a historical look at education in America, you find that, sadly, our system was founded with the goal of creating a society of dutiful, obedient foot soldiers, based on the German model. Thom Hartmann makes a persuasive case for this in his insightful book *Beyond ADD*. He takes us to early nineteenth-century Prussia (now Germany), renowned for its merciless and efficient army—until the Prussian army suffered a staggering defeat at the hands of Napoleon. This so shocked the leaders of Prussia that they went on a mission to find out why their soldiers had gotten so soft. German philosopher Johann G. Fichte, in his "Address to the German Nation," indicted Prussia's school system, saying schools had failed to produce compliant pupils. These brash, undisciplined students, he asserted, went on to become disobedient and rebellious soldiers.

In 1819 the king of Prussia established a universal compulsory school system with the goal of producing dutiful children who would follow orders and later become winning soldiers. This strategy worked, at least initially. Over the next five or six decades Prussia became a leading industrial and military power, due largely to an efficient, although uninspired, workforce.. Prussia became the object of world envy, with governments sending representatives overseas to study what it was doing right. Horace Mann, one of the most influential leaders in American education, was among those summoned to Prussia; he returned raving about how Prussia's disciplined school system could be useful in America to cure social ills, tame the Wild West, and provide quality workers. Not surprisingly, American industrial leaders embraced the concept of a system that would provide colonies of compliant worker bees to labor in factories and on railroads. In the words of Hartmann, "So began the dumbing down of America."

As we know, Germany, model for the American education system, was paying a price for its short-sighted educational priorities. The same system that produced meek, compliant children also produced meek, compliant adults so desperate for leadership that they embraced the fanaticism of Adolf Hitler. They were wired from childhood to look the other way when faced with the horror of the Holocaust. Erich Maria Remarque states in *All Quiet on the Western Front* that Germany's defeat was caused by the "tricks of schoolmasters." And theologian Dietrich Bonhoeffer claims that the defeat of the German army in World War II was the "inevitable product" of the German educational system.

While certainly not *all* American schools and teachers are left-brained, education seems to draw more than its share of individuals who value compliance, order, and sameness. Charlotte's an example of a primary school teacher who is by far the most left-brained individual I've ever met. She was fascinated with a lecture I gave on differing learning styles because she'd always assumed that everyone learns the same way.

Charlotte told me of her obsession with making lists, organizing her house, and running an impeccable classroom. She admitted she had very little creativity, but she went on to say that there's a lot to be said for her punctuality, neatness, and reliability. Charlotte said she dreams in black and white, and her dreams are not particularly symbolic of anything that's happening in her life. Charlotte was amazed that there are actually people who can spell by visualizing; she said she could never see a snapshot of a word in her head. She said the only way she can spell is to break words into phonetic pieces, each two to four letters. She was stunned when I multiplied twenty-seven by eighty-nine in my head. She shook her head and said, "I could never do that."

Charlotte's reading comprehension was average; she went slowly and repeated the words in her head. She was teaching her special ed students to read using phonics, the method that makes sense for her. She was puzzled that many of her students failed to catch on with this approach. One deficit of the left-brained population is that they generally have difficulty getting out of their own heads and seeing things from another's perspective. They lack the spatial ability to see the validity of the way a right-brained child learns. In the words of Dr. Dorry, "Their comprehension of the learning process is so distinctively left-brained that they have no concept that somebody else could have a different way of processing the world."

I believe there are a lot of Charlottes out there teaching our children because the educational system is a comfortable fit for left-brainers. These are individuals who enjoyed their school experience and who thrived in the orderly, left-brained classroom with its emphasis on rules and neatness. They appreciate the predictability and familiarity of the school environment. They flourish on making lesson plans, correcting penmanship, and grading homework. They want to give back to the system that so richly rewarded them.

Dr. Dorry points out that it's no accident that the majority of teachers are women: Females are more likely to have a left-brained, linguistic form of intelligence. This can be traced back to elementary school, when, it's well documented, girls develop speech and language skills much earlier than boys.

Unfortunately, many people go into teaching by default. They can't find another career that inspires them; they may not have confidence in their skills to be successful in science, business, or mathematics professions. Louis S. Levine writes, in an article titled "The American Teacher: A Tentative Psychological Description," that one of the prime motivations for entering teaching is "simply lack of interest in any other field." Teaching is an easy choice because it's familiar. Right-brained people, on the other hand, tend to shy away from the teaching profession. They tend to associate school with negative experiences, so the last thing they want to do is become part of the system that made them feel inept. Right-brained individuals who do pursue teaching usually do so in order to change the system; they get into education with a crusader's perspective to right all the wrongs that have occurred. Unfortunately, they quickly become disillusioned with the rigidity, paperwork, and politics of education, and move on to other, more rewarding professions.

My experience with public school teaching began in 1972 when—eager and idealistic—I took a job as a high school instructor in Cherry Hill, New Jersey. Full of energy and ideas, I quickly earned a reputation as a tough but innovative teacher. For example, instead of assigning a series of book reports to my philosophy students, I orchestrated a lively classroom debate on the differences between Jungian and Freudian schools of thought. I was pleased that my pupils attacked this challenge with such passion and vigor.

I remember thinking: I have what it takes to be a great teacher! Apparently, my department chairman didn't agree. My success in inspiring students to learn philosophy went unnoticed; he chose instead to reprimand me for being one day late in distributing PTA handouts to parents. This particular administrator was also put off by my nonconformist attire (I wore a turtleneck and sport coat instead of a coat and tie) and my less-than-perfect record keeping. I was also considered a maverick because of my interest in long-distance running. I ran every day after school, prompting this admonishment: "It's very unprofessional for a teacher to be seen in shorts!"

Perhaps my biggest shortcoming—in my supervisor's eyes—was that I related well to my students, who often sought me out for advice on personal problems such as divorce or difficulties with parents. While my behavior was always friendly and supportive, this rapport was perceived as "unprofessional," undermining the distance that must be kept between pupil and teacher. Because I was different, it was assumed I was "difficult"; my one-year teaching contract was not renewed.

Because most teachers are left-brained, and because they tend to teach the way they learn, it stands to reason that they will reward left-brained, linear intelligence. Evidence of this abounds in current literature on children with ADD and other learning disabilities. Thom Hartmann correctly notes that lectures and reading assignments— left-brained teaching methods—are still the norm, even though our children are being conditioned from birth to learn through visual means. The result, Hartmann says, is that our teachers are speaking English but may as well be speaking Greek. "Until our children are again taught to be good auditory processors (not likely to happen in any home that has a TV), or our educational institutions begin to offer far more visual and stimulating forms of education (not likely to happen in these days of budget crises), there will continue to be an epidemic of children who seemingly just can't learn. And they are often diagnosed as having ADD."

There was a time, perhaps a generation ago, when it was possible and even probable to find middle and high school students who had teachers they admired and respected. This is, sadly, a rare occurrence nowadays. I'm observing a rising tide of students who say they cannot relate to their teachers. This isn't just the case for underachievers and dropouts, it's true of pupils who are on the honor roll. I work with many adolescents who have a grade point average of 3.5 and higher, and almost without exception they are a cynical lot. Not a day goes by that I don't hear comments like "My teachers are all freaks," "I've never met a teacher yet who isn't a total geek," or "Why don't they teach us something, *anything*, that isn't a lot of mindless crap?" These are seventeen-year-old cynics who are getting good grades—not because they like school, but because they need a respectable GPA to get into college or get a job. Many of them simply don't want to disappoint their parents.

I can honestly say I have rarely, in all my years working one-on-one with gifted, right-brained, and ADD children, heard a child or adolescent state that his education was useful, inspirational, or joyful. Quite a shift from one generation to another. Many students of my generation found education a wonderfully fulfilling experience that instilled in them the joy of learning. These are the students who went on to college and graduate school, becoming students for life. That our educational system is now perceived as worthless by the very students who are excelling in it is the ultimate indictment.

Ground Rules for Working with the ADD Child

Instead of thinking of your child as . . .	Think of him as . . .
hyperactive	*energetic*
impulsive	*spontaneous*
distractible	*creative*
a daydreamer	*imaginative*
inattentive	*global thinker with a wide focus*
unpredictable	*flexible*
argumentative	*independent*
stubborn	*committed*
irritable	*sensitive*
aggressive	*assertive*
attention deficit disordered	*unique*

—DR. THOMAS ARMSTRONG, *The Myth of the ADD Child*

Now that you have a clear picture of the special qualities of the ADD, right-brained child, we'll begin work on harnessing his strengths. The beauty of this program is its simplicity: You need not be a professional educator to work with your child at home and help him discover what he does well. You can also show this book to your child's teacher or tutor and ask him or her to try these methods with your child. While all children learn at their own pace, you can expect to see tangible results within just a few work sessions if your child has a visual, right-brained learning style and you observe a few basic rules.

Don't Pressure

We all want the best for our children, and we want to push them to reach their potential. But for children with ADD, too much pressure has the unintended effect of sabotaging learning. Andrew and Jay are good examples of what happens when very sensitive, right-brained, ADD children are pressured by well-meaning parents and teachers.

Andrew is a charming seven-year-old blond who is small for his age and slight of build. He is a very bright second grader who, despite his teacher's diligent efforts, is not reading. Andrew has a very involved mother who praises him constantly for his memory and intelligence, and points out to all her friends what a gifted child he is. Andrew, however, interprets his mother's boasting as pressure to live up to his "giftedness." Bright boy that he is, he has become adept at finding ways to avoid reading and any other tasks that he might not do perfectly. He reasons that he can't fail if he isn't really trying.

I have been working with Andrew once a week for several months, teaching him to read using the visual method I'll describe later in this chapter. I have thrown phonics out the window, capitalizing on Andrew's wonderful memory. He has learned to enjoy reading and and has become quite good at it. Sadly, the story doesn't end here, because the pressure from his mother has simply shifted to other areas. She is constantly harping on him to finish his homework, get perfect scores on spelling tests, and score the most goals on his soccer team. Andrew can never meet his mother's high expectations.

At age eleven, Andrew goes so far as writing a suicide note and carrying his father's loaded gun into his bedroom. His mother intervenes before he can harm himself, shrieking at him for considering such a foolish thing and locking up all the weapons in the house. When I later ask him why he wants to kill himself, Andrew responds, "Life sucks. No matter what I do, it's not good enough. I'm such a loser."

Jay, age nine, brings home a report card with all A's and one B. Instead of acknowledging his success, his father says, "What's with the B? With a little more effort you could get all A's. Just work harder next time." Jay responds by getting all D's and F's the next semester. When I ask him about it, he shrugs and says, "If my dad criticizes me for a B, what hope is there? I might as well get all F's. They'll say the same thing, only louder. At least I don't have my hopes raised and then dashed again." What Jay is saying is that if you can't make your father proud of you, make him ashamed of you. Be the best at being the worst.

One of my students, sixteen-year-old Ben Sotelo, is labeled ADD and hates school. Ben wrote this bitter and poignant poem to express his powerful feelings about having ADD.

The Outcast

I have always been the outcast,
The one to be made fun of,
The one picked last,
The one singled out by the teacher,
The one to be cast out first,
The one never to be loved.
I have hated who I was since birth,
I have always known I was different,
I would always be the last to be loved,
Everyone knew it,
But no one ever cared.
I have always hidden from the Truth,
I never wanted to be Alone,
I never wanted to be thrown to the wayside,
I have hated the outside world,
I cannot stand the presence of another.
I have been struck down,
But never got up to fight back,
I have always turned the other cheek,
Brushed myself off,
Only to be thrown down again.
I have concluded
That there is only one way I can escape,
This tortuous life,

Is to end it. . . .
To be looked over a whole life,
Is devastating,
It's horrible for a child,
To live with these burdens,
It's taken a long time,
To face these problems.
Now I am angry at those who have crossed my path,
And will destroy any who do it again.

Such anger! Ben, Andrew, and Jay are extreme examples of what labeling and parental pressure can do to children, particularly children as sensitive and intelligent as these are. While some children do respond well to pressure and enjoy the challenge of trying, failing, and overcoming, it's rare to find them within the ADD/right-brained population.

Jacqulyn Saunders and Pamela Espeland write of the crippling effects of perfectionism in their book *Bringing Out the Best: A Resource Guide for Parents of Young Gifted Children:* "Many high-ability children confuse their ability with their self-worth and define themselves in terms of their accomplishments. They become perfectionists—prisoners of their own success for whom nothing but the best is good enough."

In working with your child, recognize from the outset that he is already a perfectionist and is extremely hard on himself. Coercion will not work with these kids, nor will pointing out their every mistake. As difficult as it may be, repress any expectations you may have of your child. He's highly perceptive and hates to disappoint you. The fear of failure may overwhelm him if he senses your expectations are too high. He will give up rather than run the risk of trying and letting you down.

Thomas G. West notes that people with dyslexia and other learning disabilities tend to reach a crisis stage in adolescence and early adulthood. They are wrestling with the internal conflict of knowing they have great talents but also substantial difficulties. It's the difficulties, of course, that get all the attention. "This condition may be especially intensified with the most highly gifted," West writes. "They feel the wrenching conflict of knowing they are really brilliant, at least in some areas, while their ability and measured performance in other areas may be decidedly poor. They feel they have something to give but have not yet found a way to have their work accepted. Too often, the special talents may be totally obscured by their deficiencies and the inexplicable difficulties. And throughout, their teachers and parents can see the confusing pattern only as stupidity, laziness, or willful contrariness."

To minimize pressure on your child when beginning this program, be nonchalant. You might suggest, "Johnny, why don't we sit down after dinner tonight and do some special reading—just you and me?" You might promise a reward afterward, perhaps something your child enjoys doing with you, such as a game of table hockey or checkers. Your friendly and casual manner will let him know that there's no agenda, no expectations.

Finally, reinforce—whenever you can—how much you love your child, no matter what. *Bringing Out the Best* offers one game that I find especially appealing. It's called "I-love-you-because," and it can be played anywhere, including waiting rooms and on long car trips. The authors advise, "Start by saying to your child, 'Do you know why I love you? I love you because_____.' Fill in the blank with anything appropriate. Then the child gets a turn, and it's back to Mom or Dad. Reasons for loving should cover a wide spectrum—from having freckles, to taking baths, to being good at numbers or reading. They can even be silly: 'I love you because the sky is blue' is child-sized humor, but it also implies that your child is worth loving just because he or she is part of the scheme of things, like the sky.

"The game ends when you say, 'I love you because you are_____.' Fill in this blank with your child's name."

Use Positive Reinforcement

Especially at the outset, reward effort, not results. The results will come later, after your child's confidence and enthusiasm for learning build. Always praise, don't criticize your child. If your child makes a mistake, as hard as it may be, gloss over it for the time being. The time to correct mistakes (gently) is after he has completed the task and you've gushed with enthusiasm at his effort.

There is a right way and a wrong way to praise. Try to avoid making sweeping statements like "I'm so proud of you," "You're such a genius!" or "You're going to be the smartest kid in your class." These comments, while well intentioned, can be misconstrued by your child as more pressure. It is much better to validate specifically what your child is doing well: "I love the way you're able to focus so well," "You really put a lot of effort into that math problem," "I'll bet it feels really good to spell that hard word!" Take yourself out of the picture and let your child own his successes. This will internalize his drive to excel and keep you out of the nagging role. Help your child understand that he's accomplishing things for himself, not to please you.

Positive strokes are especially important for right-brained children, who really do *feel* more. Left-brained children don't have as much of a tendency to internalize criticism; they'll more logically cope with corrections and suggestions without taking them personally. The right-brained child, who is more emotional and sensitive, will magnify the criticism and be unable to learn from the experience. If you tell him ten good things about his work but mention one minor area that needs improvement, that one negative comment is what he'll remember and blow out of proportion.

Aim High

Believe in your child's abilities, and he will go to the moon for you. ADD and right-brained children don't learn in a step-by-step manner, so it's possible to jump ahead to more difficult concepts to build confidence, with surprisingly good results. An example might be attempting seventh-grade algebra with your fourth grader. You might say, "This is *so* hard. There is almost no chance that someone your age could do it, so don't worry about getting it wrong. Most people would get this wrong anyway. Go ahead and try. No one expects you to get it right the first time."

Most students, especially those who are right-brained, savor a good challenge. A far cry from the stereotype we've given them, today's children are not "slackers"; in fact, revealing new research finds they want *more* challenges in school. A 1996 national survey called "Getting By: What American Teenagers Really Think About Their Schools" asked thirteen hundred students about their attitudes toward teachers, homework, and discipline. The study, from the nonprofit agency Public Agenda, found that *half* of high school students say their schools fail to challenge them to do their best. This yearning for a tougher curriculum is consistent among all socioeconomic groups, rich and poor, white and minority, suburban and inner city. Jean Johnson, one of the study's authors, says, "The kids themselves are clearly saying they are asked to do relatively little and could do a lot more. They have a high regard for teachers who are demanding, and there is almost a hunger to be pushed further."

So don't be surprised to discover that this technique works almost every time. The child who was reluctant to try even grade-level work will rise to the challenge of an "impossibly hard" task and do remarkable things. One reason this strategy works is that in the face of difficult tasks, children with ADD can hyperfocus, which allows them to visualize. They tend to trip up more on easier tasks, during which their minds wander and they lose their powers of visualization. But once your child is confidently doing seventh-grade math, he'll find it far less intimidating to go back and fill in the gaps, tackling fourth-, fifth-, and sixth-grade math concepts with greater ease.

Make Tutoring a Priority

We all lead such crazy lives, it's difficult to find time for what really matters. But if you can set aside ten minutes a day for your child, it will pay off in huge dividends. Skip your habitual after-dinner TV show or incorporate tutoring into bedtime story time.

You know your child's rhythms and temperament better than anyone else. Choose a time to work when he's feeling happy, energetic, and willing to try new things. If your child is tired, hungry, and frustrated at 5:00 P.M., it's not a good time for a tutoring session. If possible, try to work the same time each day to give your ADD child the structure and consistency he needs, while making this special time a part of your daily routine.

Pick a Quiet Place

For obvious reasons, the ideal place to work with the ADD child is one with minimal distractions, such as the child's room or your study. Make sure you're away from television, the telephone, siblings, and any other tantalizing diversions. Experiment with different locations to see which works best. Working with your child is your highest priority, so treat it as such. Let your answering machine or voice mail pick up the phone. Shoo brothers and sisters away, and make it clear to everyone that this is uninterrupted time for the two of you. It's only ten or fifteen minutes a day, so make it count!

Don't Insist That He Sit Still

Especially if your child is ADHD (with hyperactivity), he literally needs to move to think. He can still be listening and learning even if he's wiggly or moving about the room. Some teachers of ADD students give them two chairs in the classroom and the freedom to ricochet back and forth from one to the other. It sometimes helps to do something physical with an ADD child, such as stretching or shooting a few hoops, before settling down to work. This helps him burn off excess energy and prepare to focus.

I often work with children who play musical chairs around the dining room table or even crawl under the table during lessons. As long as your child is paying attention, don't get into a power struggle over his hyperactivity. You may be surprised to find he's actually absorbing what you're saying while he's doing his Energizer Bunny act.

Choose Material That Is Novel and Relevant

I'm continually amazed at children who are labeled ADD and hate lectures, textbooks, and worksheets at school but can focus for long periods of time while putting together Legos at home. It seems that when the child finds work interesting and relevant, he doesn't really have ADD at all. In fact, even the most distractible child has the ability to hyperfocus if the material interests him. Your challenge is to find subject matter he enjoys: If your child is fascinated by sharks, pick a book on sharks to work on reading. If he's into Matchbox cars, use cars to illustrate simple math concepts. You're only limited by your imagination!

It's important that the curriculum for children who are right-brained and/or ADD be not only relevant but stimulating. It may seem a paradox, but children with ADD actually need *more* stimulation to learn than does the average child. Dr. Thomas Armstrong, in *The Myth of the ADD Child*, says ADD kids are not overstimulated but *underaroused:* "[ADD children] appear to require a larger dose of stimulation from the environment than the average person, and if they don't get it, then they attempt to create it by making their own stimulation (i.e., through hyperactive behavior)." The best curriculum for the right-brained child includes hands-on and experiential activities such as building models, measuring things, performing science experiments, and going on field trips. Remember: Learning doesn't just occur in the classroom.

Give Him the Big Picture

This is a critical point to remember: The holistic, right-brained child will find it much easier to attack a task if he knows where he's going first. Think of how he, and most kids like him, learned to walk. Rather than going through a tedious process of trial and error, the right-brained child is more likely to observe walking for months, then suddenly get up and go. He may pick up sports in the same way, watching other children swim or play hockey and then taking the plunge into the pool or on the ice before he has learned the intermediate skills. He doesn't learn to ride a bike by being told, "Put your left foot on this pedal, now the right on this pedal, now push down and then stroke up." He jumps on and rides, and only later does he figure out how to work the gears and the brakes. Look out!

Barbara Meister Vitale has a good illustration of this point in her book *Unicorns Are Real: A Right-Brained Approach to Learning*. She tells of some children who had difficulty with puzzles and were labeled as having severe eye-hand motor coordination problems. "I watched these kids and they were movers. They were up and down, in and out, and they'd rather draw pictures along the side of the Dittos than anything else. They were having a great time. They just couldn't put puzzles together. So I took the puzzle and put it together for one child. Then I had him take one piece at a time, move it to one side, and put it back in place again. He had no trouble. Next I dumped the puzzle onto the desk and he put it together beautifully. Why? Because I had shown him what it looked like when it was all put together."

Another example of whole-to-part learning comes from Jacqulyn Saunders and Pamela Espeland in *Bringing Out the Best: A Resource Guide for Parents of Young Gifted Children:* "Imagine the ski instructor who teaches children to ski by first having them practice putting on ski equipment. Once they can manage this, the instructor has the children move on to learning to ride the lift, and afterward to stationary drill-and-practice in the configurations required for turning and stopping. Only then are the children allowed to go down an actual hill —provided they haven't yet retired permanently to video games in the chalet. Those few children who do persist may never feel the kind of exhilaration essential to developing a love of skiing."

Your right-brained, ADD child needs to know the final destination before you hand him a road map and directions on how to get there. If you're building a model plane, show him the finished product on the box *before* handing him the step-by-step instructions (many right-brained kids don't need the directions anyway). Fill a bottle to illustrate the concept of volume before hitting him with the formula $v = lwh$. This holistic way of teaching is congruent with the way right-brained people think.

Use Humor

It's no surprise that studies have found that healthy families laugh . . . a lot. We tend to take life so seriously sometimes as we face daily the pressures of work and running a household, in addition to parenting a demanding child. It's certainly normal to feel low if you have a child who is unhappy and is doing poorly in school. Remind yourself every day to lighten up, to look for humor in everyday situations, and to enjoy a belly laugh with your child. Right-brained, gifted, and ADD children tend to have a sophisticated sense of humor, "getting" the jokes and puns that go over the heads of other children. Use laughter liberally during tutoring sessions to help your child relax, let down his walls of perfectionism, and enjoy being with you.

Kids find it hilarious that I dress like them and imitate their lingo and mannerisms, slapping them "high fives" when they do a good job or poking fun at myself for being "phat" (the '90s teen word for cool). While you don't have to go this far and regress to being a teenager, using humor and slang are great ways to break the ice and help your child understand from the get-go that this is *not* the same old way of teaching to which he's become accustomed.

Laughter is, indeed, the best medicine. Liberal doses of laughter have been shown to actually boost the immune system and give us a better sense of well-being; it's certainly one of the best ways I know to forge a better bond with your child.

Teach Him How to Make a Picture in His Head

As I've explained, my years of experience in tutoring ADD and pseudo-ADD (right-brained) children convince me that, without exception, these children are visual learners with amazing powers of memory. Therefore, as Dr. Armstrong says, "students can be helped to look at their 'inner blackboard' (for some kids labeled ADD it may be more of a mental movie screen or other highly dynamic image). They can place onto their mental screen spelling lists, times tables, math formulas, or other material to be learned." Once a child masters this concept, he's entering an arena of strength (visual memory) rather than trying to improve on a corresponding area of weakness (phonics, auditory processing).

If your child is right-brained, for him reality is a series of pictures that are random, usually colorful, and, in extreme cases, devoid of sound. I find it fascinating that the same child who cannot recall one word of a teacher's lecture on World War II has total recall of a television show on dinosaurs. The trick is to take this innate visual ability and "aim" it at concepts such as math, reading, and sequencing.

To give your child a feel for what it means to visualize, tell him to close his eyes and make a movie in his head of himself completing a string of tasks you might describe (not to actually do them). Give the instructions slowly to allow him time to turn them into a picture. The directions might go like this: "Get up from the table. Go down to the car. Open and close the driver's side door three times and the passenger side door once. Come back upstairs. Go into the refrigerator and get out a carton of milk. Pour the milk. And don't forget a root beer for me. Bring both of these drinks to the table. Put them down. Walk to your room. Bring me a *Boys' Life* and turn it to page thirteen." If your child can "play back" the movie or repeat the instructions back to you, he's visualizing. Note that even when given *auditory, sequential* instructions (an Achilles' heel for people with ADD), he can recall them perfectly *as long as he takes the time necessary to turn them into a picture.* This is an extremely valuable skill for right-brained children and forms the foundation of the future work that we will do.

Here's another exercise that's very effective in helping children turn verbal instructions into mental pictures: Give a sequence of numbers, such as "four, seven, three, two," and ask your child to visualize the numbers in his head and give them back to you in reverse order, "two, three, seven, four." As long as you give the numbers slowly and allow your child time to visualize, four digits are quite easy for most right-brained students. Once your child masters this with four digits, move on to five, and so on. Then have *him* give some numbers and see how well *you* do! Keep going until someone misses. Some very right-brained adolescents can start out with seven or eight digits and work up to twenty or more, given in groups of four.

Your right-brained child should excel at this game over his left-brained friends because if he focuses, he has the ability to hold images in his head for longer periods of time. Your child will enjoy demonstrating this skill to peers and teachers who haven't yet recognized this special quality.

Spelling

◱ It's wise to choose spelling as the first subject area when working with a right-brained child. The reason is simple: The child will gain a tremendous amount of ground in a short time. This not only builds confidence and makes learning fun, it allows him to glimpse what might happen if he applies his visual memory to other subjects as well.

In teaching spelling to your right-brained/ADD child, forget about all the "rules" we learned in school. Our education system is designed for left-brained children who have an auditory learning style. In other words, these kids are able to sound out consonants and vowels from left to right to form words.

While traditional schools are bombarding kids with phonics, right-brained children struggle to spell that way. Children with ADD may discern consonants to some degree but typically lack the ability to fine-tune their hearing enough to differentiate between subtle vowel sounds. I myself cannot hear the difference between the short *i* in the word *big* and the short *e* in the word *step*. But I can hear consonants and some of the long vowels, such as the *o* in *overt* or the *u* in *use*. There is a strong correlation between how poorly a student responds to phonics and how well he does in visualizing whole words.

Children who are ADD and right-brained are "spatial" in their processing, which makes them more prone to inversions (reversing letters). It's not all that unusual to see them write their names in a perfect mirror image. This would be fine if your child is learning Chinese, but it makes English a real challenge. Because of your child's visual and spatial way of thinking, he may also write his name in a circle or a square. His ability to visualize in three dimensions allows him to rotate a word like cat in his head, seeing it from above, from underneath, or as a mirror image. This ability, while an asset for artists and architects, can be a nightmare for children trying to nail down words and reproduce them in left-to-right fashion on a lifeless page. I believe that this is at the core of what is labeled dyslexia.

Use Color

Our left-brained schools teach spelling in black and white, usually using white chalk on a blackboard. So for right-brained children we're going to be more innovative and make liberal use of color. Sydney Zentall, a professor of special education at Purdue University, has found that color can capture the attention of children labeled ADD and improve their skills in copying written material. She also finds that when ADD children see letters on a screen, they're much more likely to pay attention if the letters are in color. I've been using this technique with right-brained and gifted children for years, and I can attest that color *does* make a difference.

Let's begin our first spelling lesson with some white unlined paper and colored pencils, crayons, or markers. Choose a word that is slightly more difficult than what your child is presently capable of spelling.

Write out the word—for example, *cartographer.* Instead of writing the whole word in a single color, aid your child's power of visualization by breaking the word into syllables and using a different color for each syllable. *Car* might appear in red, *to* in blue, *gra* in yellow, and *pher* in green. Write the word in big letters, filling the entire page.

Hold the paper at least one foot away from your child. Direct him to look at the word until he can see it in his mind. He may see just the letters, or he may see the word *and* a picture of what it represents. Both will help his ability to spell. Some children prefer to close their eyes or to look at the word and then away until they can remember what the word looks like. It's important not to rush this step. Ask your child to take as much time as he needs to get a picture or a snapshot of the word in his mind. I insist on at least twenty seconds of processing time.

Once your child has had time to see the word in his head, turn the paper facedown. Instruct your child to spell the word *out loud.* The reason we begin with oral spelling is that while writing the child is looking down, which is not optimal for retrieving visual images. Your child will be much more likely to succeed with spelling initially by spelling out loud.

If your child is successful at this task, ask him to spell the word backward. If you have a truly right-brained child, you'll be amazed that he can spell backward as easily, or almost as easily, as forward. Many of my students are able to spell words such as *existentialism* and *microbrainscanology* forward and backward without missing a beat.

Once you've gotten your child's attention, it's easy to move on to other words and inject some variety into spelling by asking questions such as, "In the word *cartographer*, how many *a*'s are there?" "How many *r*'s?" "This word has twelve letters. What's the ninth letter?" Constantly express amazement when your child is able to come up with the correct answer. Let him know that many kids who get all A's in school could never hope to remember long words like this. This taps into your child's perfectionism and drive to be the best, and can make even the most reluctant speller enthusiastic in just one session.

Spelling this way is no big deal for the right-brained, ADD population, although left-brained spellers may consider it somewhat freakish. The visual learner simply remembers the way words look. Just as nature gives him a powerful memory, it takes away from his auditory processing. The same child who can spell *collaboration* forward and backward will have a difficult time trying to spell it the way it sounds.

Some lucky individuals have the ability to do both visual and auditory spelling, but most of them will lack either the tremendous ability of the extremely right-brained person to visualize or the finely tuned phonetic success that left-brained spellers can achieve.

After working with your child on individual spelling words—perhaps three or four each day for one week—switch to easier words, adding more of them. For example, for a typical third grader you might write in different colors:

gentle
lion
return
tender

Use the same visual technique as described before and watch him build on his successes. Again, *it's important to tell your child not to attempt to spell the word unless he can "see" it.* Never stray from this principle. If the child isn't getting a picture of the word, he's most likely being distracted and is not visualizing.

The next step in spelling is to have your child select several words from a favorite text. Instruct your child to underline the words, study them, and spell them forward and backward.

After a half-dozen sessions of visual spelling from a text, your child is ready to take the word from his visual memory and commit it to paper. Pick an appealing book, such as *The Hobbit*, and underline several words, each about eight or nine letters long. Ask your child to look at the words one at a time, then all at once. Say, "Can you see all of them? If so, spell them."

It's important to instruct your child to keep visualizing the word and "go back into the picture" before writing each letter. Visual spelling is such an acquired skill and is so rapidly developed in your right-brained child that it will soon become obvious to all that this works much better than the old-fashioned method of painfully trying to sound out words. It's amazing to see a child who hates spelling and misses half the words on his tests suddenly get hundreds in spelling and actually look forward to learning new and more difficult words!

At this stage it's no longer necessary to have the child spell backward. Spelling backward is a tool that is used early in the process to get the student to focus more intently on the visual image. A child cannot spell backward easily unless he's truly seeing the words. Spelling backward is also a novelty skill that can boost a child's confidence and help him realize that, at least in this arena, he's better than most students.

Spelling Games

Since most right-brained children are competitive, have a good sense of humor, and enjoy novelty, you'll get a lot of mileage out of playing spelling games with them. Spelling doesn't have to be drudgery!

Pick up a good book, dictionary, or encyclopedia. Decide in advance how long the words will be, depending on your child's level. Select a word for your child to spell. Let him either write out the word or study it on the page, with no time limit. Then have him attempt to spell the word out loud from memory, both forward and backward. Give him one point for correctly spelling it forward, and one point for correctly spelling it backward. Keep score. Then let the child pick out a word for *you* to spell (it can be harder if you want to handicap the contest). This is not only a fun game to play with your child, but it will also give you a good feeling for how visual and right-brained *you* are. For many parents this is quite a revelation.

I often play this spelling game with fourteen-year-old Tim, an exceptional artist who creates brilliant computer graphics but used to insist that he couldn't spell anything. When I started to work with him, he was labeled ADD and doing poorly in school.

One day Tim and I decided to pull names of cities randomly from an atlas. He pulled *Helsinki* for me; I spelled it forward and backward. I pulled *Shigatse* (Tibet) for him, and he easily spelled it both forward and backward. The score was tied at 2–2. Tim was so good at this game, we decided to try spelling two words at a time, then three, then four, and so on. The game went on until we both reached five words, including names of obscure Siberian villages and isolated Turkish hamlets. I didn't have to let him win; Tim always beats me because he's more right-brained than I could ever hope to be. But in the meantime, we'd turned a mundane study session into a fun half-hour that has not only taught Tim spelling and visualization but has increased his understanding of geography to boot.

Another fun and educational spelling game you can use is much like the hangman game we played when we were kids. Jon, age sixteen, is a high school sophomore who is weak in spelling and has a list of twenty spelling words he needs to memorize by Friday. The words range from *assembly* to *xenophobia*. We have the spelling list in front of us for this exercise, but we don't use pencil and paper. It's all done in our heads.

Jon chooses a word from the spelling list (it's *cacophony*, but I don't know that) and tells me that the word has nine letters. I get just three or four guesses. "Does it have an *a*?" I ask. He responds, "Yes, there is an *a*. It's the second letter." My second guess is, "Does this word have an *n*?" He answers, "Yes, there is an *n*, and it's the eighth letter." I successfully guess that the word is *cacophony*, and I get two points for figuring it out with no wrong guesses.

Now it's my turn to choose a word for Jon. I pick *mammogram*, telling Jon that my word has nine letters. He first guesses *i*, and I respond that the word has no *i*. However, his second guess is *a*, and I'm cornered. "Yes, there are two *a*'s, one in the second place and one in the second to last place." Jon now knows the word is *mammogram* and gleefully gives the answer. He gets one point instead of two because he had a wrong guess. However, I let him redeem himself and get the second point for spelling the word backward, which he does effortlessly. With fifteen or twenty minutes of this game, Jon has completed memorizing his spelling list, and on Friday he aces the test.

One variation on this game that works well with younger children is to give a series of clues to help them visualize words. For example, twelve-year-old Evan has a list of fifteen words to memorize, varying in difficulty from *appreciation* to *township*. I say to him as I pick *township* for my word, "Okay, Evan, I'm thinking of an eight-letter word that starts with a tall letter. It has a vowel in the second place and a vowel in the second to last place, and it ends with a long letter with a tail on it. What is it?"

Evan gets just one chance to guess the word and must interpret my auditory directions in order to successfully identify the word. Once he figures out that the word is *township*, he's asked to spell it both forward and backward. You can take turns playing this game, handicapping it according to your abilities. For example, while I may give Evan three or four clues for each word, he has to give me only one. Because Evan is highly competitive by nature and knows he has a chance to beat me at this game, he'll give it his all and will do a remarkable job paying attention, even though he's been diagnosed with ADD and his teachers say he can't focus in class.

The following exercises are also useful in teaching spelling to right-brained, visual, and kinesthetic children:

1. Have your child trace words with his finger on a table or on a blackboard. Have him say the words out loud as he traces them.

2. Make a "spelling tree" by anchoring a small branch in a flower pot with plaster of paris. Every time your child has a new spelling list, cut out circles, leaves, or flowers, write a word on each one, and tie it to the tree. Use the tree as a decoration in your child's room.

3. Help your child better visualize the shape of spelling words with this easy exercise: Have him print each of his spelling words on a page. Then ask him to draw a box around each word. Have him study the shape of the box in addition to the letters inside it.

4. Ask your child to type out spelling words on a typewriter or computer keyboard. Make sure each word is spelled correctly, then print them. This exercise not only teaches spelling, it helps teach or reinforce keyboarding skills.

5. Play a tic-tac-toe spelling game with your child. You can use a blue marker, and have your child use a red marker. Instead of writing X's and O's, each of you spells a different word in each square. Watch your child score in spelling as well as in tic-tac-toe!

Invented Spelling

When I first heard about "invented spelling," I remember wondering wistfully why it couldn't have been in vogue when *I* was a kid! This is a bizarre approach to spelling because what matters isn't that the child spells the word right but that he has the ability to express himself freely and creatively, unencumbered by spelling rules. Proponents of invented spelling certainly have the best of intentions: When a first grader picks up a pencil and musters the courage to write his very first sentence, you're not going to harp about misspellings.

But allowing this free-form spelling method for right-brained children beyond the initial stages of composition can have disastrous results. Because right-brained children have such a good memory, they may have difficulty relearning the correct spelling—for example, spelling it *because* after writing *becuz* too many times. Even after learning the appropriate spelling, they may still revert back to *becuz* if they're under pressure, such as in a timed testing situation.

The parent and teacher need to strike a balance between encouraging self-expression and learning spelling rules as the child masters writing skills. Once your child is writing with confidence, you can introduce correct spellings by using one of two approaches: First, encourage him to ask you how to spell any unfamiliar words before attempting to write them. Second, if he still makes a mistake, praise him first for his diligence and great ideas, then mention—with no pressure—that "in case you'd like to know for next time, here's the way to spell *because*. It's a pretty tough word."

Reading

▣   Michael, age seven, is struggling with reading. Despite an IQ in the upper 130s, he can't seem to grasp the meaning of all those strange symbols on a page. He thinks he must be dumb because he looks around the classroom and sees other children reading out loud. To protect himself from the disappointment of trying and failing, he looks bored. He yawns frequently during class, looks around the room, and searches out other diversions.

Michael is typical of many right-brained and ADD children who find reading, particularly reading out loud, a tremendous source of frustration and embarrassment. They are faced with the challenge of seeing words, turning them into pictures in their heads, then verbalizing them. Because they tend to be more distractible and to process information more randomly, their eyes may jump ahead or behind the word they're supposed to be reading. The result is choppy, nonfluent reading. They may miss the "little" words, skip lines, and generally be poor oral readers. Yet these same children can be exceptional silent readers once they understand the concept of turning words into mental pictures.

Barbara Meister Vitale writes about our traditional classroom approach to reading in *Unicorns Are Real*, noting that "today, most reading instruction is aimed at the left hemisphere. It is logical and sequential. Phonics is built on part-to-whole, on sequence. Learning the sounds is done part-to-whole, in sequence.

"But what happens to the children who have to learn whole-to-part? What happens to the child in school who cannot learn phonics, who can learn only the whole word? He stays in phonics until the third grade—and he still cannot read! He's started on his career of failure in school."

Does late reading make him a failure? While you may be wringing your hands over your child's reading difficulties in first and second

grade, it may be reassuring to know that there is no association between early reading and high IQ and/or later academic success. Many
late bloomers take comfort in the fact that Albert Einstein was inconsistent at best in his early school years; some writers and researchers
have considered this great man to have been dyslexic. As Thomas G.
West writes, "Einstein had trouble learning and remembering facts,
words, and texts, but he was a teacher to the world. He was slow to
speak, but in time, the world listened."

George S. Patton, one of the best-known military leaders in American history, was a late reader who showed many signs of dyslexia as a
child. When Patton entered the Virginia Military Institute in 1903
to prepare for West Point, his father wondered how he faked his
reading of the "no hazing pledge." In spite of Patton's poor reading,
spelling, and grammar skills, he later became an accomplished military
strategist with an uncanny feel for timing and spatial relationships in
battle.

The great poet William Butler Yeats was also a late reader who had
atrocious handwriting, was a poor oral reader, found silent reading
utterly baffling, and never did learn to spell. Yeats writes, "Several of
my uncles and aunts had tried to teach me to read, and because they
could not, and because I was much older than children who read
easily, had come to think, as I have learnt since, that I had not all my
faculties. . . . My father (one Sunday) said if I would not go to church
he would teach me to read. . . . He was an angry and impatient teacher
and flung the reading-book at my head, and next Sunday I decided to
go to church. My father had, however, got interested in teaching me,
and only shifted the lesson to a week-day 'til he had conquered my
wandering mind."

Anecdote after anecdote suggests that many brilliant people learn
to read late in their grade school years. One might ask, What difference does it really make *when* your child learns to read? Well-known
educator Carlton Washburn did a famous study in the 1930s of children in the public schools in Winnetka, Illinois. He compared classes
of children who were introduced to formal reading instruction in first
grade with those who weren't introduced to reading until second
grade. The children who started earlier had an initial advantage on
the reading test used to chart pupil progress. But the advantage totally

disappeared by the time the children were in grade four. The most revealing part of the study came years later when the subjects were in junior high school. The evaluators didn't know which children had been in the first-grade reading group and which were in the second-grade group. Observers were asked to look at all facets of the students' reading behavior. The study reached a very dramatic conclusion: The adolescents who were introduced to reading late were more enthusiastic, spontaneous readers than those who began reading early.

These data are also supported by educational research from other countries. David Elkind writes in *The Hurried Child,* "In Russia, formal education and instruction do not begin until children are age seven. And yet Russian children seem far from intellectually handicapped. Early reading, then, is not essential for becoming an avid reader, nor is it indicative of who will become successful professionals."

Elkind says forcing children into early reading can actually have *detrimental* long-term effects on children's academic performance and enthusiasm for learning. He asserts that children who are pushed to read before they have the requisite abilities to do so can develop long-term learning difficulties. Elkind theorizes, "It almost seems as if reading had been foisted upon them, at great cost in time and effort, without their having any real understanding of the value of what they were learning. They showed the apathy and withdrawal that are frequent among children who are pushed too hard academically."

Before we became obsessed with fast-tracking kids and forcing everyone to read in first grade, right-brained children learned to read in their own good time at about eight years of age. In years past, we didn't make such a fuss about the child who failed to read until third grade. Perhaps in our more agrarian society a higher premium was placed on children's mechanical skills and abilities to do spatial tasks. We weren't as likely to label children who were late readers as "slow," "learning disabled," or "late bloomers."

I have found, as a general rule, that no matter what reading approach is used, most right-brained children somehow learn to read by third grade, probably by building a decent sight vocabulary. What is it about third grade that produces this transformation? I have personally witnessed this and have heard stories of remarkable "cures" for reading difficulties that took place during this pivotal year. Usually the improvement is dramatic and comes about as the student does more silent and less oral reading. I believe the student finally understands the relevance of reading, realizes there's no way he can avoid it, and figures out how to "crack the code."

One key way to tell whether or not your child truly has a learning disability such as dyslexia is to see what happens during third grade. If he gets through the year and is still not reading, then you probably have a child whose learning style deviates from the norm enough to justify being labeled dyslexic or learning disabled.

Phonics Versus Whole Language

Why isn't phonetics *spelled the way it sounds?*

—*Mark Lowry's Fun Stuff*

There is perhaps no greater controversy in education nowadays than the debate over whether phonics or whole language is the best way to teach our children to read. Phonics represents the traditional method of teaching reading by breaking words into sounds. Whole language is embraced by so-called progressive educators who want to instill children with a love of reading and comprehension first, then worry about filling in the details (like spelling and grammar) later. My opinion may draw rancor from both sides of the debate: I believe that phonics is the best approach for students who are left- or whole-brained. For most children with ADD or dyslexia, however, phonics is a left-brained solution to a right-brained problem. It wouldn't have worked for such famous right-brained dyslexics as Edison, Einstein, and da Vinci, and it won't produce significant results with most right-brained children today. On the other hand, whole language—while wonderful in theory—has failed miserably in practice. Once an educational fad, it's now falling out of vogue, with the pendulum swinging back toward phonics.

Many experts who believe in a "one-size-fits-all" teaching approach are convinced that we'd all be better off if children received only the phonics method. While phonics worked well during our generation—when more children were sequential, auditory processors—it's not congruent with the rewired visual brains of twenty-first-century children. The more right-brained a child is, the less successful phonics will be; nonauditory learners have trouble filtering subtle sounds (particularly vowels), which makes phonics a constant struggle.

Many experts believe phonics is the best way to teach mainstream children to read and view it as *the* first line of attack for dyslexia and other reading difficulties. Yale pediatrician Sally E. Shaywitz advocates a heavy dose of phonics (or phonological processing instruction) for children between the ages of four and six as a way to remediate problems associated with dyslexia. This fails to recognize and apply the strengths of these children, who are made to feel inferior because phonics doesn't make sense for them. Shaywitz and many educators like her view these children as flawed; her writings are peppered with terms such as "impaired" and "deficits."

Yes, phonics will produce some positive results with considerable time and effort, particularly if the child receives individual instruction. But as a front-line approach for right-brained reading difficulties, phonics makes no sense; it relies too heavily on an area of weakness. To ask a child who thinks randomly and pictorially to learn to read using a method that's sequential and sound-oriented is handicapping him from the start. It may work, but it's more sensible to apply a method that's simpler and more congruent with the way he thinks. Using phonics for right-brained children is like teaching a blind child to ski by holding his hand. He may get to the bottom of the slope, but it's far better to teach him to capitalize on his remarkable hearing so he can ski on his own. He "hears" the subtle changes in snow conditions by tuning into the sounds of his instructor's voice and skis. In the same way, we can teach visual children to read and spell using methods that tap into their natural visual abilities.

While proponents of whole language understand the drawbacks of phonics, in many ways the cure has been worse than the disease. Popularized in California in the 1970s and '80s, whole language embraces the philosophy that individual words don't matter as much as instilling a love and appreciation of reading. This "anything goes" approach makes it okay for children to mispronounce and misspell words; what really matters is that they have comprehension and understand the value of reading. These are noble goals, yet whole language has been misapplied by well-meaning but left-brained instructors. Reading levels in California have declined at an alarming rate since whole language became the primary method of teaching reading. Children are ill-prepared to take standardized tests, which emphasize difficult words and their synonyms and antonyms.

My primary criticism of whole language, as now applied in our schools, is that it turns reading into a guessing game. The student is often asked to sound out an unfamiliar word without help from the teacher. This is when the excellent memory of the right-brained child becomes a curse. He looks at the first few letters of a new word, hazards a guess, and misses. Now his photographic memory associates the letters on the page with the wrong word. If the teacher catches him and tells him the correct word, his brain files that away in addition to the erroneous information. The next time he encounters the same word, he's likely to blurt out the wrong pronunciation again, especially if he's under pressure. I've seen this happen over and over again with visual, right-brained students. Just as pathways in the brain are wired and reinforced by correct spellings and pronunciations, they can be wired with inaccurate ones that are difficult to erase. It's critical to catch right-brained readers *before they make a mistake.*

Another criticism I have of the way we administer whole language is that the child isn't given enough time to process the material. If he's feeling rushed or is overwhelmed by too many sight words without enough time to visualize them, he won't remember them.

Finally, proponents of whole language make the same mistake as advocates of phonics: They believe that one or the other will work best for *all* children. My years of experience tell me that some children respond better to phonics and some to whole language. I often start the right-brained student with a sight word approach to reading that eliminates any guessing; I make sure I read any new words first. Once he's well on his way to reading, I add a dose of phonics as a finishing technique. This is the way today's emerging right-brained population should be taught to read.

Oral Reading

Schools tend to value oral reading because, at least superficially, it gives teachers a barometer of how well a child is reading. The logic goes that if a child can read out loud at the appropriate level, with a reasonable amount of fluidity, he must be comprehending the material. This couldn't be further from the truth. Oral reading has very little to do with silent reading, so as a measure of reading skills, it misses the mark for right-brained children. Remember that oral reading, while highly prized by our teaching system, is hardly a skill that most of us will use extensively in our adult lives (unless you're a radio or TV news announcer). What matters in the "real" world is how well we can master silent reading skills.

Our schools not only place a premium on oral reading, they further add to a child's humiliation and distress by doing it in a very public manner. Remember Michael, the seven-year-old who didn't get phonics and wasn't reading in first grade? Kids like Michael are already uncomfortable with reading out loud to a parent or teacher. Imagine the humiliation they feel when asked to read in front of their peers. That is why reading groups can be so disastrous. Michael reads painfully slowly, tripping over words and blushing as he makes mistakes. He's embarrassed and humiliated; he'd rather be anywhere else. Flustered, Michael tries to hurry through the passage to end the ordeal as quickly as possible. But rushing makes the problem worse. Michael is only in first grade, yet he already thinks of reading as something to be avoided at all costs.

To get your child back on track with oral reading, find a book he's familiar with that is about one to two years below his current grade level. Ask your child to read it out loud as much as he can, *slowly* using your finger as a visual guide, so you control the pace. Point directly under the words you want your child to read.

This method keeps your child's eye focused on one word at a time, so he's not jumping ahead or behind. More important, it slows down the process, allowing time for visualization to occur. If your child is very right-brained, chances are he's not only seeing the word on his mental blackboard, he's also seeing an image of what it represents.

Check him periodically to make sure he's getting both—for example, that he's seeing not only the word *dog* but an image of his neighbor's black Labrador retriever. If he says he isn't getting a picture, gently suggest that he close his eyes and visualize the word and the dog in his mind. If he's right-brained, he should be able to do this easily because this is an area of strength for him. And as we have said, this is why right-brained readers have a tough time with words like *from*, *though*, and *then*. There is no corresponding visual image for these words.

In *The Gift of Dyslexia*, Ronald D. Davis refers to these little words as *trigger words*; they have abstract meanings or a number of different meanings. He tells us there are more than two hundred of these troublesome little articles, modifiers, and pronouns in the English language. They trip up visual thinkers because they do not symbolize a visual object or action. Davis has had success in getting dyslexics to master these trigger words by using an interesting visual-kinesthetic approach: He directs students to roll out pencil-thin lines of clay to form words and then to visualize what's been created. He'll also ask children to make clay models that help them picture the word. For example, a creative youngster can depict the word *and* by sculpting a clay child, then adding another child who is holding his hand. For *the*, a student might sculpt three pieces of fruit, such as a banana, an orange, and an apple, with a clay arrow from the word *the* to the orange. Davis finds that this method helps the visual learner create a picture where before there was none.

Reading should be fun, so rather than insisting that your child "concentrate" (which most kids associate with something slow and painful), ask that he pay close attention, particularly to those pesky trigger words that may trip him up. This next step is critical: Tell your child that when he comes across a word that he has a chance of missing, *he should allow you to read it for him*. He may tell you he's having trouble with the word, or if you notice he's struggling with it, you can jump in. This serves three purposes: It takes the fear and anxiety out of having to guess at hard words; it keeps your child from blurting out the wrong word, which imprints on his brain and is more difficult to undo later; and it helps your child commit more difficult words to visual memory as you read them to him.

Since Michael cannot stand making even one or two reading mistakes without shutting down, I will preread everything, then pick words or phrases at random for him to read selectively out of context. If Michael misses a word, instead of correcting him, I pretend I didn't hear him quite right. For example, if the sentence reads, "I like horses," and Michael says, "I like *houses*," I'll interject, "You did say *horses*, right, Michael?" His reply: "Oh, yeah . . . I did. Horses it is."

While I don't confront Michael with his mistake, he still knows he misread the word. This simple face-saving technique is a key strategy in working with children like this. Some parents and educators have criticized me for this nonconfrontational approach, arguing that it enables the student in his perfectionism. I don't see perfectionism as something a child needs to—or can—be "broken" of; rather, it's an essential part of who he is, no matter how much we wish we could change it. On the positive side, perfectionism can be a marvelous asset in academics if harnessed correctly. The key is to allow students to get past their fear of failure and learn to build on their successes.

At the end of your session, after praising your child's effort and improvement in reading, review the list of words that your child did not read himself. This reinforces his visual memory and the correct pronunciation. You might say, "Now we're going to review the words that I read for you. Watch as I point at the word, and listen as I read it." It's not necessary for your child to read or repeat the word, only that he pay attention.

The next day, begin by reviewing the passage that you read the day before. But this time have your child read the passage *entirely by himself,* including the difficult words that you read the day before. You'll be amazed at what he can do! Your child will confidently read even the toughest words, retrieved from his wonderful visual memory. You are, step by step, building his sight vocabulary. Watch for the fluency; what you'll notice is the smoothest reading you've ever heard from your child.

Continue with a new passage in the same book, again reading for him the words he can't easily read himself. Keep a running list of new words that your child has learned, and pull it out from time to time as a reminder of his success. Or you may find it useful to use a high-lighting pen to mark words your child has had difficulty with and subsequently mastered. Whenever you see one of these new words in another context, whether it be in another book or on a road sign, point it out to your child. This will reinforce his accomplishment as well as establish the importance of reading in our everyday lives.

It's not necessary to work with your child on oral reading for more than five to ten minutes each day. I find that reading longer than this results in decreased performance. This type of reading is very difficult for ADD and right-brained children, requiring intense focusing. Five to ten minutes of reading with the right technique is far more valuable than two hours of using the wrong one.

Remember, your goal over time is to reinforce your child's strength —his powerful visual memory—to cover a weakness, phonetic decoding. If your child is right-brained, you and he will be rewarded with remarkable improvement. This is one of the reasons I continue to work with children one-to-one, because the rewards of teaching right-brained children to read visually come so rapidly and so dramatically.

Michael, once he tasted a little success, became an avid reader. He was tested before I began working with him and had a sight vocabulary of fewer than five words. After just a dozen sessions his reading level is mid–second grade. He can read sentences such as "The cat meowed loudly throughout the evening." He still cannot sound out words, but his parents and teachers help him by reading unfamiliar words for him. After seeing them just once, Michael commits them to memory.

Freed from the pressure of guessing at words, Michael relaxes, pays more attention, and is able to enjoy reading. His delighted parents report that he now pleads with them to read to him and even gets out a flashlight under the covers after bedtime, sneaking a peek at his favorite stories!

Silent Reading

While right-brained, ADD children may have difficulty reading out loud, nature again gives them a compensating strength from which to work: They can be excellent silent readers and speed-readers. After all, their minds work visually and often at a feverish pace. It's fascinating to observe how the most right-brained student, the child who flounders while reading out loud, is the one who is most likely to excel at silent reading. That's because reading is about comprehension, and comprehension is about visualization, a strength of the right-brained population.

The left-brained child who can read a literary passage fluently has the ability to decipher words from page to brain to mouth, but his oral reading skills are rarely associated with good comprehension. For the left-brained child to really understand what he's reading, he needs to read silently and slowly, carefully saying the words in his head. His comprehension improves if he reads deliberately, savoring each detail, pausing between paragraphs to let it sink in. Children with this learning style do well to take copious notes (they generally have good handwriting), storing the information in an organized manner, such as in a notebook or on index cards.

The right-brained child, however, is practically another species when it comes to reading. His style demands that he read quickly, scanning key words on the page, in order to produce a detailed picture in his head. The right-brained child may eschew note taking, learning more effectively by skimming the text several times and visualizing the material. His memory banks become the notebook. The first reading will give him a thumbnail sketch of the plot; subsequent readings are like brush strokes that fill in the vivid details. In many ways, it can be said that *under ideal conditions* your right-brained child has a definite edge in reading comprehension because he visualizes so much better.

Keep in mind, however, that your right-brained child is, unfortunately, highly distractible, which works against visualization and comprehension. He doesn't have the left-brained student's ability to filter out noise, which is why in a busy classroom setting he often finds himself struggling to conjure up images from words on a page. All those distractions—the student sharpening his pencil, the note being passed, the second hand sweeping around the clock—are so much more interesting!

Miguel, age thirteen, is a seventh grader at a middle school in suburban Denver. An extremely bright and creative boy, he has been diagnosed with mild ADHD and dyslexia. He's a constant drain on his teachers, is fidgety in the classroom, and is struggling with reading. Miguel is placed in a special remedial reading group in which he's subjected to daily phonetic exercises and workbooks. The constant drill kills his spirit and convinces him that he's stupid. Miguel is told repeatedly that if he wants to better understand what he's reading, he'd better slow down and read more carefully. What Miguel really needs is quite the opposite: to *pick up the pace*. (More on speed-reading later in this section.)

My mission is to put Miguel on "fast-forward," to convince him that if he rapidly scans the material, his reading comprehension will improve. I choose a book at his grade level, in this case a Hardy Boys mystery or an article in *Sports Illustrated for Kids*. If Miguel comes across a word he doesn't know, I ask him to either figure it out from context or ask me what it means.

I tell him to imagine that his mind is a TV screen; that he should be getting a clear picture in his head, just like on TV, as he reads. If he's not getting a picture at any time, I instruct him to stop reading and look away, then return to the text and try hard to "clear the snow out of the picture." As long as he's visualizing, he's reading, I tell him, and I challenge him to go as fast as he can while still maintaining that all-important picture. If Miguel reads briskly, his alert mind is hyperfocusing on the text and has less opportunity to wander.

As Miguel reads, I watch over his shoulder, occasionally asking him questions about the pages to check his comprehension. He's getting it! I smile knowingly as Miguel devours the material several times, getting a sharper picture in his mind with each successive reading. He has a natural ability to speed-read, and a light bulb goes off in his head as he understands what it means to visualize while reading. After just five tutoring sessions, Miguel can read a 150-page book in just ninety minutes, with keen comprehension. Even his oral reading improves, although that will never be a strength for him. Miguel develops a love of reading and is a prime example of what happens when we tap the right-brained child's visual potential instead of allowing it to remain dormant.

To begin work on your child's silent reading skills, start by reading to him. Instruct him to take your words and turn them into mental pictures. It might help to ask him to visualize a TV show or a movie running in his head. Once he understands the concept of visualization, tell him that it's the same way when he reads to himself: He should be getting a picture in his mind also. It might not be as detailed as the one he gets when you read to him, but he should be getting a picture nonetheless.

Then give the child a book that interests him. Tell him, "We're going to read silently now. Just do it in your head. Don't 'mouth' the words as you go." Next, preview any difficult words in the passage. Say, for example, "I'd like you to read this paragraph. You might notice these words here. This is *electric*, this word is *notorious*, and this one says *fiendish*." Again, this serves the dual purpose of reducing the pressure to decode tough words and aiding your child's visual memory without imprinting the wrong words.

Tell your child if he loses the picture anytime while reading to let you know and to hand the book back to you so that you can read to him for a short time. Once he gets the picture back in his mind, he can resume reading. Check his progress periodically, asking him to give you details about the picture in his mind.

This process helps your child make the association that reading is about visualizing. Tell him over and over, "If you're not getting a picture in your mind, you're not reading." The so-called little words like *the*, *from*, and *that* become unimportant. This is the kind of reading your child was born to do. It frees him to use his vivid imagination to take him anyplace he wants to be, and he can do it within the confines of his own mind.

More Reading Exercises

The following exercise works very well for the student who is just beginning to learn to read. Like so many others I use in my practice, it is in the form of a game. You might start by writing perhaps eight, ten, twelve, or more words on an unlined piece of paper in some form of a pattern, such as:

ask		learn
smoke		and
tomorrow	○	molar
mile		animal
today		goose

Draw a small circle in the middle of the page, give a pencil to your child, and then say one of the ten words clearly at least twice. His job is to draw a line from the center circle to the correct word. As he ponders the task, ask your child such leading questions as "How long is the word?" "What letter do you think it starts with?" "What letter or letters does the word end in?" This forces the child to look at the whole word instead of looking only at the first letter and guessing at its pronunciation.

It is important to make certain that you're using words which are somewhat similar in length and sounds, but always include a few words that will be easy for the child to distinguish. Begin with one of these to give him a good start on the exercise.

Many children enjoy CD-ROM programs, like Reading Blaster, which give points for correct answers, so I like to create a similar reward system, assigning a given number of points per correct answer and a bonus for getting them all right. For example, you might give your child fifty points per correct answer and five hundred bonus points for getting them all correct. It is then possible to go to a harder level in which you are limited only by your creativity in selecting words. It is important to include a mix of simple words, such as *to*, *for*, and *from*, with some long, difficult words, such as *existentialism*, *claustrophobia*, and *sartorial*. Praise your child liberally when he successfully identifies one of the difficult words you call out; be sure to point out that these are college-level words.

A benefit of this game is that it works on focusing the child to look at the whole word and apply whatever phonetic skills he has to the task of identifying individual words. I usually repeat the word several times after the child has successfully identified it, with comments such as, "How smart of you to know that *claustrophobia* begins with *cl* and has a *ph* in it, which sounds like an *f*." The reality is, your child probably knew none of that but did catch the *c* sound and figured it out because it was the longest word on the list. What you're doing is giving the child your method of word identification while sneaking in some phonics. You also put the child in a position in which he can learn without having much probability of making a mistake.

Once your child has the ability to focus on individual words, here's a technique to train his eye to look ahead a word or two, to produce more fluid reading. Begin by placing a pencil or pointer directly under random words on the page that you want your child to read. Choose both little and big words. Move fairly rapidly from one word to another, doing perhaps five or ten words per page for two or three pages. The speed will vary, but you should always allow two to five seconds for your child to decode the word in his mind and say it out loud. Most of the time you'll find that your child will be able to identify the word more quickly than that.

Next, tell your child that you're going to point at a word, and you want him to read the word *immediately following it*. When he's comfortable with that, try having him read the word that's two words away. This exercise trains his eye to go slightly past the word that he's on, which makes oral reading more fluid and gives him the ability to scan the printed page silently and efficiently.

Here's another exercise that works for both oral and silent reading: Pick an unfamiliar page from a book that's the appropriate grade level for your child or one that's slightly more difficult. Skim over it yourself first, searching out words that might pose a challenge for your child. Write them down in small letters on a piece of paper. Try to form the words as closely as possible to the way they appear on the printed page. If the text is appropriate for your child's level of reading, there should be fewer than ten words on your list.

Before handing the book to your child, go over the word list with him, pointing to each word as you say it. When you're finished, go back to the beginning and have your child read the entire list out loud to you as you continue pointing. Don't worry if it takes two or three tries before he gets them all right. Jump in to help if he's hesitating. It's imperative that he know all of these words before you move on.

Next, have your child read the text himself, either silently or out loud. Preface the reading by saying, "There are no words on this page you can't read." If he's reading aloud, slow him down and watch him revel in the realization that he has a good chance of flawlessly reading every word on the page!

If he's still having difficulty with the words you preselected, check to make sure you're writing them as they appear in the book. It may help to print the word list using a typewriter or computer. If you're making block letters or the letters are too large, your child won't make the connection.

After the first page is read correctly, repeat this process for the next two or three pages. Remember, your child tires easily with reading, so be watchful for signs that he's not concentrating and has had enough. At the end of the session, go back and review the entire list of words. Even if you've compiled an impressive list of thirty or forty words for more advanced readers, you'll likely find that your child remembers most or all of them, particularly if you've run interference and helped him learn the word before he stumbles on it and pronounces it incorrectly.

Speed-Reading

I suspect that if the Evelyn Woods speed-reading program gave refunds to dissatisfied customers, the vast majority of them would be left-brained. Right-brained people, almost without exception, make the best speed-readers. I discovered this quite by accident when I was studying for my master's degree in education. One night while cramming for a final the next day, I was quite surprised to find that reading quickly actually *improved* my comprehension. Just one reading would give me general concepts; when I needed more detailed retention of the material, I would scan the material three or four times.

I was amazed to find that I could read a four-hundred-page book in just one hour and scan it three or four times in a two-to-three-hour study session. By the third reading the book was mine; I could quote it chapter and verse. While at the time I assumed I was some sort of "freak" for having this ability, my work with right-brained children has shown me just how many other "freaks" are out there and how universally this reading technique can be applied.

I strongly believe that if schools could identify and use these methods with right-brained children, beginning in grade school, rates of illiteracy would plummet. Illiteracy is largely the result of teachers using improper techniques for students who are right-brained, visual learners. These children are pressured inappropriately to read at the preschool or kindergarten level, before their brain is wired to read. They fail and become frustrated. Remedial programs make the mistake of telling these kids to slow down while reading, which only makes the problem worse. In the book *Strong-Willed Child or Dreamer?*, Drs. Dana Scott Spears and Ron L. Braund make a good case for this in discussing teaching styles for different modes of learning: "Many parents assume that if a child is not understanding a concept, a slower step-by-step presentation is the answer. But if a presentation has been ineffective once, going slowly is more likely to frustrate the boredom-sensitive dreamer than to teach the concept."

While right-brained children need to slow down to read out loud, quite the opposite is true for silent reading. Oral reading is a distinctly different skill and should be taught differently. When reading orally, it is extremely important to get the child to slow down and emphasize each particular word. For oral reading, comprehension is not the main goal, but for silent reading, it's the whole ball game. Right-brained learners are not limited to reading every word and repeating it in their head, as left-brained people must do to attain good reading comprehension. Their minds move quickly and visually. They can speed-read as soon as they can master a few hundred words by sight. Once your child is able to read within one year of grade level, speed-reading should be introduced.

To get your child to speed-read, tell him to scan the page—go *fast!* —and let the words give him a picture. To determine the optimum speed for your child, first have him read at his normal oral speed, only silently. Instruct him not to mouth the words as he goes but to read the words in his head. Most of the time, especially if you're working with an ADD child, you'll find that he has a strong tendency to drift away from the material so that other thoughts and images can creep in, interrupting the visual image that the text is supposed to produce.

Next, tell your child that you want to see if he can read better, as far as understanding what the text is trying to say, if you can speed him up a bit. Tell him that he doesn't have to bother with the little words but that he should quickly scan the material, slowing down and reading word for word only when he thinks something important may be happening in the story. A good technique that I often use is that I preview the material first. Then, as the child reads it, I ask specific questions from the text. For example, I might question him about who the characters are, what they're wearing, what the setting is, and the time of day. The idea is to help focus the reader and direct his attention back to the text if his mind is still wandering. Remember that you're dealing with either an ADD child or a right-brained child with exaggerated sensitivities, and he will have a strong tendency to be distracted, especially if he has a history of reading problems. He will probably be in withdrawal mode until he achieves some success. It's up to you to create that scenario.

Especially at the outset of working with any child with reading problems, remember the key tenet is to make sure you get success, no matter what you have to do to achieve it. It is critically important that the first time you work with your child on speed-reading, you impress him with the concept that when he reads faster, his visual picture improves. Explain to him that silent reading is *really* reading, and that oral reading is mostly used as a way for adults to gauge how well children are reading. In his own language, talk about how oral reading is not an accurate indicator of how he reads. Silent reading, however, is what he will be doing for most of his life, and how well he does with it is what counts in the long run.

This reading program covers virtually all aspects of reading and is more congruent with the right-brained child's learning style than any other method being used today. These are simple, proactive techniques that don't have to be used for a prolonged period of time. The aforementioned reading techniques can be applied to not only primary students but secondary students and in most subject areas, including science, history, geography, and sociology. For middle school and high school students who are applying these reading techniques to specific subject areas, my advice remains the same:

1. Study in short bursts.
2. Speed-read the material first, going for general concepts.
3. Reread the material several more times, filling in the details.
4. Constantly monitor that you're getting a visual image as you read.

To increase your odds of success with this program, it's important that you *model good reading behavior yourself.* Banish the television from your living room; instead, keep a healthy assortment of reading materials for both adults and children on your coffee table. Have regular discussions with your child about the latest book that you—and he— are reading. Set aside some special time before bed to read a story or poem out loud to the whole family. Join a book club or reading group. If your child's school has a book club program, become a frequent buyer. Get your child a library card and make regular trips to the library with him, checking out books for both of you. Many libraries have summer reading programs that reward children with certificates and other prizes for reading. Once your right-brained child picks up on your love of reading, he, too, will find it feeds his vivid imagination and sets his mind free.

Math

◨ I've worked with many a child who struggles mightily with times tables, flops at flash cards, and fails to finish a set of problems as easy as 2 + 5. Yet after only a handful of tutoring sessions, these right-brained, ADD children can be doing complex addition and multiplication problems (74 × 3 or 156 + 398) *in their heads*. The reason many bright students are failing in math is simply the way that it's taught: through drill, repetition, and timed tests. It's assumed that hammering math facts over and over again is the best way for all children to learn, but the truth is, this method only works for students who are left- or whole-brained.

Traditional methods of teaching math bypass the right-brained child's greatest strength: the ability to access and hold images. Flash cards, it turns out, are fine if you take the "flash" out of them. They're visual, which helps children with a right-brained learning style, but they're a nightmare for ADD kids because they demand quick processing, which is not congruent with their learning style. Rush a visual learner, and he's out of his game.

Some schools, such as those using the Montessori approach, will use "touch" math techniques such as money counting, the abacus, and bead frames, which work infinitely better to illustrate math concepts for right-brained kids than memorizing long lists of equations. But even the more innovative programs usually involve timed tests and massive amounts of repetition. Because they don't learn this way, right-brained children associate math with negativity and failure. Yet if they can get past the simple computations and equations stressed in the primary grades, they often excel at the more abstract and difficult concepts introduced in geometry and calculus.

How interesting that young Albert Einstein hardly shined at simple arithmetic. His sister writes that in primary school Einstein "was considered only moderately talented, precisely because he needed time to

mull things over and didn't respond immediately with the reflex answer desired by the teacher. Nothing of his special aptitude for mathematics was noticeable at the time; he wasn't even good at arithmetic
in the sense of being quick and accurate, though he was reliable and
persevering. Also, he always confidently found the way to solve difficult word problems, even though he easily made errors in calculation."

For many brilliant and creative math thinkers, the area of strength
is mathematical *intuition*, but doing simple arithmetic calculations remains an area of weakness. The trick is to captivate and entice these
children with complex mathematical concepts—negative numbers,
squares, square roots, powers, and cube roots—*before* they're saddled
with the necessity of learning basic math facts. Once they have a solid
understanding of math and are intrigued by the concepts, they'll be
more willing to master basic processes such as simple division or
multiplication as a means to an end.

Right-brained children have a deep, innate need to know *why* they
are learning something. Almost without exception they will ask, even
at an early age, "Why am I doing this?" It's not enough to say to them,
"It'll be clear to you in time." Relevance is everything, especially
relevance to their everyday lives. Giving your child an allowance and
having him open a savings account is a great start. Encourage him to
save up for that special Lego or computer game he really wants. Have
him shop with you at the supermarket; point out the prices of various
items and ask him to help you stay within your budget. Let him weigh
your produce, figuring out how much the grapes cost based on price
per pound. Compare how much it costs for the small versus the large
box of Cheerios. All this will sharpen your child's mathematical skills
and illustrate the importance of math in our lives.

You can certainly go beyond computational math in coming up with
"real life" examples. For geometry, teach your child about perimeter
and area as they relate to building a fence in your yard or building a
tree house. Invent a problem that calculates the volume that a Coca-
Cola bottle can hold. Children enjoy word problems, such as those
having to do with how far planes and trains can travel in an hour at a
given speed. Cooking is also a wonderful way to make math come
alive. Measuring cups and spoons can be used to help your child
understand such concepts as fractions, volume, and multiplication.

I'm working with Todd, age twelve, a sixth grader who is lagging behind in math class. He is extremely bright, with an IQ of 135. The only child of affluent parents, Todd is slender, freckled, athletic, and very popular with peers but not with teachers. He has a lot of leadership qualities and is worshiped by many of his classmates, but he has a mean streak, too—the product of repressed anger about his poor academic performance—which he often directs at "safe" targets such as peers with physical or mental disabilities. He tells me right off the bat that he "hates math" and doesn't understand why he needs to learn it. While he's smart enough to understand most math concepts, Todd labors with simple computation, such as 64 ÷ 8, or 9 × 7.

My first step is to take the pencil out of Todd's hand. When he's concentrating on writing numbers on paper, he's not visualizing. If he balks at giving up the pencil and paper, I might coax him by saying, "Almost anyone can do math on paper. But I suspect what makes you special is that you—and kids like you—can do it in your head. Let's give it a shot." I begin with the number 8. There's nothing magical about this number—I could have picked 12, 16, or even 114—but because Todd thinks he's bad at math and finds problems intimidating, I start with a simple number.

I begin by saying, "Okay, Todd, we're going to do some head math. Forget about writing anything down. And don't bother counting on your fingers. Just relax, take your time, and go into your head to solve these problems." I give him the commands verbally, usually in two or three steps at a time, pausing several seconds between equations. I instruct him: "Divide 8 in half . . . now add 3. . . . Next, double that number."

Todd gives me the correct answer of 14; I play scribe and dutifully write 14 on a piece of paper. We continue: "Now, Todd, divide 14 in half . . . add 3 . . . and square that number." Since Todd doesn't know what "squaring" means, I tell him to multiply his answer by itself. When he arrives at the correct answer of 100, I write that number on my page, crossing out the 14.

Todd relaxes since this is pretty simple stuff for him. There's no time pressure, the computations are well within his understanding of math, and he doesn't have the added burden of having to write his answers legibly. Should he give me an incorrect solution, I might make light of it: "That was a good answer—it's close. Let's go back and retrace our steps to see if we can get the right number this time." If Todd is still struggling, I use simpler equations, writing the solution to each step.

Since Todd is doing well right now, we move on to a third set of computations: "Take 100 . . . subtract 12 . . . and divide by 2 . . . and again by 2." When Todd gets the right answer, I write down 22 and we continue: "Now subtract 5 . . . and double that number."

Todd is really getting the hang of this. I can tell that he's visualizing because he's not writing or counting on his fingers. He begins to smile and eagerly anticipates the next question. I instruct him to multiply 34 by 3, and when Todd gives me the correct answer of 102, I proceed: "Now divide 102 by 2 . . . subtract 3 . . . and divide that number by 2." When Todd arrives at the correct answer of 24, I again write down the number.

This mental math exercise involves auditory sequencing and also tests Todd's ability to add, subtract, multiply, and divide. The beauty of this lesson is that it shows Todd how to bypass a weak area (auditory processing) and turn it into a strength by using his remarkable powers of visualization. This drill also frees Todd to harness his visual skills without the hindrance of having to write or show his steps. I've found that when children are writing, it's more difficult for them to visualize because they're looking down at the page. Since so many right-brained children have fine motor difficulties, the very act of writing requires tremendous concentration, which takes away from the ability to focus on the task at hand.

Todd grows to enjoy this exercise, impressing his parents and teachers with his computational skills. His father reports that on long car trips, one of Todd's favorite games is "mental math." He just can't get enough of it! This success gives Todd a shot of much-needed confidence so that he has the courage to try more difficult math in the classroom. Todd's improving esteem also has the effect of making him a much more agreeable child, both at home and in school. His anger diffused, he no longer acts out his frustrations by picking on his classmates. His success in math has a ripple effect on all other aspects of his life.

You, too, can use this simple "head math" drill with your right-brained, ADD child. It makes for an excellent warm-up exercise for a tutoring session and, if your child enjoys it, a good closing exercise as well.

Addition

Once you've used this exercise as a warm-up to unleash those powers of visualization, move on to simple addition. I always begin with addition regardless of the child's grade level because it's the simplest concept to master and is the most basic building block of math. Later, you can attack subtraction as the opposite of addition, and multiplication as a shortcut to addition.

Run a string of numbers vertically down a page, such as:

$$
\begin{array}{r}
5 \\
5 \\
3 \\
2 \\
+1 \\
\hline
\end{array}
$$

Tell your child to add the numbers in his head, *not on paper.* If he's reluctant to give up the crutch of writing everything down, stress that you're trying something new and what really matters is that he try, not that he get it right the first time. Sometimes I use a sports analogy: "When you're doing math on paper, it's as if you're playing on the road. You can do it, but the deck is stacked more against you. When you do math in your head, it's like playing with the home field advantage."

Again, discourage your child from counting on his fingers because this tends to bypass visualization. Tell him that time is not a factor; you'll wait as long as it takes for him to do the computation. His speed will improve as his confidence level and visualization skills improve.

Once your child has mastered simple addition in his head, move on to more difficult problems, such as adding two-digit numbers and carrying. Ask him to add columns of numbers, starting with numbers that end in five and zero, such as:

```
   15
   20
   30
   45
   75
 + 15
```

Show your child how to carry the extra digit to the first column. Gradually increase the level of difficulty, using numbers that end in digits other than 5 and 0, working your way up to three-, four-, and five-digit numbers.

Subtraction

Subtraction is normally more difficult than addition because it's easier to count forward than backward. If you can find a visual way to help the child understand what subtraction means, you'll be ahead of the game. For example, draw fourteen milk bottles on a page and have someone drink three of them, crossing off three from the page. Now ask your child to count how many remain. This teaches the child that $14 - 3 = 11$, and also gives him a good foundation for doing future word problems. Allow extra time for your child to do subtraction problems because it won't come as naturally to him as addition. Another strategy is to present subtraction problems as addition problems in reverse. For example: What number plus 11 equals 14?

Avoid overloading your child with too many problems at once since this can make him feel intimidated and defeated before he begins. Instead, work on five to ten different problems and reward him for good, honest effort. Remember, virtually all right-brained children have a strong drive to be the best. *They're not lazy!* When your child appears uninterested or exhibits "dropout" behavior, it's because he feels he can't be successful and is saving face.

Try a visual approach to subtraction: make little "sticks" next to the numbers in a subtraction problem. For example:

```
14   11111111111111
- 3   111
```

Now go back to the top row and ask your child to strike off the number of marks next to the bottom number from those next to the top number:

```
14   11111111111XXX
- 3   111
```

He'll count the remaining sticks in the top row for the correct answer of eleven.

Negative Numbers

Most public schools wait until approximately seventh grade to teach negative numbers to children, yet I find that this concept can easily be taught to children as young as first grade. To introduce the idea of negative numbers, you might use the example of numbers on a thermometer. (It helps if you live in a cold climate!) Show the child a thermometer and say, "It's 7 degrees below 0, or minus 7, and it drops 3 degrees. It's getting colder, moving away from 0. How cold is it?" You might write down $-7 + -3$. Your child should grasp the concept that adding negative numbers is the same as adding positive ones, giving you an answer of -10.

Next, you might say, "It warms up 12 degrees, so it's now above 0. What's the temperature?" When explained this way, most children can readily understand how to add negative numbers.

Multiplication

Once your child has mastered addition and is doing simple equations in his head, he's ready for multiplication. If he's proficient at mental math, he already has the foundation for doing multiplication in his head. All he needs is a system. While left-brained children may be very adept at memorizing times tables through drill and repetition, right-brained kids generally do better at multiplication by performing a series of visual steps to reach the answer. For example, if you're working with the "8" multiplication tables, most schools will drill kids with

$$8 \times 2 = 16$$
$$8 \times 3 = 24$$
$$8 \times 4 = 32$$

and so on. Left-brained children, who respond well to drill and repetition, generally learn tables just fine this way. However, there are too many numbers for visual, right-brained children to easily store in their memory banks. The short-attention-span child with ADD may not see the relevance of memorizing tables—finding them boring—and may benefit from a different approach that capitalizes on his ability to count and hold numbers in his head.

If the problem is 8×4 and your child understands that $8 + 8$ or $8 \times 2 = 16$, it's a simple leap to ask him to double 16 for the solution to 8×4. Or, if your child knows that $8 \times 5 = 40$ but doesn't know what 8×6 is, you have a choice: Tell him to go up 10 from 40, then down 2. Or if he knows that 8×3 is 24, he can double that to arrive at the correct answer of 48. This gives your child a system to solve times tables that capitalizes on his intuitive math abilities as well as his growing proficiency at doing visual math.

Continue with more of the 8's: If you ask your child what 8×7 is and he doesn't know, see if he knows that 8×3 is 24. Ask him to quickly double it, for $8 \times 6 = 48$. For the final step he can either add another 8 or perhaps more simply go up 10 from 48 (58) and subtract 2 for the correct answer of 56. This is a foolproof method that uses both reasoning and visualization. As your child practices it, he'll amaze you with his abilities. Many right-brained adults who have long since forgotten their multiplication tables may find this system useful as well!

Older children can learn to apply their powerful memory to more complex problems, such as 83 × 34. Instruct your child to break the problem down into pieces: First attack it as 83 × 3 (249) and add a zero, for the answer to 83 × 30. Have him visualize the number 2,490 until it sticks. (It may help to record the number on a piece of paper for him in case you need it later.) Next, have him multiply 83 by 4 for the answer of 332. Instruct him to retrieve the first number (2,490) and add 300, visualizing 2,790. (Ask him if he can see the numbers in his mind.) Now ask him to add 30, for a total of 2,820. Lastly, tell him to add the 2, for a final answer of 2,822. He may discover that a task that seemed impossible without a calculator is simple and fun as long as he's right-brained!

Division

Most of us probably remember the ordeal of learning long division, with its divisor and dividend—one number under the "box" and another to the left of it. Long division is a difficult process even for left-brained children. Imagine what it must be like for the right-brained, ADD child, who has a difficult time paying attention in the first place and is weak at solving problems in a step-by-step manner. The way most schools teach long division is alien to the way that right-brained children process. It's too sequential, is nonintuitive, and takes them out of the arena of visualization.

When working with the right-brained child, work from a position of strength: Apply his intuitive and visual abilities to solve complex problems. Explain to your child that division need not be intimidating; in fact, it's simply the other side of multiplication. To be successful your child needs to work in reverse—using times tables to reach the solution. For example, say the problem is 67 divided by 9. Ask your child to first run through his 7 or 9 times tables, finding the solution that is closest to but less than 67.

In this case, it would be 9 × 7 = 63. Instruct the child to take the 63, put it under the 67, and subtract. The answer would be 7, remainder 4 (if you haven't yet reached the decimal stage). This is a more right-brained variation of the way most schools teach division, which is done entirely on paper and uses a sequential logic and step-by-step approach to the discipline.

The next step in division is to work with three digits divided by one, so we're getting into more sequential processing. An example might be 135 divided by 4. Get your student in the ball park by asking a question such as, "What multiplied by 4 would get you *close* to 135?" Have him guess at an answer; most likely he'll throw out 30 or 40. Next ask, "Is the resulting number larger or smaller than 135?" We know that 30×4 is 120, and 40×4 is 160, so we now have some parameters for the solution: It's somewhere between 30 and 40. The next step involves some trial and error. Since 135 is closer to 120, ask him to pick a number in the low 30s. He picks 32, and multiplies by 4 for an answer of 128. Again, all of this is done in the child's head, with no pencil and paper. It's okay for you to jot down a number to hold after the student does the mental math, but make sure you do the writing, not him. Let him save his powers of concentration for the task at hand!

He now knows that 32 is too low, so encourage him to try something higher. He might attempt 33×4 or 34×4, doing the multiplication in his head. He figures out that $33 \times 4 = 132$, and $34 \times 4 = 136$. So the correct answer would be 33, remainder 3.

Having mastered this stage, the next step is to divide four digits by one (for example, $4,032 \div 7$) and three digits by two (such as $197 \div 16$). Use the same process, emphasizing the child's ability to hold images or numbers in his head. Stay away from step-by-step, laborious division with its complicated divisor and dividend, and work with the more intuitive tool of multiplication, with occasional use of addition and subtraction. Continue working with larger numbers as your child is ready, gradually making the process more involved, which requires more visualization. In time, your child will be able to do complex division problems in his head, using this very simple trial-and-error method of "reverse multiplication."

Algebra

Algebra can be a real bear if you're a nonsequential learner. It's the epitome of logic and orderly processing, tailor-made to fit the way most left-brained people think. Traditional teachers of algebra are very much into step-by-step logical reasoning and tend to believe the only route to a correct answer is by following the rules and applying them in order, always showing your steps along the way. This is undoubtedly true for left-brained teachers but is completely untrue for some of the gifted, right-brained mathematicians with whom I've had the pleasure of working. I've had great success teaching concepts of algebra to students as young as six or seven, knowing that when they're introduced to a more advanced subject, they'll rise to the challenge by hyperfocusing.

Here's a good way to begin: Take a marker and a piece of white paper and draw the following equation: ____ + ____ + 5 = 25. Then give your child some choices to plug into the blanks, such as 3, 5, 7, 10, and 15. He must choose the same number for both blanks. He can either write or do the math in his head, but he'll probably employ a trial-and-error approach at first. Over time, his intuition will improve, and he'll more quickly zero in on the correct solution, which is 10 in this case.

Watch the look on the face of your seven-year-old when you tell him he's doing algebra! This exercise totally demystifies the subject and rewards your child for his effort: He's doing something that's considered middle-school math. The novelty of it will capture his interest and will not only help him focus, but boost his confidence. And by allowing him to run the numbers in his head or try them out on paper, covering his guesses with his hand, you're assuring him that there's very little risk of making a mistake, an all-important concept in working with the sensitive, perfectionistic right-brained child. If he does slip up, don't make a big deal about it. Gently encourage him to try again, reminding him that this is seventh-grade math and he's not expected to get it right anyway.

Once your child has a grasp of basic algebra, make the equation slightly more difficult—for example, ____ + ____ + ____ + 3 = 42. Our schools would most likely present this problem as $3x + 3 =$

42, which is not as visual or as easy to understand as my method using blank lines. Give your child the following numbers as possible answers: 10, 11, 13, 15, and 17, and watch his mind at work. With practice he'll be able to get the right answer the first time, and you can eliminate the choices. He'll be able to find the solution easily on his own, in most cases, without ever lifting a pencil!

Jonathan, eight years old, excels in math, wowing his parents and teachers with amazing computations in his head. After just four months of working with me, he is able to solve with ease problems such as: ____ + ____ + ____ + 4 = 1,519. This little tyke has figured out a system for plugging numbers into the blanks, going higher and then lower until he gets the right answer. For example, Jonathan might start at 500, knowing that 500 × 3 = 1,500, which is close to the correct answer but too low. Next, he guesses 507, which is too high, giving him a total of 1,525. Jonathan then guesses 505, which—when he plugs it into the blanks—yields the correct sum of 1,519.

Imagine a teaching system that values the *solution*—even if it's reached in a different way—more than the process. In such a world, the linear, left-brained way of doing algebra

$$3x + 4 = 1,519$$
$$-4$$
$$3x = 1,515$$
$$x = \frac{1,515}{3}$$
$$x = 505$$

would be considered unnecessarily cumbersome and nonintuitive, with the student being sent to a learning specialist to be taught how to do it "right."

Geometry

Geometry should be an area in which right-brained students excel because it involves spatial relationships, demanding a kind of reasoning that's congruent with visual and spatial ability. However, many left-brained teachers even manage to turn geometry into an exercise in logic and sequentiality, endlessly drilling students on formulas, theorems, and proofs. This emphasis on deductive reasoning tends to interfere with the right-brained student's intuitive logic, and even if he arrives at the correct answer, he may be docked for missing or not showing all the steps that got him there.

Some teachers argue that if you cannot show your steps, you'll be unable to move on to higher levels of mathematics, such as trigonometry and calculus. What they mean to say is it would be impossible *for them* to proceed to a higher level. This is certainly not the case for the numerous gifted, spatial, right-brained students with whom I've worked, who have absolutely no difficulty with higher math concepts but struggle mightily with anything that requires sequential processing.

The following example serves to illustrate the difference between the more traditional (left-brained) and right-brained approach to geometry:

Your child is given a homework assignment to determine the degree of each angle when two parallel lines are intersected by two transversals. His task is to find the degree of each angle, A through P, with only one clue: that angle D = 120 degrees.

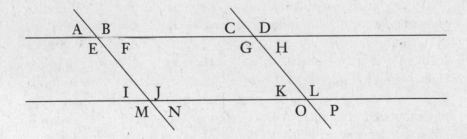

The left-brained way of approaching this problem gives us the following proof, which relies on the axiom that the sum of two angles that equal a straight line is 180 degrees:

$\angle D + \angle C = 180$ degrees
$\therefore \angle C = 60$ degrees

$\angle D = \angle B$

$\therefore \angle B = 120$ degrees

$\angle A + \angle B = 180$ degrees

$\therefore \angle A = 60$ degrees

$\angle D = \angle G$

$\therefore \angle G = 120$ degrees

$\angle G + \angle H = 180$ degrees

$\therefore \angle H = 60$ degrees

$\angle B = \angle E$

$\therefore \angle E = 120$ degrees (and so on, to solve for each angle
through $\angle P$)

A right-brained student would probably bypass this laborious, sequential method in favor of a simpler, more intuitive approach, with the same result. He may look at the problem, know from experience that alternate interior angles are the same, and quickly mark 120s throughout the figure. Knowing that his 120-degree angle has to be added to another angle to equal 180, he'll then just as easily and rapidly mark 60s on the remaining angles. He's done; he sees no need to be burdened with extraneous equations. Even though he got the correct answer, his teacher may mark his homework for failing to show his steps.

Truly brilliant mathematicians, so-called late bloomers, will generally struggle with computation and showing their steps, but if the fire remains inside of them long enough that they survive into higher math, they'll find it's in sync with their learning style. In working with right-brained children, try to instill in them a love of math and a glimpse of the big picture: that math is so much more than being able to memorize times tables or solve an equation in three or four steps. I often wonder how much loss of potential occurs because children who are potentially brilliant at abstract, conceptual math get the message early on that they are poor at this wonderful subject.

Writing

◻ There's a reason I've saved writing for last in this program for the right-brained, ADD child: Writing is, almost without exception, the most difficult subject for children with this learning style to master. The right-brained child will manifest problems with writing from the time he first picks up a crayon. His fine motor skills may be lagging during the formative preschool years, so even learning the correct way to grip a pencil can be a formidable task. His multidimensional visual orientation also makes him more prone to errors in copying letters and numbers; he may reverse them or write entire words backward. He has a difficult time bringing thoughts from his mental blackboard onto paper. It's very difficult for a right-brained child to do more than one thing at a time. As he struggles to translate pictures into words and to form letters, spell, and punctuate, his mental picture becomes distorted. Even attempting to write his name can be an exercise in frustration. He hates to fail; his perfectionism keeps him from trying again. His teacher, however well meaning, may be correcting every little mistake rather than helping him build confidence in expressing himself.

Left-brained people *think* in symbols and words, so they experience very little difficulty in translating their thoughts onto paper. It's almost as if writing was developed with the left-brained learner in mind. As Barbara Meister Vitale notes in *Unicorns Are Real*, "Handwriting tends to be in the left hemisphere. So is the ability to interpret symbols of any kind such as number and letter symbols. Most areas of language, including verbalization, phonics, reading, the ability to deal with details and facts, the ability to follow directions, hearing, and auditory association, are in the left hemisphere." It is precisely these skills, she points out, that "children must handle on a day-to-day basis in the classroom."

Another reason that writing is generally more troublesome for the right-brained child has to do with the very nature of the task: to become proficient at writing requires trial and error. But experimentation goes against the grain of the right-brained child, who wants to do it perfectly the first time. He has a hard time accepting the premise that to write well you first have to write poorly, be corrected, and try again. This process of hammering away at writing clashes with his fear of failing at something he has tried hard to do. He has a tough time acknowledging his progress; he obsesses over what he did wrong. Instead of trying harder next time, he avoids writing and the feelings of inadequacy it produces. When given a specific writing assignment, he'll either refuse to do it or will coast along, doing as little writing as possible.

Getting one of these children to write is indeed a formidable task. Your best approach is to keep tutoring sessions short, no more than ten or fifteen minutes daily. It's better to end on a positive note than to push a child too hard and leave him with the feeling that he let you down. Be totally nonjudgmental. Use praise and encouragement whenever possible. Remind yourself that sensitive, right-brained children greatly fear public humiliation. Your child hates the thought of trying his hardest and being laughed at or exposed as stupid. When he's working in an area such as writing that is difficult for him, he'll feel more vulnerable. Try to be as tuned in to his feelings as you can, and redirect the lesson or quit working when frustration sets in.

To help a preschool or kindergarten child overcome his self-doubt and fear of failure, begin by having him talk slowly as *you write his words*, letting him see what you're writing. This makes a clear association between talking and writing. Punctuate liberally, using commas and periods, explaining to your child that these breaks help you understand better what he's saying.

The next step is to gradually get *him* to write, while *you* talk. For younger children, don't start with a whole sentence but with two or three simple words, such as *and*, *to*, or *for*. Keep the tone very matter-of-fact and nonthreatening. You might preface this exercise with a statement such as, "Writing is hard for everyone. There's no way you can fail if you try." A promised reward at the end of the session—such as a treat or an extra story at bedtime—may be just the incentive he needs.

If your child makes a mistake, you have the option of either glossing over it or pointing it out to him in a friendly, helpful manner. For the child who is terrified of failing and who has only just mustered the courage to pick up a pencil, you might be well advised to let minor mistakes slide for now. What's important is that he's actually *writing*, which for many right-brained children is a major breakthrough. For the more confident, less intimidated child, you can gently correct him by making the letter the right way and saying, "I'm sure you *meant* to write it like this."

Once your child experiences some initial success with writing, have him hand the pencil back to you, while *he* dictates. Alternate in this manner, gradually increasing the number and difficulty of words that you ask your child to write. Keep a sample of his writing from each session, dating it and placing it in a folder so he can chart his progress. This gives him a visual reminder of what he can accomplish if he's brave enough to try.

For older elementary school children who are struggling with writing, try the following exercise: Pretend you both have gags over your mouths and cannot talk for five or ten minutes. Tell your child that instead of talking, you're going to have a *written* conversation. Write about anything you want; the only rule is that you won't criticize his spelling or punctuation, and he can't criticize yours. (This helps him let down his guard and introduces the notion that you might make a mistake, too, since you're not perfect, either.) Removing the pressure in this way helps even the most wary child enjoy this free-flowing exercise, while at the same time it emphasizes the connection between conversation and writing.

Follow this exercise with another in which the goal isn't creativity, but concise and precise writing. Have a friendly competition with your child in which you choose two words out of a book at random. See who can write the shortest complete sentence using those two words. For example, your child might choose *animal* and *learn*, and both of you secretly compose sentences in writing. This time, all writing and spelling must be flawless. It's understood that your child can ask any questions of you that he wants regarding spelling, sentence structure, or punctuation. If he fails to ask a question and makes a mistake anyway, give him a second chance to master the perfect writing you're seeking.

His sentence might be "Animals cannot learn," while yours might be "It's hard to teach an animal to learn." He wins, and he wins by five points because he's used just three words and you used eight. Alternate selecting words and continue to keep a running score (sneaking in a little computational math). When you think he's ready, move the exercise to a higher level: Pick three words to incorporate into a sentence, then four words, and so on. Or you can simply stay at two words, depending on your child's abilities and level of interest. This approach often captivates students since they're rewarded for writing less instead of more. What I really care about is that they're writing at all and that they're bringing a more positive frame of mind to the difficult task of writing.

As your child builds his vocabulary and his ability to write complete sentences correctly, try this lesson for variety: Make up a sentence composed of words that you know your child can spell and say it out loud—for example, "I feel good today." If he's in doubt as to how to spell any of the words, have him spell them out loud. Next, ask your child to visualize *the entire sentence*. Give him enough time so he can see all four words on his mental blackboard. Then instruct him to write from his picture, copying from his mental blackboard onto the page. If he's having trouble, simplify the process: Break down the sentence into two sets of two words or ask him to write one word at a time.

After he's doing this with ease, try this variation: Ask him a question, then have him formulate the answer in his head, turning his response into written letters on his blackboard and copying from the mental picture onto the page. For example, you might ask, "What's the most memorable thing you learned in school today?" Your child will think of a response such as, "I learned where elephants live." Help him visualize Africa or India, but also instruct him to turn his pictures into words so that he sees the words *I learned where elephants live* in his mind. Get him in the habit of taking the extra step to turn the image into words. Ask if he knows how to spell all the words; if he doesn't know how to spell *elephants*, write it for him. Finally, ask him to write the entire sentence. This exercise instills in your child the realization that he can visualize words just as easily as he can visualize pictures, and it takes the mystique out of translating mental images to writing.

The following writing technique for middle school and high school students will no doubt be controversial. Yet I defend it unashamedly, and you will, too, once you see the results it produces. If your child has a paper or book report due and is struggling with writing, you can model the correct way to do it by writing it not *for* him but *with* him.

Sit down with pencil and paper (or at the typewriter or computer keyboard) and "coproduce" the paper. Model what it's like to break down a formidable writing assignment into steps, to get him over the hurdle of getting started. For example, if your third grader is writing a report on sharks, you might say, "First, I'd like you to read this chapter on sharks. Think about what you'd like to put in your report as you go. Make a few notes if you like. Then let's sit down and you can just tell me what you remember." You can write or type while he talks. Feel free to make suggestions or to probe his thoughts with comments such as, "Tell me more about that," "What do you mean by that?" Give him permission to use his imagination and focus on the ideas while you handle the writing.

If your child is older and more research is required, familiarize him with how to dig up facts from the encyclopedia, from books and magazines at the library, or from the Internet. Don't get caught in the trap of doing all the work for him; insist that he not only observe but vigorously participate in ferreting out facts and ideas. If he's not actively involved, don't help him! Once you've gotten the ball rolling, you may be able to switch roles back and forth, taking turns with the writing and fact-searching. Explain to your child that this isn't "cheating"; remind him that he'll soon have the skills to write papers by himself.

This method may not seem intellectually honest to some, but it is far superior to workbooks in teaching your right-brained child good writing skills. For one thing, he sees their immediate relevance. He has a paper due tomorrow and is anxious to get an "A," and you have a captive audience. The disorganized, right-brained child can benefit by modeling how an adult writes, without the fear of being humiliated in the classroom. With your help he should get a good grade on the paper, which makes writing a positive experience and one that he's eager to repeat.

This isn't to say that you'll be writing papers with him until he graduates from college! Each subsequent time you work with your child, wean him from your help, having him shoulder more and more of the burden of composition. For example, if you've written most of the first paper, insist that he insert several of his own sentences into the second essay. The process continues, with you gradually taking yourself out of the writing process but always being available to offer support, ideas, and key phrases.

This "writing and weaning" technique has worked extremely well with virtually all the right-brained students I've tutored on a long-term basis. I've worked one-on-one with dozens of high school students who started out as disastrous writers and over the course of several semesters became proficient, even excellent writers.

I have to admit that when I first approach parents about using this method with their students, many are skeptical. But I always encourage them to observe as I'm working with their child. Over time they see that this method produces such dramatic results that the end justifies the means. By the time I finish working with the child, he's writing beautiful prose without me. This is what's really important, not someone else's definition of "intellectual honesty" or a teacher's concern that I'm upsetting the bell curve in the classroom. Most classrooms are already skewed against the right-brained, visual learner, and this is one way to level the playing field. Which is the greater crime: having a parent or tutor assist in writing a handful of papers for a ninth-grade history class or having a child graduate from high school without the ability to write?

Handwriting

A pharmacist friend of mine once joked that most doctors must be right-brained because they have such poor handwriting! While right-brained people can master handwriting, for most it's not a skill that comes naturally. Several studies have found that while the skills that govern drawing and even cursive and calligraphy originate primarily from the right hemisphere, printing is a left-brained task. If a child is very meticulous, always making letters the same way, priding himself on the neatness and spacing of his letters, he's almost always left-brained. These children will be lauded and will have praise heaped upon them by teachers who believe penmanship is an essential skill for survival in today's world. Kids like this are rewarded with stars and smiles on their papers, and get glowing comments at parent-teacher conferences.

The right-brained child, on the other hand, is all too familiar with red ink and frowning faces on his work. His letters may be randomly strewn all over the page, large and small, and he may reverse letters or entire words. He may write from right to left or top to bottom, forming letters and numbers in unconventional ways. For example, most of us have been taught to make the number 7 starting with a stroke from left to right, then down. A right-brained child may start at the bottom and work up.

Right-brained children also lag behind their peers in penmanship because their neural circuitry has not established a good connection between brain and hand; hence, they have difficulty gripping a pencil and making perfect letters. Being the perfectionists that they are, they'll think of any excuse not to write, lest they expose their weaknesses in fine motor skills. Even if their teachers are sensitive to their feelings, other children can be merciless, branding peers who reverse their letters "stupid" or "retarded."

To get started with your child on handwriting, once again, make a game of it. Tap into your child's innate competitive spirit with a contest entailing who can make the best letter or word. For example, "Okay, now it's time to try handwriting. Neither of us is perfect at this, but let's see who can do the best job making the letter *f*."

Then, very slowly and carefully, let your child watch as you painstakingly make an *f*, first in printed form, then in cursive. Don't do it perfectly (in my case, that's not a problem!) to take the pressure off your child. Ask him to critique your letters. Then have him take pencil in hand and make the same letters, with you critiquing his work. Don't worry if he makes the letters from the bottom up; focus on the result. Judge who did the best job. If it's anywhere near a draw, give the point to him. (If you're working with a child who rarely puts forth any effort in handwriting, you might give the point to him anyway, simply because he tried.) If you start off by letting him win, your child will probably want to play this game over and over again.

Move on to different letters of the alphabet, scoring one point for whoever wins each letter. For added variety, you might keep score as if it's a World Series: It's a "best of seven," and the first person to get to four wins. The goal is to get your child to focus on making perfect letters while at the same time analyzing and picking apart your handwriting to see firsthand some different ways of making letters or numbers. Once you've mastered the game with individual letters or numbers, move up to whole words, phrases, and sentences.

Even with lots of practice in handwriting, recognize that many right-brained children, particularly boys, will never excel in penmanship. (Right-brained girls are more likely to become proficient at handwriting, perhaps because they generally try harder to please their teachers—and certainly a way to please most teachers is to write neatly!) Count yourself lucky if your child's writing is at least legible, since this area is very difficult for him. And recognize that, despite the importance many educators attach to it, the time is rapidly approaching when handwriting will be almost completely obsolete thanks to computers, E-mail, and other electronic advances. Most of us already use handwriting for little more than jotting notes in our calendars, signing checks, and making grocery lists. Before long, voice-activated computer systems may replace keyboards as well.

There's no doubt that computers help compensate for many of the difficulties right-brained people have with writing. They remove any worries about poor penmanship, and the computerized spell checker and thesaurus make writing much simpler. Most word processing programs now correct errors in punctuation and capitalization as well. But, unfortunately, the computer keyboard is far from a panacea for right-brained children struggling to put their thoughts on paper. The reason is that keyboarding is still a brain-to-hands operation. The neural circuitry involved in handwriting is the same as that used in typing; therefore, the messaging system from thought to hand is slower for most right-brained people.

This is not to say that right-brained people can't be trained to be excellent typists, only that it's not an area of strength for them. One exercise I occasionally use with right-brained children who are struggling to learn the keyboard is to cover most of the keys so that only about eight letters or symbols are showing. Ask the child to apply his visual memory to the task of studying the letters until he gets a good picture of them on his mental blackboard. As he looks away from the keyboard, ask him questions about the sequence of letters. Continue using this method for the rest of the keyboard until he can easily remember the layout of all the letters, numbers, and symbols. He'll still have to hunt and peck for a while, but this method should lessen the amount of time it takes him to learn to type.

There are also many innovative children's computer software programs on the market that can introduce kids to mouse and keyboarding skills, such as Sammy's Science House, Bukbik's Adventure on Wonder Island, and Disney programs such as The Lion King and Aladdin Activity Centers. Once a child is familiar with the layout of letters on the keyboard, basic typing instruction is usually all that's needed to firm up his skills. Right-brained children will work hard to master keyboarding because they see the relevance of it, both in school computer labs and at home. Help your child understand that the computer can set him free, making it easier for him to express his thoughts and ideas on paper so that others can know them.

Study Tips and Troubleshooting

■ As your child gains confidence in his new skills, your tutoring sessions will be gradually replaced by study sessions. He no longer needs you to coach and coax him every day; he's ready to tackle homework on his own, with you standing by as an available resource. The following suggestions will help the right-brained and ADD child get the most out of study time, as well as establish a work ethic that he can apply for the rest of his life.

Don't nag.

Do you find yourself constantly asking in exasperation, "Have you done your homework yet?" Take yourself out of the nagging role by making a positive statement, such as, "You can go play with your friends (watch your favorite TV show, have a root beer, any other incentive) *after* your homework's done." To avoid battles, establish a routine in which homework is done at the same time each day.

Minimize distractions.

Designate a consistent, quiet study area for your child that's free from television, ringing telephones, and annoying siblings. If absolute quiet is impossible in your household, give him some "white noise" by running a fan or turning on a tape of sounds of the ocean. Make a rule that no family member is permitted to disturb him during study time unless World War III breaks out.

Have the child work in short, intense bursts.

In the absence of distractions, the right-brained child can accomplish a tremendous amount in forty-five minutes. If he works much longer, the learning curve drops and his ability to retain material will be dramatically reduced. Set a timer for forty to forty-five minutes, to keep him from constantly looking at the clock. If he fails to finish all his work, he can return to studying later when he's had a mental break.

Have the child apply speed-reading techniques to new material.

Because your child thinks mostly in pictures, he must visualize the text to learn it. Just as in your tutoring sessions, when studying he should quickly scan the pages first for the big picture. He may need to read the material three or four times to fill in the details, slowing down for the sections that are most significant. On the final reading he can jot down notes to help him remember important dates or names. Or he can use a highlighting pen to help him recall significant passages.

Have the child use visualization techniques to memorize charts, graphs, and tables.

The same visual technique that's used to teach children how to spell can be applied to something as complex as memorizing the periodic table of elements. The student should be instructed to break the chart down into manageable components (he can cover the rest with white paper), study the information for a minute or so, look away, look back to check the accuracy of his mental picture, then move on to the next segment. If he applies his powerful visual memory, he can absorb a startling amount of information in a very short time.

Have the child dive into writing assignments.

Outlines and note cards are fine for sequential, left-brained students, but for the right-brained, ADD student, they just provide another excuse not to write. He has so many thoughts swimming around in his head, it's difficult to organize them. He is better off just sitting down and reeling in some of those ideas, committing them to paper or computer. Once he gets into the groove, he can go back and put his thoughts in logical order. For a younger child *you* may have to get the ball rolling. Help him write the first line or two, then leave him alone to finish the assignment.

Follow studying with something your child enjoys.

Children can be conditioned to accept studying if they know that when they're done, they can look forward to a pleasurable activity, such as shooting hoops, playing a favorite video game, or getting a special snack.

Test Preparation

It's the moment that Noah dreads. His second-grade teacher has cheerfully announced a timed pop quiz on multiplication tables. Immediately, Noah is tense and nervous because he associates tests with feelings of failure. His palms sweat, his stomach is in knots, and he's consumed with how he's going to feel when he fails. Because Noah is so caught up in these feelings, he has nothing left to give to the task at hand. Noah will flunk this test, and the sad reality is, *he knows the material.* In his state of panic, he's unable to retrieve the times tables from his mental blackboard. He's cornered and is placed in the awful position of failing at something he knows how to do.

Tests, particularly timed tests, can be a nightmare for right-brained children, as demonstrated by research from psychology professor Colin MacLeod at the University of Washington. He compared the reading comprehension time of what he calls "verbal coders" (left-brained subjects) with that of "spatial coders" (right-brained individuals). In the research, the subject was asked to read a sentence such as "Plus is above star," and then shown a picture of a plus symbol above a star. The individual was then asked whether the statement was true or false. MacLeod timed two steps of the process: first, the time it took a person to comprehend the sentence, and second, the time it took to confirm whether it was true or false (verification time).

This research found that spatial coders took more time overall to answer the questions, particularly because of a *significant lag time in comprehending the material.* In other words, there's a processing delay in turning the written material into a mental picture. But once the spatial coders had a mental image, they were able to match the spatial images with the pictures more rapidly, so they had a slight advantage in verification time.

The following are MacLeod's results showing the average amount of time it takes two groups to comprehend a sentence and then to verify that it does or does not describe a picture:

LENGTH OF TIME IN SECONDS

Groups	Comprehension	Verification	Total
Verbal coders	1.65	1.21	2.86
Spatial coders	2.60	.65	3.25

This research, described in *The Spatial Child*, prompted author John Philo Dixon to ponder, "Are there ways in which schoolteachers should change instructional strategies to help children who rely primarily on spatial coding of information?" I would respond that certainly one way is by eliminating timed testing.

Even when your right-brained child is regularly applying his powerful visual memory to academic tasks, he can still be caught flat-footed in a testing situation. He may study for hours for an exam on World War I, able to spew out names and dates effortlessly while studying at home. But with classroom distractions and the anxiety of a timed test, he freezes and fails to retrieve the information. All of his nerve endings are on edge; he's bothered by every scratch of the pencil or rustle of paper. A high percentage of my right-brained students lament that they know the material but just don't do well on exams.

If this is the case with your child, have him use the following approach to written test-taking: First, rapidly scan the test from start to finish, as if it were a menu. Instruct your child to stop when he comes to a question that he can answer *with 100 percent certainty*. He should continue skipping around, answering the easier questions. This helps him achieve some confidence in a test situation, allowing him to relax and focus on the questions rather than on his fear of failure. This relaxation process facilitates visualization, helping him retrieve the correct answers from his memory banks for the remaining questions.

Tell your child that if he finds himself on the brink of panic during a test, he should take a "mini-vacation." Have him practice taking a few seconds to close his eyes or look upward while letting his mind briefly take him to a relaxing place, such as an ocean beach. At the same time, he should breathe deeply, relaxing his neck, shoulder, and back muscles. When he feels calm, he should return to the test, again scanning for the easier questions that he feels confident he can answer and saving the toughest ones for last. This technique should immediately improve his test performance.

Investigate whether your child is eligible for untimed or oral tests. If he has a formal diagnosis of ADD or dyslexia, you can request this of his teacher. Explain to the instructor and administrators that this exemption need not last forever; it may be needed for only a brief time until the child becomes more adept at taking tests. Often, when working with younger pupils, I will ask teachers to give students an opportunity to verbally spell, forward and backward, any words they may have missed on a written spelling test. Many teachers will accept this; students will relish the opportunity because it allows them to show off their unusual visual abilities to their shocked instructors!

Even if your child insists he doesn't need more time on exams, encourage him to at least try it once to see the difference an untimed test can make. Without the pressure to "beat the clock," virtually all right-brained children are better able to demonstrate their knowledge and understanding of the material. Untimed tests provide a more accurate barometer of what the right-brained child really knows; they help level the playing field, since the right-brained student processes more slowly than his left-brained peers.

If your child is still subjected to timed tests, don't be discouraged. Many right-brained children can, over time, train themselves to learn the tricks to surviving timed tests. You can help him prepare by doing mock tests at home, stopwatch in hand, implementing the scanning and relaxation techniques described above.

Troubleshooting

If, in spite of your best efforts, this program isn't producing the results you expected for your child, the following might help identify the problem and determine an alternate plan of action:

I can't get my child to work with me.

Many children will accept instruction from their parents, but some will dig in and would rather have *anyone* work with them than you. If your child is used to getting into power struggles with you, don't let this program become another battleground. See if your child will work with the other parent or an older sibling, who may be less intimidating starting out. A favorite aunt, uncle, grandparent, coach, teacher, or neighbor might also be enlisted to get the ball rolling. Chances are, once your child finds initial success with this program, he'll be more than eager to show you his new skills and won't be so resistant to working with you. Just remember the cardinal rules: Don't pressure your child and don't convey that you have high expectations of him. In the absence of pressure, he'll rise to his own high standards and do great things!

I'm not above offering children a small reward or incentive for their cooperation in following this program. You'll know best what works for your child. Some parents keep a sticker chart, adding a star or sticker each time the child cooperates for a tutoring session. One sticker might be good for an extra story at bedtime, five for renting a special movie, ten for a trip to the zoo, and so on. Some parents, as a last resort, will even bribe their kids to work with them, paying them a quarter or a dollar for each session. Whatever works!

My child won't sit still.

I know it can drive a parent crazy to be reading a story or explaining a math problem while little Johnny is bouncing off the walls. If you're working in his room, he may be up and down constantly, looking out the window, playing with toys—in short, anything but paying attention to what you're saying.

Consider whether, in spite of all appearances, Johnny really *is* listening. He may be one of those kids who needs to move to think. If it seems he's truly not listening, ask him a few questions to find out. You may be surprised that even while he's doing his wild child act, he's hearing everything you're saying. If not, try finding another place to work, one without as many tempting distractions. As mentioned earlier, some teachers find that setting up two desks in the classroom works for hyperactive children, allowing them the freedom to bounce back and forth between desks during lessons. You can try this approach at home as well.

The visualization exercises don't work. He's not getting a picture.

Some kids will insist that they aren't seeing anything on their "mental blackboard." First, ask yourself: Are you sure your child is right-brained? It might be helpful to review the traits of right-brained children in the first section of the book and reevaluate your child or consult a specialist. These techniques will not be nearly as effective for left- or whole-brained children.

Are you working at a level that's too difficult for your child? Try going back to simpler words or concepts.

Are there any distractions that may be getting in the way? The enemy of visualization is distractions. If there's a loud stereo in the room, or if your child is hungry, or it's late at night, your child will be less able to visualize effectively.

Are you hurrying your child? Some very right-brained children are slow processors, and it can take what seems an eternity for them to successfully visualize a word. Don't rush your child; tell him to take as long as he needs to get a picture in his head.

Are you sure he understands what it means to make a picture? This can be a difficult concept for some children (and adults). It might be helpful to review the section earlier in this chapter on teaching your child to visualize.

Where is your child looking while trying to visualize? It's difficult to make a mental picture while looking down or picking up all the detail in your peripheral vision. For optimal visualization, your child should either be closing his eyes or looking upward.

He's visualizing but isn't applying this ability to spelling, reading, and math.

Chances are one of two things is going on: Either your child is afraid of making a mistake or he's deliberately failing. Some children are so perfectionistic that they won't give an answer until they're virtually 100 percent certain it's right. Many right-brained and ADD children, especially brighter ones, feel so devastated when they make the slightest mistake that they will not risk an answer until they're sure they can answer it correctly.

Many times the child will ask for more time, or appear unresponsive, or just say, "I'll let you know when I get it." Don't rush him or interrupt this process. Allow as much time as necessary within reason. Gently remind him that what matters is that he tries. Say things such as, "This word is much harder than most words you have to spell in school. This is a ninth-grade word; if you miss it, don't worry about it. No one could expect someone your age to get it right."

There's a chance your child may be deliberately failing. Some children fail on purpose so as to lower expectations. In essence, they are saying, "I can't fail at this task because I never really tried" or "I failed on purpose because the task was boring and not worth my time." When a child acts bored and uninterested, don't take it personally. Think of it as his defensive armor, the result of being trumped in school situations. Think back to when your child was a toddler or preschooler and loved exploring his world. That's the way your child really is. If he acts uninterested or complains that school is "boring," see his behavior for what it is: a shutdown mechanism. Your child most likely brought a curious mind and lots of enthusiasm to school, only to have it squelched by a teaching system that doesn't understand him.

The reason many children deliberately fail or do not reach their potential is defensive as well. Your child may have gradually adopted an attitude of "I will keep my hopes constantly low to shield myself from the harsh reality of trying my hardest and failing." Most right-brained and all gifted children have an innate desire to excel. Your child is not really bored and is probably not lazy. What you're observing is a form of "dropout behavior," a defense against failure. Don't call his bluff; understand it for what it is and take the pressure off any way you can.

We were making great progress, but now we're in a slump.

You will have up and down days with this program. Keep your goals realistic. There will be days when you reach real breakthroughs with your child, and days when, for whatever reason, things just don't click.

If you seem to hit a prolonged slump, consider that it may be one of those vexing periods in the school year when ADD children seem to go one step forward and two steps back. In the twelve years I've been working with ADD and gifted children, I've noticed a very predictable pattern: Children who are on a traditional school year calendar seem to hit "troughs" around mid-November, February, and April. I gauge this by the number of calls I get from panic-stricken parents who wonder why Johnny is suddenly having so much trouble in school.

Children with ADD are inconsistent by nature, and it's difficult for them to put forth 100 percent effort 100 percent of the time. Even if your child is off to a good start in the school year, by about mid-November the pressure may be taking a toll on him. He hasn't had a real vacation in two months and the days are rapidly getting shorter (many hypersensitive children suffer from seasonal affective disorder), and he may be suffering from cabin fever because of inclement weather. It may seem to be an eternity until winter holiday break. Mid-November is a time when virtually *any* student can be in a rut, but for the ADD child, at the far extreme of the "sensitive" scale, it will be more obvious.

February is also a tough month for many kids because the holiday vacation is but a distant memory, and spring break is simply too far in the future to offer any hope. Again, the days are short, the weather may not allow a lot of physical activity outdoors, and the school year seems to drag on forever. April can be a rough month for students as well; spring break is over, yet it's a little early for children to anticipate the "finish line," that is, summer vacation!

The best thing you and your child's teacher can do is anticipate these slumps, talk to your child about them, and keep your cool when they occur. Many times parents or teachers overreact to setbacks, sending the child into a tailspin. If you panic, your child will pick up on your doubts and be distracted by your reaction rather than focusing on how he can get back in the game. When he's distracted, he's not visualizing, and his processing and organizational difficulties are exaggerated.

You may notice signs of a slump when your child "forgets" to turn in an assignment, daydreams more than usual in class, or fails a test he would normally ace. Your child may go to great lengths to cover up the problem, telling you he doesn't have any homework tonight. He may fail to bring home his spelling books, math binder, or worksheets. He may tell elaborate lies about his poor performance in school, in the hope you won't find out and be disappointed in him. But judgment day will ultimately come when you get the bad news via a phone call from the teacher, a parent-teacher conference, or a sorry report card.

While you may be stunned and angered by your child's poor performance and his cover-up, be very careful how you handle it. While it's important that you express your disappointment and concern, let your child know that you still love and support him. I've heard parents and teachers say some deplorable things to these sensitive, shame-filled children. Or they drag their kids to doctors, demanding drugs to "fix" the problem. The result is that many of these kids are so hurt and humiliated, they refuse to try again and never claw their way back out.

To head off such a crisis, it's vital that you have a good line of communication with your child. Let him know he's safe in telling you things, even things you don't want to hear. If November, February, or April are rolling around and you sense a slump, be proactive. Say, for example, "I know school can sometimes be difficult and boring for you, and you've been at it a long time now without a break. I want you to know that if you have any problems with missed homework or failed tests, or if you find your mind wandering a lot in class, it's okay to tell me. I'll go with you to talk to your teacher, and we'll work it out. I won't think any less of you because you have a tough time in school sometimes. I want you to know how much I appreciate that you keep it together so well most of the year. It can't be easy, and I applaud you for doing as well as you're doing." This kind of honest, unconditional acceptance will work miracles with the perfectionistic, sensitive child who needs to know that someone close to him understands his dilemma. If he lies about his poor school performance, most likely it's because he'd rather do anything than let you down.

Be there for your child; be his advocate. Insist on a meeting right away with his teacher to talk about the reasons for his setbacks. If he suddenly went from A's and B's to D's and F's, see if he can get himself back on track by doing some extra-credit work or a makeup test. Do what you can to minimize the failures and give him a chance to save face. When he begins to emerge from his slump, it's a good time to lavish him with compliments, rewards, and positive strokes.

It's sad that left-brained parents and teachers too often assume that kids see F's and zeros as a "wake-up call" to motivate them to get back in the game. On the contrary, many right-brained students will seize on the zeros as a reason to give up. They may reason that since one or two bad grades can drag down their final average, what's the point in trying now anyway? They'll appear bored or uninterested, and make comments like "Okay, I did lousy, but I don't care. The system sucks, the teachers suck, and everything is against me, so why bother?" They quit so they won't feel as if they failed. Don't be fooled by this defense mechanism. Recognize it and combat it. The price is high if you don't. When these adolescents get backed into a corner, they choose the only path they know to avoid more pain: They give up—not only in school but in other areas of their lives.

I'm reaching "parent burnout."

Just as you take the pressure and the nagging off your child, you should take it off yourself. As the parent of a right-brained child, you may be right-brained and perfectionistic as well. You're not perfect and you're going to make mistakes, but remember that you're working with a child who has been very difficult to parent since birth. Add to that the challenge of chipping away at a defensive wall around your child that most likely has been years in the making. It's not easy to erase the shame, frustration, and humiliation that most of these children have endured since preschool.

When you feel yourself approaching parental burnout, take care of yourself. You need a deep well of love and patience when parenting a hypersensitive ADD child, so it's important that you take time to replenish the well. Take breaks from your child with the help of your spouse or by negotiating regular time to yourself with a day care provider, sitter, or sympathetic friend or relative. Find a challenging or relaxing new activity for yourself so you don't become obsessed with your child's problems.

I can't promise the journey will be an easy one, but with time, love, encouragement, and unconditional acceptance, you can empower your child to discover the strengths that lie within. You'll find no investment of your time more rewarding. You are changing the world by changing the life of a child.

In Search of the Ideal Classroom

Here's to the kids who are different,
Kids who don't always get A's,
Kids who have ears
Twice the size of their peers,
And noses that go on for days,
Here's to the kids who are different,
Kids who bloom later than some,
Kids who don't fit,
But who never say quit,
Who dance to a different drum,
Here's to the kids who are different,
Kids with the mischievous streak,
For when they have grown,
As history has shown,
It's their difference that makes them unique.

—DIGBY WOLFE

Flash back to your third-grade classroom. Chances are that most of the time you're a passive observer, sitting at your desk as you're told, watching your teacher talking and writing on the blackboard. Sometimes you're asked to read to yourself, then answer questions on a worksheet. The emphasis is on quiet and order. Your teachers are cast as the givers of knowledge; you and the other pupils are little sponges waiting eagerly to soak it all up.

So many facets of our lives have changed as a result of research and improved technologies, it's amazing that a generation later our classrooms remain largely the same as they were in the '40s, '50s, and

'60s. While there are some exceptions, most classrooms are uninspiring places in which frustrated teachers are trying to reach a growing number of "unreachable" kids. Information is still being presented auditorily, and assignments are given in the driest, most repetitive fashion imaginable. A typical assignment is to read ten or fifteen pages, then answer a set of predictable questions that largely call for regurgitating facts rather than thinking creatively.

Even such subjects as science and history, which are ripe for visualization and hands-on exploration, are often taught in this dry, boring fashion. The result: These subject areas attract only left-brained, sequential children or those who can survive the presentation. It's no wonder the classroom is losing out to television and video games.

Thom Hartmann, in his wonderfully conceived book *Beyond ADD*, discusses the progression of teaching throughout the history of mankind. Primitive man told stories around the fire, and for many thousands of years the oral tradition (lecturing) was the preferred way of passing on information. Even today in our visually oriented society, educators are still standing up in front of classes giving speeches.

Like me, Hartmann has talked with many teachers who agree that kids today are "wired" differently from kids a generation ago. "Could it be that this difference is real, and that what it's really about is the transition people are making from an auditory to a visual learning style? While some educators point to the 1960's as the time when our schools 'collapsed' or became too permissive, that period of time also coincides with the first generation of children raised with TV."

As our children are becoming more restless, more visual, and more right-brained, their learning style is colliding with that of our teachers, who are generally left-brained and thrive on order, neatness, and repetition. The problem is more acute than ever simply because a growing number of children are being pushed to the right on the learning style continuum. As the gap between the way teachers teach and the way students learn becomes wider, schools are failing our children at an increasing rate.

The repeated calls to get "back to basics" represent nostalgia for a time when life was simpler, when the rules made sense, when more of our children were left- or whole-brained. It's a well-intentioned but misguided attempt to make sense out of chaos. Back to basics is wonderful for children who are left-brained "teacher's pets," but for kids who are right-brained and ADD, it's like trying to put round pegs into square holes. Most of the proponents of basics are left-brained themselves and have the same Achilles' heel common to this population: They generally lack the ability to see things from others' perspectives. Right-brained children don't need to be "broken" of their learning style through more structure, more drill, and more discipline; they need an educational system that captivates and challenges them, helping them access their many strengths.

While they are in the minority, some emerging teachers and schools are experimenting with more innovative teaching methods, which appeal to right-brained children. Your job as a parent is to find them or, in the absence of any good choices where you live, to do the best you can by working with your child and by showing this book to teachers, school administrators, and decision makers. You can make a difference!

Pick up most popular books on Attention Deficit/Hyperactivity Disorder, and you'll find pretty standard advice on selecting the ideal classroom setting for your ADD child. While well meaning, this advice is akin to rearranging the deck chairs on the *Titanic*. While seating ADD children closer to the teacher certainly can't hurt, it's a far cry from what's really needed: a revolution in education.

Twelve Suggestions for Creating Right-Brained Classrooms and Schools

1. Require all teachers to take classes, both in college and through regular in-service presentations, on differing learning styles. Understanding the many ways that children learn is critical to an instructor's effectiveness in the classroom. Our teaching colleges place far too much emphasis on how to write lesson plans or construct behavioral objectives, and far too little emphasis on how to determine and work with the learning styles of students. There is more than one kind of intelligence; in fact, Howard Gardner writes in *Multiple*

Intelligences that there may be anywhere from "seven to several hundred dimensions of mind." Yet our schools have, at best, paid only lip service to these various intelligences. Gardner says, "If anything, education has proceeded according to the opposite assumption —there is one way of teaching, one way of learning, and individuals can be arrayed in terms of their skill at this mandated form." If we have any hope of reaching the growing population of right-brained children, we have to start by understanding how they think and learn.

2. Test all children for their learning style at the start of second grade. By this time a child's learning style will be mostly "hardwired," and it would be a simple task for schools to determine a child's preferred style of learning and where he is on the left-right brain continuum. This would be a simple thirty-minute test, which could be administered at very little cost to school districts. I would take the dollars that are now being spent on meaningless in-services and redundant standardized tests and redirect them to this vital learning styles inventory. We could work more intelligently and efficiently with limited resources by taking a short time *up front* to identify a child's learning style and then accommodate it. It's certainly less time-consuming to catch a dyslexic child or visual-spatial learner early and teach to his strengths than to deal with the costly staffing of a "learning disabled" child years later.

I foresee a day when we have left-brained and right-brained classes at a given school, with a smattering of whole-brained learners in each to balance class sizes. While these groups would be taught to read, write, and spell using a different approach, there would be opportunities for the classes to interact, such as for field trips and special school events. It's important that students have contact with other children who have different learning styles so they can understand how other people learn. This would help foster more cooperation and understanding among people with different learning styles.

It may take years before our schools identify and understand how to teach this new breed of child; the best thing you can do for your child *right now* is to bypass the sluggish educational red tape and establish a good rapport with the person on the front lines: the classroom teacher.

Most teachers really do want to help children. They may feel as frustrated and impotent as you do when a seemingly bright child is struggling in their classroom. Until now, they simply haven't been given the tools to help right-brained and ADD children harness their many strengths. My experience as an advocate for these students has taught me that many classroom teachers are intrigued and enthusiastic about trying visual teaching methods if they're approached in a manner that's helpful and nonthreatening. Start by sending a note to the school requesting a half-hour meeting to share with his teacher or teachers what you know about your child's learning style. The tone should be upbeat and nonthreatening; you want the teacher to feel part of the team that's helping your child, not under attack. It may be helpful to bring your child along, particularly if you've been tutoring him successfully and he can demonstrate his visual abilities.

Your approach might be, "This is all pretty new stuff, so how could a teacher be expected to know it?" Explain that you're now aware that different children have different learning styles and that you strongly suspect your child is a visual, right-brained learner: He has to turn everything into pictures in his mind in order to process and retrieve that information. You might ask the teacher to look at a picture on the wall and turn it into words. For most, it's a struggle. You can say, "This is what my child must do all day long in school."

Without going into great detail, explain that this right-brained problem of translating pictures to words is a double-edged sword: It produces some weaknesses, such as in oral reading, phonics, and timed tests, yet your child also has some great strengths, such as a powerful memory, creativity, and the ability to think holistically.

This would be a good time to produce some examples of the work you've done with your child, such as words he can spell forward and backward. Briefly demonstrate the method you're using, with colored letters on white paper, that's worked so well for your child. If the teacher has never seen this before, it can be quite a powerful experience. Watch the look of satisfaction on your child's face as he shows his teacher that—when taught in accordance with his learning style—he's smart after all! This almost always piques a teacher's interest, providing the perfect opportunity to offer to lend her this book and suggest she read others in the recommended reading list provided.

"You will like Mr. Woofard. He has an attention-deficit disorder."
Drawing by Booth; © 1991 The New Yorker Magazine, Inc.

You've laid the groundwork for what will be, it is hoped, a rewarding and lasting dialogue with your child's teacher. You may also be helping many other right-brained children for years to come.

3. Place children with a teacher who either has a corresponding learning style or has demonstrated that he or she understands it and can effectively teach these children. If you have a child who's been formally diagnosed with ADD or another learning disability, *ask to pick his teacher.* I frequently suggest this to parents, and many schools are willing to accommodate this request within reason. It's vital that you find the right teacher for your child because, as discussed earlier, right-brained and ADD children will do much better in a classroom setting if they feel their teacher understands and respects them. Right-brained students will almost always excel with an instructor who expects good work from them and who has a tolerance—even an admiration—of their uniqueness.

The following checklist will be helpful in choosing this "miracle worker." It's a good idea to bring your child along with you when you observe the classroom and interview the instructor so that you can gauge your child's response as well.

Is the instructor left-, right-, or whole-brained? (This may take a little detective work with questions from the left-to-right brain continuum because many teachers don't know.) Obviously, a right-brained child will function best in a classroom with a right- or whole-brained teacher.

What knowledge does the instructor have of alternate learning styles?

Can the instructor give examples of how she has worked with children who have ADD or visual learning styles?

What is the instructor's attitude toward ADD?

How does the instructor deal with kids who have a short attention span? Who are unruly? (Look for a teacher who is flexible, offers creative solutions, and who doesn't want "cookie cutter kids.")

Is the teacher's style to lecture/read/fill out worksheets or to engage children with projects and activities?

Does the classroom appear to be an appealing and stimulating place?

What is the instructor's philosophy regarding homework?

How does the teacher feel about untimed and verbal tests for children with ADD?

Does the instructor seem to have a lot of energy and enthusiasm for her job? A sense of humor?

When you visit, does the teacher talk only to you or does she speak directly to your child? Does she speak warmly to him, kneeling down to his level?

How does the instructor feel about your being very involved with your child's education?

Would *you* want this person as *your* teacher?

Later, you might ask your child the following questions:

Did you like the teacher? Why or why not?
Did you think the children in the classroom seemed happy and
    interested in learning?
Imagine that you're in that classroom. Tell me how you feel.

Strongly consider your child's input, but ultimately the decision has
to be yours. Keep in mind that the stronger the rapport between your
child and his teacher, the more conducive the environment will be for
learning. It's important that all children like their teacher, but it's
critical for children who have ADD.

Once you've made your choice, put your request in writing and
direct it to the principal. Let him or her know that you and your child
have invested a lot of time identifying the teacher who best fits his
needs. Discuss your child's learning style and his corresponding
strengths and weaknesses; emphasize that you believe the most important variable in his education is the teacher. State in an understanding and nonthreatening way that you realize the school can't grant
every request but that you hope they give your plea strong consideration, given the fact that your child has a different learning style or
formal diagnosis of ADD. While many principals balk at allowing
teacher selection as a general rule, most have your child's best interest
at heart and will grant your request. If this approach fails, you have
some recourse, which will be discussed later under your legal rights.

In the worst-case scenario, if your child is stuck with a less than
desirable teacher, don't give up. Request regular meetings with the
teacher, ask her to observe you working with your child, and continue
tutoring him as much as possible. If the relationship between your
child and his teacher is especially strained, give him regular "mental
health days" off from school. If, after all is said and done, you're still
dealing with a teacher who insists "It's my way or the highway," you
should opt for the highway. Seek a more suitable teacher or school for
your child.

4. Limit pupil-teacher ratios to no more than 15 to 1. While I
recognize that lowering existing ratios will be costly, I believe taxpay-
ers would be willing to pay for it *if* we finally see some positive results

coming out of education. We can spend more for education and less for police protection, courts, jails, and drug treatment centers. Ronald Kotulak, author of *Inside the Brain*, says studies show that for every dollar spent on early childhood development, we save five dollars down the road in social services, mental health services, prisons, and other programs that deal with the aftermath of low esteem, violence, and aggression. Dr. Bruce Perry of Baylor College of Medicine, a leader in research that explores the effects of the environment on the brain, says, "Developmental experiences determine the capability of the brain to do things. If you don't change those developmental experiences, you're not going to change the hardware of the brain and we'll end up building more prisons." Let's invest the money up front when we can still change lives rather than paying a heavy price for our shortsightedness in the future.

If your child is in a classroom with twenty-five or thirty other students, you may have to be creative to get him the more individual attention and challenges he needs. One mother of a gifted, right-brained child arranged for the elementary school guidance counselor to take him out of class periodically to play chess with him. See if your school has a chess club or competition that focuses on knowledge, such as Odyssey of the Mind. Continue to stimulate his mind and satisfy his intense curiosity with regular trips to the library and museum. Challenge him with new concepts during your tutoring sessions.

5. Provide a stimulating, experiential environment. It's interesting that most ADD handbooks recommend that children be placed in very stark, lifeless classrooms so as to "minimize distractions." This advice misses the mark by a mile. Children who have ADD and who are right-brained need to be captivated to learn. In a dull environment they simply tune out and daydream. As Ronald D. Davis writes in *The Gift of Dyslexia*, "If a teacher does not appeal to the curiosity of a student and has failed to make the subject being taught the most interesting thing in the environment, the teacher has created the perfect environment for ADD."

When walking through your school in search of the best classroom for your ADD child, look for the classroom with lots of visual appeal. Bypass the tidy, sterile room with its perfectly aligned desks in favor of the one with lots of life and *controlled* energy: The classroom should be decorated with colorful art projects and be an enticing place of workstations, book corners, and fantasy play. Look for the high-energy, playful teacher with a twinkle in her eye.

This is not to say that children with ADD should be in a totally chaotic environment. In fact, the "open classroom" setting can be disastrous for students with ADD. When left unattended to design their own curriculum and start and finish their own projects, the child with ADD finds himself at a loss as to where to begin. He lacks the internal self-discipline to be his own instructor. Instead, he needs to be given choices of specific activities while being closely monitored along the way.

Children today not only need a structured, "high-stim" atmosphere to hold their attention, they need to see the relevance of academic tasks. Therefore, help create an academic environment that takes children *out* of the classroom and brings interesting people *into* the classroom. Sign up to be a room mother or classroom volunteer, offering to make arrangements for special trips and speakers. Do a survey of occupations of other parents; invite one in every month or so to talk about his or her career. Children who are just starting to think about "what I want to be when I grow up" are fascinated to learn about different occupations. Students should also spend at least a couple of days a month in the "real world," whether it be a field trip to a fire station for little ones or a career day for a middle or high school student.

The right-brained child will work harder at his studies if he understands that school can help him reach a goal. So if your high school junior wants to be a deejay, light the fire in him with a job shadowing project at his favorite radio station. Include an interview of a station employee, with specifics on what skills are necessary to land a job in radio. Once the student recognizes *why* he needs to have good writing, communication, and technical skills to fulfill his dream, he'll never look at high school English or speech in the same way.

Let your child's interests guide him toward appealing classes and extracurricular activities. If his passion is chess and your school doesn't have a chess club, offer to organize one. Suggest a before- or after-school computer lab; distribute sign-up sheets so other parents can get involved. With many people clamoring for basics, we should resist the urge to do away with extracurricular activities and so-called elective courses; these provide an oasis for right-brained children in left-brained schools. As Howard Gardner writes in *Multiple Intelligences*, the ideal curriculum should nurture all types of intelligence, not just the verbal/linguistic and logical/mathematical modes that are so prized by our schools. The remaining intelligences include visual/spatial, key for builders, artists, and architects; musical; bodily/kinesthetic, used by dancers, athletes, and surgeons; interpersonal, which helps us relate to others; and intrapersonal, which is used in writing, philosophy, and our conversations with God.

Get involved in your school's curriculum development efforts. Regularly attend school board meetings, being vigilant when it comes to efforts to ax so-called frills in lean budget years. ADD expert Dr. George Dorry rails against the "nepotistic bureaucracy" that looks to art, music, and shop classes as the first programs to go when budgets are cut. He states, "Our educational system doesn't place value on visual-spatial learning. We want to turn out lawyers and accountants, instead of architects and individuals who can deal in three dimensions." Dorry's point is well taken: The basics are important, of course, but under my program, children can master reading, writing, and math skills *without having to sacrifice other subjects that give them tremendous joy*. In many cases it's the elective courses that provide the incentive for the marginal student to stay in school. Electives such as art and music develop intelligences that have as much validity as learning how to solve an algebra problem. Who says we can't have it both ways?

6. Employ longer lessons that integrate a variety of subjects. Why is it that most classes are forty-five to fifty minutes? This is a long-standing academic tradition that no longer makes sense. For the right-brained, ADD child who has difficulty starting tasks and shifting gears, short classes can be a tremendous source of frustration. Just as he's becoming engrossed in building a papier-mâché volcano, the bell rings and he's forced to put it all away and move on to the next totally unrelated subject. Learning is compartmentalized (a left-brained characteristic), with students toting around separate notebooks and folders for history, science, math, English, and art. Heaven forbid that the subject areas should overlap or that an effort be made to synthesize the material (a right-brained approach) and demonstrate how it inter-relates. Dr. Jane Healy writes in *Endangered Minds* that "one of the biggest gaps in children's experience these days is in seeing connec-tions between all the bits of information they have accumulated; teachers are frustrated because their students have difficulty linking ideas together meaningfully. A fragmented curriculum does nothing to remedy the situation." You might discuss a more integrated curricu-lum with your child's teacher, or at least seize opportunities to make connections in talking with your child about what he learned in school today.

Students can be captivated for large blocks of time *if* the subject matter is relevant and varied. For example, if the class is studying Africa, students might study the geography, language, culture, music, and biology of Africa during a two- to three-hour time period. Incor-porate into the lesson a variety of teaching materials that appeal to auditory, visual, and kinesthetic learners. Show a short wildlife video. Have students put together a puzzle, naming and spelling all the countries in Africa. Ask a group of children to build a model of Victo-ria Falls. Have another group use the computer to research efforts to save the black rhino. Pull out musical instruments and perform some African music. Delve into the history of Africa. Serve an African lunch that day or plan a Kwanzaa celebration. You'll find that so-called short-attention-span kids may not have such a short attention span at all if classroom material is interesting, multisensory, and relevant.

Dr. Healy writes admiringly of a fourth-grade class that used this "big picture" concept with phenomenal success while studying Egypt. "In addition to reading from many background sources, discussing, making projects, and collaborating on simple research reports, the students were also reading books of children's fiction related to the study at hand." She observed that each day the children were asked to make a journal entry and discuss what they read. "In the discussions, skillfully moderated by the teacher, the level of interest was high," Healy notes. "Each child had different views and different comments. I found myself astonished by the depth of understanding these young students showed. . . . Clearly this was a good teacher at work." Clearly we should expect *all* our teachers to be this good.

7. Make homework more meaningful. Tim, an eighth grader at an affluent suburban middle school, has an IQ of 130 and is failing most of his classes. Tim has a formal diagnosis of ADHD but refuses to take his medication. He has a habit of forgetting homework assignments and

CALVIN AND HOBBES © 1987 Watterson. Dist. by UNIVERSAL PRESS SYNDICATE.

regularly gets D's and F's on timed tests. His esteem is low; he takes up pot smoking and drinking as forms of self-medication and recreation.

Tim quickly grasps math concepts in class, yet each night he is sent home with fifty to sixty problems to drive the points home. Solving problem after problem works well for Tim's left-brained peers, who find that drill reinforces general concepts. But for Tim this homework is irrelevant "busy work," extinguishing whatever spark of interest he may have had. After completing eight problems, Tim sighs. Bored, he finds himself seeking out a diversion—any diversion will do—to save him from this mundane task. He puts on a rap CD or surfs television channels, looking for something more entertaining and stimulating. Chances are that Tim will never finish his homework. If his mother or father intervenes and insists he can't watch TV until his math is done, he'll race through his work, making careless mistakes. Homework simply has little value to him—and Tim isn't alone: A 1996 survey of teens by the nonprofit agency Public Agenda finds most students struggle to find a meaningful connection between today's homework and tomorrow's professional aspirations.

Too many children go home with backpacks filled with dull, tedious problems. This kind of homework doesn't test a child's knowledge of a particular concept; it tests his ability to complete a meaningless assignment while overcoming extreme boredom. Homework should not extinguish a child's love of learning; it should be considered a tool to reinforce concepts and keep the spark ignited outside of the classroom. For students like Tim, repetitive, mundane homework should be *greatly reduced*. Most schools that work successfully with ADD students recognize this and have virtually eliminated homework, understanding that most homework is repetitious and a left-brained effort to hammer concepts into children's brains.

If your child's school is not among them, talk with the teacher about incorporating more long-term projects and research papers into the curriculum. See if you can arrange for some trade-offs: Instead of asking your child to do fifty math problems each night, perhaps he could complete ten of the most difficult ones. Instead of asking him to do one book report each week, suggest that he do a much longer— and more complex—report at the end of the month.

If your school doesn't already have one, organize a science fair. This serves several purposes: First, it's more academically challenging for a student than repetitive homework. Your child will respond better to the novelty of a difficult task than the repetition of the familiar one. When challenged, the right-brained, ADD child can visualize better, which enhances learning. Second, project-based learning lends itself to more quality involvement from parents. Instead of bugging Mom or Dad for help with quadratic equations (which most parents won't remember anyway!), the child can involve his parents in projects from conception to final product. This is a way for parents to participate in their child's education in a meaningful and fulfilling way, which is in turn the most important predictor of a child's success in school.

Lastly, this type of learning more closely reflects the challenges we face in adult life. Not many of us bring home repetitious "busy work" from the office night after night that has to be completed the next day. Instead, many jobs demand that we juggle several long-term projects at once. We have specific deadlines, and we have to budget our time accordingly. Asking students to complete assignments in a similar manner is great training for the real world. In *Multiple Intelligences*, Howard Gardner writes, "In our view, most productive human work takes place when individuals are engaged in meaningful and relatively complex projects, which take place over time, are engaging and motivational, and lead to the development of understanding and skill. . . . Most of productive life consists of projects—projects that are mandated by others, projects that are initiated by the person herself, or, most commonly, projects that represent an amalgam of personal desire and communal need."

Assigning a series of long-term projects works well for most children as long as several mini-deadlines are set along the way so that the procrastinator doesn't become overwhelmed at the last minute. For example, in one week the student must turn in a paper outlining the project; in two weeks he must bring his work-in-progress to show to his classmates, and so forth. If a project is broken down into manageable steps, with easily foreseen deadlines, the organizationally challenged child can still keep up.

8. Reform testing. Do you remember history tests when you were a child? Most likely you were asked to recall a bunch of names and dates in a variety of formats: multiple choice, true or false, or fill in the blank. The emphasis was on minutiae rather than general concepts. Unfortunately, it still is in most schools. We have a whole generation of students who hate history because of the way it's taught.

For example, a traditional left-brained test on World War II might query: "On what date did the Japanese bomb Pearl Harbor?" "Name three German concentration camps." "What was the name of the plane that dropped the bomb on Hiroshima?" Left-brained children are very good at remembering names and dates, but struggle more with the big picture. A more right-brained test would assess mastery of *general concepts:* "What was the turning point of the war?" "When did the Germans and Japanese begin to sense the tide was turning against them and why?" "Discuss the psychology of how the war shifted to the Americans' favor." Details and dates are significant, of course, but without a broad conceptual understanding, what do they matter? As Howard Gardner says, "When it comes to assessment, educators need to make it clear that merely taking a temperature over and over again does not heal a patient and that a person who can only spit back facts cannot be expected to solve an unfamiliar problem or create something new."

A more enlightened approach to history testing might be to ask essay questions on movements and general concepts the first week, then quiz students on specifics such as dates and names the following week. This process helps global, whole-to-part thinkers get the big picture first, before saddling them with details. As I've said before, right-brained children are more eager to learn the particulars of a subject once they've mastered broader concepts.

In addition, while left-brained children are generally good at expressing ideas on paper, many right-brained children may be better at demonstrating mastery of subject material through oral testing. Oral testing may be a backup option when the teacher believes a child knows the material but has failed a test anyway. During a verbal exam, the teacher can probe and explore concepts with a child in addition to asking him about names and dates. Often, right-brained children will offer very insightful and creative slants on things, ideas that don't lend themselves to fill-in-the-blank responses. To recognize and praise the right-brained child's different perspective is very validating of his unique intelligence and gives him the realization that there is a place for his way of thinking in school and in life.

The reason schools don't do more oral testing of students is obvious: It's too time-consuming and teacher-intensive. In the factorylike atmosphere of our schools, it's so much easier for stressed-out teachers to check off multiple choice answers than to take the time to really *talk with* our children. If oral tests are a luxury we simply can't afford, teachers can develop other alternatives to test children who think in pictures, such as asking them to give a speech, develop charts and graphs, prepare an audiotape, or create a diorama. Many visual, right-brained students will also test well on the computer (more on the computer to follow).

I support open-book testing, particularly for older students, because it takes time pressure off the child. When a right-brained child is under the gun, he's not visualizing and does a poor job at retrieving information. Open-book testing is also excellent preparation for the real world, in which we draw upon available resources to write research papers and prepare for presentations. What's important in most careers isn't how much material you can cram into your brain but how easily you can *access* key information and apply it to the task at hand.

Timed tests are a relic and should be banished from schools. They take the visual, ADD child out of his game. To lobby your child's teacher for an exemption from timed testing, explain that visual students take longer to retrieve information from their mental blackboard; therefore, timed tests are an unnecessary handicap. If your child seems to know the words going into a spelling test but misses them anyway, suggest that he be tested individually using a nontimed, verbal test. In other words, the teacher gives the word and allows the child plenty of time to visualize and then retrieve it from his mental blackboard; in spelling bee fashion, the teacher then listens as he spells the word out loud. Most teachers will agree to this, particularly if the student agrees to spell the word both forward and backward during verbal testing. The child who correctly spells backward can convince even the most stubborn teacher that he's not getting an unfair advantage. What you're seeking is not special treatment but a level playing field.

If timed tests are being used for computational math, explain to the teacher that for most right-brained children, timed tests work against visualization and against the way they process. Urge the teacher to either eliminate or minimize timed testing, reminding her that timed tests are not necessarily a good indicator of how well a right-brained child knows the material. Timed tests are also unrelated to our success in adult life. How many of us have to spit out information with a stopwatch running to succeed in our jobs or careers?

If the teacher insists that children show their steps during a math test, ask that this be waived as well. Many right-brained children know the frustration and injustice of getting the answer right on a math problem but having it counted wrong because they didn't demonstrate how they got there! Ronald D. Davis laments in *The Gift of Dyslexia* that as a child he was a victim of this ridiculous left-brained mode of teaching: "In algebra, I correctly answered every problem in the book, every problem the teacher put on the blackboard, and every problem on the tests. Yet I failed the class. The teacher explained that the purpose of the class wasn't just to get right answers; it was to learn how to do the problems. I hadn't done a single one of them. All I had done was write down the answers." Instead of requiring the student to show his steps, the teacher might ask him to explain, one-on-one, how he arrived at the answers. It's intriguing to discover the many creative and unconventional approaches these children use to solve problems.

I also believe our system of grading is a dinosaur; grades are entrenched in our culture but are a subjective, arbitrary, and lazy way of quantifying how a child is doing in school. Many parents will resist abolishing letter grades because *we* grew up with them and apparently have an obsession with labeling each child an "A student" or a "D student." But in many cases letter grades merely reflect how well a student can regurgitate material under time pressure. "Teacher's pets" typically get the A's; children who challenge the teacher or have a different take on things get C's or worse. Letter grades are another remnant of an antiquated educational system that was designed to produce obedient yet unimaginative foot soldiers. Grades perpetuate the notion that the teacher is the absolute authority, and the child exists only to parrot the instructor's thoughts and ideas.

As an alternative, I propose that parents be given *detailed written evaluations* of their child's progress on a regular basis. Many of the more enlightened public and private schools are doing this already. The written evaluation provides the parent with infinitely more information than a letter grade ever could; the written report should then be followed by a private conference with the teacher.

As a result of abrogating letter grades, colleges will be forced to be more inventive in student selection, requesting portfolio applications and even suggesting, in some cases, that applicants visit the campus for face-to-face interviews. Many institutions of higher learning are already deemphasizing ACT and SAT scores, recognizing that a student's performance on achievement tests is generally not a sound predictor of how he or she will do in college.

It's critical that we see testing as a tool to help us chart a child's progress and identify areas of strength. It should not be used to label or shame children. Achievement tests can be useful in terms of measuring a child's academic progress, but they say nothing about what your child is *capable of learning*. Certainly no achievement test can measure a child's ability to solve problems or can measure how creative and intuitive he is.

Bringing Out the Best: A Resource Guide for Parents of Young Gifted Children by Jacqulyn Saunders and Pamela Espeland sums up my thoughts on testing well: "Just remember that even the best test can reveal only how a particular child performed particular tasks on a particular day." In other words, while testing can certainly give us valuable information, it should never be viewed as the final word about a child's potential to succeed. The authors conclude, "Would you want *your* future to be decided by a group of powerful people who knew nothing about you except your score on a 200-item test you took a month ago? Of course not, and neither would your child."

9. Eliminate IQ testing. I strongly believe that IQ testing has done more to mislabel and discourage children than it has ever done to identify learning problems and help kids. All too often in my work I hear parents and teachers make such ignorant comments as, "How can I expect this child to achieve? His IQ is only 90" or "My son Rick wants to be a doctor, but his IQ is only 107. I'd better talk him into doing something more realistic." I recently heard the parent of a very bright and creative little boy lament, "I always thought Forrest was gifted because he's so good at art and music. But he's not. We had his IQ tested, and it was only 120." Now Forrest is sentenced to spend his school years in a typical classroom, which harps on his weaknesses and ignores his great strengths.

There's also the case of Sarah, a Russian girl whom Laurie adopted at age five. Sarah rapidly picked up the English language, and her new mother was curious about her intellectual capabilities in other areas. When evaluated by an "expert" after just nine months in the United States, Sarah was proclaimed to be borderline mentally retarded. Upon closer examination it was revealed that the test had many questions Sarah couldn't possibly have answered because of cultural differences and the effects of spending her first five years in the deprived environment of an orphanage. When asked in one exercise to match a dog with a bone, Sarah shrugged and couldn't answer because she'd never seen a dog before! Fortunately, Sarah's mother didn't buy into the test results, and later IQ testing revealed that she was of at least above-average intelligence.

IQ testing came into vogue in the early 1900s when the French psychologist Alfred Binet was asked by Parisian educational authorities to invent an instrument to effectively predict which students would survive in the public schools and which would not. When word of this novel test that could measure intelligence spread to the United States, people in positions of power became quite excited about its potential. IQ testing was applied not only as a vehicle to measure scholastic preparedness of elementary school children, but it became a way for bureaucrats to quantify an individual's intellectual value in many facets of life, including military service. By the 1930s, IQ tests were widely used in America, with the underlying belief that they were an accurate measure of intelligence and that intelligence was something one inherited, not a trait affected by the environment.

IQ testing has a dark side in our history, having been used as a means to justify racism and discrimination. Some "true believers" have suggested that people of varied races and ethnicities score lower on IQ tests because they're inherently less intelligent. IQ tests are also used to promote one culture's superiority over another's (such as Japan over Mexico). This is ethnocentrism and left-brained, linear thinking taken to its most absurd extreme.

There are many types of IQ tests out there, some better than others. These tests are given by licensed psychologists who receive special training in how to administer the tests and interpret results. IQ tests can be given from two years of age through early adulthood, with most children taking them from ages five through twelve. Most IQ tests are made up of several subtests; for example, the test might have a section on putting together blocks, finding symbols or shapes within a picture, working puzzles and mazes, reading comprehension, providing antonyms and synonyms, and answering mathematical and computational questions. While some IQ tests at least make an attempt to quantify right-brained forms of intelligence (the Wechsler Intelligence Scale for Children, third edition, or WISC-III, has a visual-spatial component), on balance most commonly applied IQ tests today are biased toward mathematical, logical, and linguistic forms of reasoning.

Right-brained children are generally at a disadvantage in timed IQ testing situations because they need more time to turn the visual pictures in their minds into the written answers required on a test. Many children who do poorly on IQ tests do so because they panic under time pressure and fail to translate or retrieve the information in their heads. Once a sensitive, right-brained child gets off to a bad start in a test situation, his old fear of failure kicks in and he falls apart. His worst fear comes true.

Thankfully, nowadays the application of intelligence tests is rapidly on the decline as we become more enlightened about their limitations and more sensitive to their costs ($200 to $600). These days as few as one in four schoolchildren will ever take an IQ test. Teachers are hesitant to recommend them except for children reading one to two years below grade level or students who appear to be very bright but are not performing well in school.

While there are some promising tests now being developed, they're not yet widely applied and they are typically very costly. Until a far better test is devised, such as an untimed test derived from Gardner's model of multiple intelligences, we should put IQ tests on the back burner. They are subjective, shaming, and often a deterrent, keeping students from following their dreams—the last thing they need.

If your child's teacher or a learning specialist suggests an IQ test, you might spare him the indignity of appearing less bright than he really is by politely declining. Because most IQ tests are designed for left- or whole-brained children, the results will be meaningless for your right-brained child. Say you'd rather wait for an IQ test that measures *his* kind of intelligence.

10. Avoid retention of students. Retention, or being "held back" a grade, can be devastating to any child, particularly a hypersensitive right-brained individual. No matter how gently the news is broken to him, how much it's "for his own good," he'll still come away with the message that he's stupid and inferior. Certainly retention is warranted in extreme cases, but I wonder how many right-brained, ADD children are being held back in the early grades unnecessarily, simply because they're late bloomers.

Schooling is too often based on the faulty assumption that early reading, writing, and computational skills are associated with intelligence and later academic performance. Right-brained children simply have a tendency to pick up these skills later in their school careers, but this does not mean that they're flawed or that they're not smart. In fact, these late bloomers will frequently surprise their parents and teachers with how much they shine once they progress beyond the third grade.

If the school suggests retention for your child, see if you can propose a middle-ground solution. It might be that you hire a special tutor for the summer or tutor him yourself in a manner that's congruent with his learning style. Set reading goals for him over the summer instead of letting him watch a lot of TV. Inquire about some form of small group remediation for your child when school resumes. Remember that retention is rarely justified; if the school insists on it and you strongly disagree, consider changing schools.

If you have a right-brained child who's already showing late-blooming tendencies as a toddler and preschooler, it might be advisable to consider delaying his entry into kindergarten, particularly if he has a summer or fall birthday and is right on the cusp of the academic year. It is better for him to be among the oldest in his class than the youngest, especially given his proclivity to develop later than the left- or whole-brained child.

11. Eliminate tenure. One of the most destructive forces in public education today is teacher tenure. It invites mediocrity and works against the introduction of new and refreshing ideas. Tenure perpetuates the status quo and makes it next to impossible to weed out bad teachers.

In 1995 only one teacher was dismissed in the entire state of Colorado. Bill Cisney, a member of the Littleton, Colorado, public school board, notes that in his district *not one teacher has been fired in ten years:* "The process that we have to go through in order to terminate a teacher is absolutely mind-boggling. It takes lots of time, an enormous amount of work, it's very expensive because of the litigation, and we're highly unlikely to win that process, because all of the burden of proof lies with the district." Cisney has been advocating legislation to do away with teacher tenure, supporting a bill that was introduced by Senator Tom Blickensderfer in the 1997 state legislative session. Blickensderfer points out that it's children who suffer if we keep substandard teachers in the classroom: "There's nothing worse for a schoolchild than to have a bad teacher. It can turn them off learning."

In a free marketplace under the voucher system, tenure would most likely be the first thing to go because it works against quality education. A competitive system would produce recruitment of quality teachers at higher levels of pay. The best teachers rise to the top and are compensated accordingly. With financial incentives for being the best, teachers have even more reason to excel—and good riddance to those teachers who are simply punching a clock until retirement.

I've worked in many schools where four or five wonderful teachers, out of a faculty of fifty or more, are in high demand, with parents lobbying intensely to get their children placed in these classes. Imagine a day when schools are *filled* with excellent teachers, and think of the ripple effect it would have on our children, our families, and our society.

12. Foster more competition among schools. If we want a higher standard of education for our children and an alternative to left-brained, assembly-line schools, we have to be willing to introduce more competition in education. Our schools have to rise to the challenges outlined in this book; we can no longer settle for mediocrity. I envision a system that gives parents and children of *all* socioeconomic groups the opportunity to attend a school that best fits their learning style, values, and ambitions. I strongly believe the time is now for school choice in America.

American education is terminally flawed, and what's necessary is a radical change to take it off life support. With a voucher system we would no longer have the traditional, two-tiered educational structure in which your child either attends a public school or you pay through the nose to send him to an exclusive private school. If it costs $4,000 per child today to educate your child in a public school, the voucher system would give you a credit for a portion of that amount to use for the school of your choice as long as the choice is approved by the state department of education. Imagine the possibilities!

Vouchers would transfer control of education from bureaucrats to parents. Educators would be forced to compete for vouchers, to cater to the demands of the consumer. Only those schools providing high-quality education at a reasonable cost would thrive. Injecting more competition into education would force administrators and teachers to become more innovative with their methods and more sensitive to the needs of their students. Teachers and schools that don't cut it wouldn't survive because parents would pull out their kids and shop elsewhere. Schools that did make the grade would have long waiting lists, compensate their teachers better, and provide greater incentives for bright, creative individuals to go into teaching.

Vouchers would also lead to a broader menu of choices that would be available to a wider spectrum of children. We'd most certainly see more schools that focus on gifted and talented children, back to basics, dyslexic students, ADD, and outcome-based education. *You'd* get to decide what best suits the needs of each of your children, so potentially you could have three children in three separate schools. You could send your budding artist to a magnet school that emphasizes art classes, your dyslexic child to a school that's staffed by specially trained professionals in the field of dyslexia, and your left-brained, gifted geology fiend to a specialty school that's renowned for its natural science curriculum. As the parent of a right-brained child, you could apply the voucher credit toward sending your child to an innovative school for right-brained and/or ADD children.

At the present time, almost no one wants these kids in their schools. When I discover a school that does an especially good job of teaching right-brained kids and I begin referring children there, it never fails that, within a short time, I receive a phone call from the principal asking me to stop heralding her school as a good place for students with ADD. I have not found any large public or private school system that comes close to serving the needs of this growing population.

Yet under the voucher system, schools for right-brained, ADD children could become all the rage because these students are a growing share of the market and no one else knows what to do with them. A school for the right-brained ADD child would eliminate all the things that aren't working for these students, such as timed tests and massive amounts of homework. This visionary school for the ADD child would be based on an experiential curriculum that applies visual teaching methods, making liberal use of cutting-edge technologies such as computers and virtual reality machines to captivate its pupils.

Perhaps the greatest beneficiaries of a voucher system would be children of lower- and middle-income parents. While wealthy kids can afford to attend private schools, disadvantaged children have no choice. It's no wonder that minority constituents are more likely to support competition in education. One Gallup poll has found that while 70 percent of Americans support full educational choice, the figure is even higher for minorities surveyed: A whopping 86 percent of African Americans opted for choice, along with 84 percent of Hispanics. A voucher system will help level the playing field in education, giving disadvantaged and minority children greater opportunities.

Breaking up the current monopoly stranglehold on education is perhaps one of the most proactive, visionary things we can do to help our children and our children's children. Imagine a system in which schools are held accountable not by a set of arbitrary, standardized test scores but by parents and students who directly receive their services and are free to leave if they're not satisfied. We can have such a system; write to your state and federal lawmakers urging them to draft and pass legislation encouraging more educational options.

School choice is *the* political/educational issue of the twenty-first century.

Your Legal Rights

Now that you better understand and appreciate the strengths of your right-brained child, you may be feeling some outrage at how he may have been labeled and shamed by our left-brained schools. Filled with righteous indignation, you might be tempted to storm into the principal's office, slam this book down on the desk, and demand change. Or you may want to make a lot of noise at a school board meeting. With this approach you're likely to be dismissed as just another "difficult parent" who is placing demands on an already overstressed and overworked administrator or school district.

I've witnessed this hundreds of times. Parents who pressure schools to do a better job educating their kids are labeled controlling, enabling, or troublemakers. They're accused of making excuses for their kids. Yet, to my way of thinking, these parents are unsung heroes. Why don't schools attack the *real* problem parents—those who don't even show a passing interest in their child's education? Don't let this fear of being labeled a wacko dissuade you. You are watching your child's innate love of learning flicker out because of substandard teaching. You have a right to demand more; your child's future is at stake.

While most instructors genuinely want to help your child and will agree to some modifications in the classroom, expect to lock horns with some teachers. My experience has taught me that about one in five teachers will adopt a defensive and closed-minded attitude, bristling at any suggestions that might imply "special treatment." Resistance usually comes on two fronts. The first goes something like this: "I'm not going to change the way I teach an entire class to meet the learning style of one kid." If this happens, suggest that most likely there are many other students in the class who share the same learning style and who would benefit from an alternative teaching method. If you can devote the time, offer to volunteer several hours a week in the classroom as a teacher's aide, working in a small group with right-brained children. Or offer to demonstrate the methods described in this book to a teacher's aide who can integrate them into the mainstream classroom.

A second defense from unyielding teachers might be: "I'm not going to coddle these kids. Sooner or later they're going to have to face the real world." What these teachers fail to recognize is that their so-called real world is not the same world these children will enter upon graduation. As our world becomes more random, visual, and right-brained, we need to adjust our methods of teaching accordingly.

If you're up against a teacher who is somewhat skeptical about modifications for your child, try to be understanding. State that you know the classroom is the teacher's domain and that your goal is to help her run things more smoothly. Reiterate that you're not seeking special treatment for your child, you're asking for modifications that are in sync with his learning style. Stress that you're not just asking the teacher to adjust, that in exchange you and your child will pledge to meet her halfway. The result of your discussion might be a simple, nonbinding agreement that goes something like this:

Sample Agreement

We recognize that [name of child] has a diagnosis of ADD and has a right-brained, visual learning style that requires modifications in teaching. These modifications include:

- that [name of child] will be exempt from all timed testing
- that in math class [name of child] will not be required to show his steps, but will instead be required to explain verbally to the instructor how he arrived at his answers
- that in spelling [name of child] will be allowed to spell words verbally (both forward and backward) for the instructor in lieu of writing them down
- that [name of child] will be given the option of being tested one-on-one with the teacher as long as the request is made at least 48 hours before the test

> In exchange for these modifications, [name of child] agrees to comply with all rules of the classroom and to put forth his best effort to learn the material.
>
> These modifications will be in place for a finite period of time (usually two or three months) to allow [name of child] to achieve success, build confidence, and catch up with other students. This agreement will be reviewed at that time.

A written agreement probably won't be necessary for a teacher who is eager to work with you, but for the reluctant teacher it can provide a good middle-ground solution before you roll out the heavier artillery. You—and the teacher—may find it comforting to have your understanding on paper where it can be reviewed from time to time. Many teachers also prefer to have everything documented, and this serves that purpose. A written agreement also has more weight and validity than a handshake; it is more likely to be adhered to because it has the feel of a legal document even though it's not.

If you've exhausted all your options—meeting with the teacher, suggesting a contract, requesting a different teacher, or changing schools— it may be time to become educated about your legal rights as the parent of a child with ADD. My experience has been that parents rarely have to pursue legal recourse; school administrators often acquiesce to parental demands once they realize the parents know what they're doing and are digging in for a fight.

Section 504 of the Rehabilitation Act of 1973 states: "No otherwise qualified individual with handicaps (disabilities) in the United States shall, solely by reason of her or his handicap, as defined in section 706 (8) of this title, be excluded from the participation in, be denied the benefits of, or be subjected to discrimination under any program or activity receiving Federal financial assistance." (29 U.S.C. Sec. 794)

Written in typical left-brained, bureaucratic verbiage, this paragraph provides you with ammunition when working with public schools in making special accommodations for students with ADD. In this section, individuals with handicaps are described as those with any physical impairments as well as those with "any mental or psychological disorder, such as mental retardation, organic brain syndrome, emotional or mental illness, and *specific learning disabilities*" (italics added). A September 1991 policy memorandum from the U.S. Department of Education confirms that this applies to children with Attention Deficit Disorder.

Section 504 provides for the following adaptations in the regular classroom: "Providing a structured learning environment; repeating and simplifying instructions about in-class and homework assignments; supplementing verbal instructions with visual instructions; using behavioral management techniques; adjusting class schedules; modifying test delivery; using tape recorders, computer-aided instruction, and other audiovisual equipment; selecting modified textbooks or workbooks; and tailoring homework assignments." Other provisions include reducing class size for children with ADD as well as providing special tutoring, classroom aides, and note takers.

Section 504 gives you clout if you have a right-brained, ADD child, but his difficulties are not severe enough to qualify for special education services under IDEA, the Individuals with Disabilities Education Act. If your child is denied special ed services and has a diagnosis of ADD, ask to see the school district's Section 504 plan to determine his eligibility under that statute. It's important to note that schools are required to provide for the needs of children who are diagnosed with ADD, even if these students fall under their regular education programs. A child doesn't necessarily have to be designated as "special ed" in order to qualify for certain modifications in the classroom. The eligibility requirements are broader for Section 504 than for IDEA.

Which designation would be most helpful for your child? Attorney Matthew D. Cohen at Loyola University Law School says if your child is eligible, there are several advantages to the IDEA qualification. He says, "The IDEA has far more specific provisions with respect to the range of services to be provided, how the child's education plan is developed, and the procedural safeguards which are available if there are disputes with the public schools." Cohen, who's litigated many landmark special education cases, points out that once your child has an Individual Educational Plan under IDEA, the school cannot modify or discontinue the plan without giving you, the parent, notice and the right to due process. Section 504 is not as specific, however, about educational services and your rights of appeal.

On the other hand, Section 504 contains some significant provisions that do not apply to IDEA. For example, in addition to filing an administrative hearing request with the school district, you can file a complaint with the U.S. Department of Education's Office of Civil Rights. This agency has the authority to *independently* investigate violations of Section 504 and to find schools in noncompliance. Section 504 also allows you to recover damages if you ultimately file a civil action against the school. IDEA does not provide for monetary damages except under extraordinary circumstances.

If you're confused about whether your child qualifies for IDEA or Section 504, or neither, you're not alone. Many school districts are struggling with these issues as well, some more enlightened about ADD than others. Cohen says, "Parents and professionals seeking services for children with ADD should recognize that there is wide variability in how school districts will respond to these requests. The awareness of school districts will range from a complete understanding of their obligations to serve children with ADD under both the IDEA and Section 504, to only a limited understanding of how children with ADD fit into the overall eligibility scheme provided by the statutes." You may need to take matters into your own hands and, with the Section 504 statute in hand, educate your school administrators about your rights. Again, I always recommend approaching your child's teacher first instead of tackling the entire school bureaucracy from the top down.

What should you do if the teacher throws obstacles in your path, dismissing you as another meddling parent? I would suggest the following plan of action: First, try to enlist the support of a learning specialist or special ed instructor at the school. Plead your case and see if that person can act on your child's behalf. Then arrange a meeting with this individual and the principal at which you detail the meetings you've had with your child's teacher and your dissatisfaction with the outcome. Be sure to emphasize (politely, not hysterically) that you're brokenhearted as you watch your child's love of learning slowly wane. Give examples of how this teacher mismatch is affecting your child (such as crying, depression, stomachaches, refusal to get up to go to school). Ask the principal to meet privately with the teacher and special ed instructor to see if they can develop a consensus on how to best help your child. Give it one or two months to see if this approach works, while you continue to work with your son or seek special tutoring outside of class.

If a month or two passes and nothing has changed, your next move is to follow up with another meeting with the principal, this time requesting another teacher. Make the request in writing. Many principals will realize at this juncture that you're not going away and will make an effort to accommodate you. If this fails, too, your choices are clear: You can withdraw your child from the school and find a more acceptable classroom environment, you can opt to home-school your child, or you can bring the lawyers into the fray.

I see legal action as a last recourse, one that should not be taken lightly. Litigation can be costly, lengthy, and put the child in a state of legal limbo. It may be sufficient to contact a lawyer and have the individual write a letter to the principal (on official firm letterhead, of course) saying that you have exhausted all channels of remediation to help your child and are now contemplating legal action. In most cases, that's all it takes to get the attention of the powers-that-be, and you may find the district more willing to work with you.

In Search of the Ideal School

■ We're moving past the era of the "one-size-fits-all" school. With a growing awareness of children's learning styles as well as parental preferences regarding discipline, structure, and academic subject areas, we're moving toward an era of greater educational choices. Even without vouchers or open enrollment, parents now have the choice to home-school their child or send him to a neighborhood school, a charter school, a parochial school, or other private institution. As we approach the twenty-first century, the number of choices will increase, which requires you to do your homework in determining the best environment for your child. The following checklist may guide you in making the best decision for your ADD child:

Do the school administrator and teachers have an understanding of alternate learning styles?

Does the school have regular in-service programs for teachers that address learning styles?

What is the ratio of students to teachers? (Fifteen to one or less is ideal.)

Is the teaching approach challenging and relevant, without being too structured or too overstimulating?

What is the school's attitude toward ADD and other learning disabled students? What is their track record in working with these children? (Ask for some specific case histories.)

What percentage of students are taking Ritalin or other stimulants? (More than 10 percent may indicate a bias toward medication.)

How does the school feel about parents who are very involved and proactive? Does the school encourage or even require parents to volunteer in the classroom?

What is the range of compensation for teachers? Are good teachers given extra bonuses or incentives? What is the turnover rate for teachers? (Above-average salaries and low turnover are not always a predictor of quality but are certainly one indicator.)

Does the curriculum include subjects that appeal to right-brained children (such as art, music, shop, mechanics, and graphic design)?

Are traditional subjects taught using approaches that appeal to right-brained children (project-based, hands-on, experiential)?

How are students tested? Can allowances be made for untimed or oral tests for special needs students?

Is the emphasis on disciplining students or on giving them built-in incentives to comply with school rules?

How much is the tuition? (Do not assume that a private school is a better choice for your right-brained child simply because you have to get a second mortgage to send him there. My experience has been that many pricey private schools and academies are ill-equipped to teach children with different learning styles and will actively purge children who are labeled as or suspected of having ADD.)

Join an ADD support group and seek recommendations from other parents about schools that are better than others for children with ADD. Most states have public and/or nonprofit groups representing parents of learning disabled children; contact these agencies and groups for suggestions on the best educational match for your child.

Don't select a school based on its elite reputation, slick brochure, or the impressive credentials of the administrator. What really matters to your child is the quality of the individual teachers. Remember, if you're struggling with the decision of where to send your child, your number one consideration must be finding the instructor who will be the best match for him. He doesn't care if the school has a long-standing tradition in the community, that it costs $12,000 a year to go there, or that it has the highest average test scores in the state. What matters to him is that he can relate well to his teacher—period.

Magnet and Charter Schools

Until we wake up and implement a national school voucher system, we have some middle-ground options that are already in place in many school districts: magnet schools and charter schools. As the name implies, magnet schools are designed to draw students from outside their normal attendance area by offering enticing academic programs organized around particular themes. For example, a magnet school might specialize in math, science, foreign language, or remedial education. About one in three magnet schools base admission on established criteria, such as high academic performance. The remainder admit students on a lottery or first-come basis. It is not unusual to find parents camping out for days, waiting to register their children for the better magnet schools. Obviously, this sends a strong message to school boards that schools with long waiting lists should be replicated.

Originally, magnet schools were used as a desegregation device, but they are now gaining favor as a way of offering *public* school choice. They're gaining popularity as Americans seek out more and better choices in education. The latest data show impressive gains from magnet schools; the U.S. Department of Education reports 80 percent of magnet schools in fifteen urban districts showed higher achievement scores than their district averages. Magnet schools provide an excellent way to introduce competition within the public education sector.

A charter school is viewed as a way of bridging the gap between public and private schools. It's a public, taxpayer-supported school created and operated by teachers or other qualified individuals and is largely free from district oversight. It differs from a magnet school in that it's more autonomous and is created by a group of "outsiders" who share a common vision for education. These nonsectarian schools are assured of government funding as long as students achieve at levels specified in the school's contract with the local school board. Several states now have charter school programs, including Arizona, California, Colorado, Georgia, Kansas, Massachusetts, Michigan, and Minnesota. Colorado, for example, passed sweeping charter school legislation in 1993. It gives up to sixty schools the ability to apply for charters from their local districts. Under this legislation, many of the new schools must target "at risk" students, those identified as having behavioral or academic problems. There are now dozens of charter schools in Colorado. The list is diverse and includes schools that emphasize basics, arts and sciences, self-directed learning, global issues, and less traditional classrooms.

A Model Right-Brained School

I've had the pleasure of being associated with one charter school, Sci-Tech Academy in Littleton, Colorado, which I consider a model for right-brained children. Sci-Tech was founded in 1994 by a long-time teacher and his wife who saw a need for a school for bright but underachieving students. Not surprisingly, of its 135 students in grades 6 through 12, fully 83 percent are considered at risk, with 17 percent carrying a formal diagnosis of ADD.

Several things set Sci-Tech apart from other public schools in the Jefferson County School District:

- Sci-Tech Academy has a low student-teacher ratio, with fifteen pupils per teacher. Students receive more individual attention and therefore are more likely to excel.
- Sci-Tech spends less on administrators and more on teachers. This school has just *one* administrator, its director, and is consequently able to pay above-average salaries to attract better teachers.
- Sci-Tech has designed a curriculum that has a special emphasis on computers, science, technology, and graphic arts, all subject areas that captivate today's right-brained students.
- Sci-Tech embraces a philosophy of assigning specific, finite tasks *during school hours*, while requiring very little homework. Each student is given a series of challenging assignments to be completed by the end of the school day, so there's little time for goofing off or getting into trouble. Sci-Tech assigns a daily point system to represent each student's work ethic. For each of eight

class periods, pupils are awarded up to ten points for demonstrating good behavior and staying on task. Those who fail to earn at least seventy-two of the eighty total points must attend the extended hours, from 3:15 to 5:00 P.M. that same day.

If this pattern continues throughout the week and the Sci-Tech student receives less than 80 percent of possible credit for assignments and projects, he must report to Saturday school, from 9:00 A.M. until noon each Saturday. Obviously, this system provides a strong incentive for a strong work ethic and for following school rules!

- The school's curriculum is very hands-on and experiential in nature, providing students with a plethora of experiments, field trips, and fascinating guest speakers from all walks of life.
- Sci-Tech invests its shoestring budget wisely on regular teacher education programs addressing learning styles and multiple intelligences.
- Sci-Tech Academy demands that parents get involved, requiring them to volunteer in the classroom or in another capacity for sixty hours each semester.
- Testing at Sci-Tech is done on a fairer basis than at most public schools. The work is individualized, based on each student's abilities and interests, and testing is done in a variety of ways, including verbal, written, and project-based evaluations.
- Sci-Tech's director, John Le Tellier, is a genuine advocate for his students. While he has a no-nonsense attitude and believes strongly in motivation and accountability, he's almost universally liked by his students. His philosophy: "We offer structure and accountability, but it's friendly and versatile. We empower kids to make good decisions." Le Tellier realizes that to manage an experimental school such as this, he needs to be actively involved with day-to-day issues. For example, in a dispute between a student and a teacher, he takes the time to listen to the student and will bend over backward to be fair to both sides.

It's significant that Le Tellier's roots are not in traditional education and school administration; he was once the director of a head injury center in which he worked with children with special needs. He understands that each child is different and that we can work with the strengths of the brain to do remarkable things.

While Sci-Tech is certainly not perfect and has experienced growing pains, it serves as an example of a courageous school that's venturing into virgin territory as it strives to meet the needs of today's emerging right-brained population. Sci-Tech must be doing something right, since it has a growing waiting list. Even though four out of five students are considered at risk, the school's test scores are above average for Jefferson County schools. In 1996, Sci-Tech high school students scored in the 69th percentile in reading on the Iowa Test of Basic Skills (versus a 60 percent district average). Math scores were 61 percent for Sci-Tech students and 60 percent for the rest of the district. Middle schoolers at Sci-Tech earned 56 percent reading and 68 percent math scores, versus district averages of 56 percent and 60 percent, respectively.

Providing greater school autonomy, such as that found at Sci-Tech, is a proven catalyst toward improving education. In 1990, John Chubb and Terry Moe made waves with their book *Politics, Markets, and America's Schools*, which attacked the *structure* of the system as being the fundamental flaw in education. They asserted that the way we govern public schools has created a bureaucracy that treats teachers as nothing more than mindless civil servants, which stifles autonomy and lowers student achievement. One reason these researchers drew so much attention was that they were working out of the Brookings Institution, a prominent *liberal* think tank.

Their main finding: "All things being equal, a student in an effectively organized school should achieve at least a half year more than a student in an ineffectively organized school over the last two years of high school. If that difference can be extrapolated to the normal four-year high school experience, an effectively organized school may increase the achievement of its students by more than one full year."

Just what is the model for Chubb and Moe's school? The ideal school would eschew top-down management but instead would treat teachers like professionals, not government bureaucrats. This school would respect teachers' opinions, giving them more freedom to make decisions and encouraging them to work as a cohesive team. Chubb and Moe's research found that effective schools have 20 to 50 percent *less* interference from superintendents and district-level administrators than do ineffective schools, particularly in the area of curriculum development and the hiring and firing of teachers. They note, "The more school decision-making is constrained by superintendents, district offices, unions, and the rules and regulations they promulgate, the less effective the school organization is likely to be." Private and, to some degree, charter schools have fewer bureaucratic constraints because they're not at the mercy of political battles and turnovers in elected leadership. Chubb and Moe argue that our democratic system of education administration is ruining the nation's schools, a sobering conclusion from two researchers who have devoted their adult lives to studying government institutions.

Montessori

As you explore educational options for your child, you'll no doubt encounter Montessori schools, some of which can provide a sound alternative to the traditional classroom for children with ADD.

Pioneered by famous educator Maria Montessori, the Montessori teaching method uses a rich kinesthetic and experiential environment that helps children "learn to learn." Much of the philosophy centers around developing the independence of the child while creating a sense of cooperation and community. A typical Montessori classroom is filled with interesting "works," projects or activities that relate to practical life, language, math, and social and physical development. Emphasis is placed on manipulating materials, which certainly taps into the strengths of the kinesthetic learner.

Most Montessori classrooms have a low student-teacher ratio, which is a big plus. It's common to find just six to ten students per teacher; rarely will you find a Montessori classroom with a higher ratio than 15 to 1. This is essential to the students with whom I work, who need to get to know and like their teachers in order to learn. I appreciate the stimulating yet orderly structure of a Montessori classroom; Maria Montessori was certainly ahead of her time when she said, "The task of the educator lies in seeing that the child does not confuse good with immobility and evil with activity, as often happens in the case of old-time discipline."

Many Montessori classrooms are bright, appealing environments with a variety of quality materials, many of them kinesthetic. The Montessori philosophy is to provide children with a variety of choices so that (within limits) students can follow a general work plan and self-direct their activities. As some children work independently, others are receiving instruction either one-on-one or in small groups with the teacher. This approach allows the student to take a more active role in learning. For hyperactive children, the greater freedom of movement in the Montessori classroom is an enormous relief. Again, these children literally need to move to think.

While Montessori schools are light-years ahead of traditional classrooms, and I support them as a refreshing alternative to repetitious, rote-oriented learning, they're not perfect. Unfortunately, tuition can be sky high, and Montessori proponents haven't done a very good job of making clear how their approach differs from that of open schools. There's also no guarantee of uniform standards among schools, so there are good Montessori schools and bad ones.

I have also noticed that many unenlightened Montessori schools continue to use the sounding out of words as the preferred approach to reading and spelling for all children. This clashes with the right-brained child's learning style. If Montessori could effectively use sight words and visualization techniques to teach children to read, it would be an ideal classroom setting for most right-brained children. Unfortunately, Montessori schools, like many other schools, tend to attract teachers who are sequential and left-brained.

When I've come across Montessori instructors who are more right-brained, they can be wonderful with ADD and right-brained children. Their schools can be a safe haven for children with different learning styles. But, again, not all Montessori schools are alike. I've worked in some that label, shame, and purge right-brained children because of their nontraditional learning styles. It really boils down to the philosophy of the director and the appreciation and understanding by individual teachers of the subtleties of how children learn.

Back to Basics

Back to basics is being touted as *the* antidote for declining test scores, lower literacy rates, and higher dropout rates. In the United States, a return to basics is the driving force in education today. Charter schools and private schools abound with the lure of uniforms, phonics, a focus on the three R's, structure, lots of homework, and strict discipline. While back-to-basics proponents share my disdain for what's happening in our schools, I see basics as a simplistic answer to a complex problem. It's wishful thinking that we can go back to a simpler time when children grew up in two-parent families and were not exposed to drugs, crime, television, and sex on the Internet. While useful for left- and whole-brained children who learn auditorily and sequentially, basics is unquestionably the wrong approach for children with ADD, dyslexics, and bright, right-brained students.

The one thing that back-to-basics education does offer for right-brained children, to a degree, is structure. The right-brained child, particularly a child with ADD, lacks internal discipline and impulse control, so he needs more external limits on his behavior. The back-to-basics insistence on classroom decorum, with the teacher doing most of the talking and not tolerating many questions or interruptions, works in the ADD child's favor. He will perform better in a controlled setting than in an open school where anything goes. Comfort can be found in predictability and routine if the child has trouble filtering out stimuli. For children with ADD, structure, no matter how demeaning, is often better than no structure at all.

Open or Alternative Schools

While so-called open schools offer a refreshing choice for left- and whole-brained students, their unstructured environment makes them a poor choice for the child with ADD.

The roots of the open classroom can be traced to the Summerhill School in Suffolk, England, where, amid great fanfare, an experimental school was established that was the opposite of the traditional, rigid classroom. The Summerhill philosophy actually began at the Jacques Delacroze School in Hellerau, Germany, in 1922, under the directorship of Alexander Sutherland Neill. At the time, a local newspaper gave this description of the school's philosophy: "The center of school life will be social life. There will be no dictatorship from above. . . . Psychologically the school is founded on the belief that the child is good, and no punishment or rewards will be given."

In 1923, with gunshots of revolution in nearby Dresden, Neill moved the school to Austria. He soon clashed with Austrian authorities over his refusal to teach religion, so within a year Neill moved the school to England, calling it Summerhill in honor of the boardinghouse it first occupied on the southern coast. The school continues today with a relatively small student body in a location about one hundred miles northeast of London.

Neill believed that children should be allowed total freedom, so long as they didn't disturb the peace of others. He said that education should reflect a child's passions. "When a boy makes a snowball, he is interested," Neill would say. "There is more to education in making snowballs than in listening to an hour's lecture on grammar." So in the Summerhill School, students actually *choose* to attend lessons, or they can opt for something else, including play. Students select subjects of interest, exploring them in great depth, using the outdoors and museums, theaters, and galleries as classrooms, not worrying so much about such details as spelling, punctuation, and computational math. No homework or tests are given at Summerhill.

The Summerhill philosophy of freedom for children gained popularity in the United States in the early 1960s when it was fashionable to rebel against structure and authority. Open schools based on the Summerhill model cropped up throughout the country; many of these schools are still in existence today. Interestingly, this approach does have some merit for left- and whole-brained children, who are more able to handle the stimulation, unpredictability, and distractions of open classrooms since they have an internal sense of structure and order. But the freewheeling, touchy-feely, open classroom setting based on Summerhill is an unmitigated disaster for most hypersensitive right-brained children, particularly kids with ADD. Bombarded with sensory input, choices, and erratic scheduling, these children will choose by making no choice. They find it impossible to choose a task and stick to it. Such is the catch-22 of being a right-brained, ADD child. He needs to be stimulated in order to learn, yet he often needs someone to help him get started, and he requires constant guidelines and prodding to finish anything.

Lindamood-Bell Therapy

If you're limited in your choices of schools for your ADD child, you may decide to supplement his classroom experience with private instruction. Many different methods can be applied by parents or specially trained tutors. One such method that's growing in popularity is called Lindamood-Bell Therapy, an alternative program to teach reading and spelling to students who are dyslexic or who are failing to read when taught in traditional ways. Pioneered by Patricia C. and Phyllis Lindamood and Nanci Bell in San Luis Obispo, California, it's a highly touted intensive program that's being applied by teachers and tutors in several parts of the country. Its cornerstone is the Lindamood Auditory Conceptualization Test, which measures the student's ability to register and sequence phonemes, the building blocks of language. Literature from Lindamood reports that while 4 percent of the population are color blind and cannot discriminate colors, fully *30 percent* of us have auditory conceptual problems that are moderate to severe.

The Lindamood method is certainly superior to back-to-basics phonics remediation for right-brained and learning disabled children. I generally like the approach, particularly its tenet that reading is about comprehension and visualization. What sets Lindamood-Bell apart from what I do is its combination of visual and kinesthetic techniques. Kinesthetically, children learn to read out loud by experiencing the way vowels "feel" when they say them. In other words, vowel sounds are taught by the way they are felt in the mouth and vocal cords as the student exaggerates the sound. Literature from Lindamood states that "feeling the action of tongue, lips, and mouth shape in producing speech sounds gives the sounds an additional dimension." Students are also asked to trace letters in the sand or feel colored blocks or pieces of fabric as they form sentences, another use of kinesthetic or hands-on sensory learning.

Lindamood-Bell Therapy has had some promising results with children ages five through twelve who manifest early reading difficulties, for medicated children with ADD, and for dyslexics for whom nothing else has worked. It clearly has some effectiveness, if for no other reason than the child responds positively to one-on-one attention. While it doesn't work for all students and is certainly not a "cure" for ADD, it may be among the better alternatives we have right now. Unfortunately, Lindamood is too costly for most people (averaging $3,500 a month) and may become diluted through franchising. I worry that as the Lindamood method catches on, the program will expand too fast and lose its essence. The program is only as good as the teacher who implements it.

While Lindamood-Bell Therapy is certainly superior to phonics for right-brained children and will produce results with almost any child, I feel it's unnecessarily costly and will remain primarily an option for the upper class. Universally implementing the visual teaching methods that are described here will reach virtually all right-brained students regardless of income level.

Home Schooling

Given the sorry state of our schools, it's not surprising that home schooling is one of the fastest-growing movements in education today. An estimated 1.2 million children, more than 2 percent of the population, receive educational instruction at home, an almost *hundredfold* increase in the last two decades. Home schooling is legal in all fifty states, although the state laws that regulate it vary widely. While home schooling is still associated with religious conservatives, a growing percentage of home schoolers have other motivations. As our schools reach a shrinking percentage of children, many desperate parents are taking matters into their own hands and becoming at-home teachers, not an easy task. Until our schools are better able to reach right-brained and at-risk students, I see home schooling as a viable option and admire and encourage the parent who chooses to do it. After all, you know your child better than anyone else does, and you have the time and commitment to work with him one-on-one.

Children with learning disabilities and ADD thrive on individual instruction, particularly if their instructor understands how they learn. At least one recent study—from home-schooling advocate Dr. Brian Ray—has found that, on average, home-schooled children score much higher on standard achievement tests than public school children.

Should you choose to home-school your child, it's critical that you be familiar with his learning style. If he has ADD, he'll be a visual learner, and you will most likely find success with the methods outlined in this book. Use this program as a trial to see how you interact and how much you accomplish together. You don't have to spend seven hours a day working with your child. In most cases he can learn more with a capable parent in one and a half to three hours than he can in seven hours in a classroom with twenty-nine other students. Work in short, intense bursts on a subject area until you notice his attention is wearing thin. At that point, take a breather, then return to the subject later, trying a different approach, or move on to another subject altogether.

To be successful in home schooling, once again I would emphasize the importance of being totally nonjudgmental in working with your child. He will sense your expectations and frustrations, and will either "check out" or refuse to work with you. Don't let home schooling become a test of wills; if something isn't working, try another approach.

Since you have a right-brained child, you must find creative ways to get his attention and hold his interest. Instead of limiting your work to a desk or table, choose appropriate activities outside of the home, such as taking him to museums, plays, and art galleries, to keep learning fun and exciting. Make liberal use of the computer; this fits his learning style, and there are a number of wonderful CD-ROM programs out there to enhance his education, such as Microsoft's Dangerous Creatures, David Macaulay's The Way Things Work, and any of the programs from The Magic School Bus series. Check out the home-schooling support groups on America Online: They have everything from lesson plans to online teachers who can answer questions in most subject areas. There's no doubt that technology will be a catalyst for the growth of home schooling.

If you find yourself hitting a barrier with your child, consider getting outside help. It might make sense to hire a tutor for a short time to introduce a difficult new concept or address a specific subject area. Seek a trained high school or college student, or a public school teacher looking for summer work. Don't do it all yourself! Join an organization for parents who home-school their children. Many groups schedule regular sporting events and field trips. This can provide you with support as well as give your child the opportunity to socialize with other kids.

Investigate whether your child is eligible to participate in some extracurricular activities sponsored by local public schools, such as athletics, chess clubs, or computer labs. About one-third of states allow this, although the majority of districts say it's not fair to give positions on sports teams to kids who aren't enrolled. Some home-schooling parents argue that because they pay taxes, their children should be allowed to take public school classes "à la carte," but most school districts balk at the idea, saying state funding is based on full-time enrollment. Perhaps our legislators will consider modifying school funding formulas to accommodate part-time students so that the home-schooled child can go to the neighborhood school each day for an art, physical education, or music class.

Certainly home schooling will continue to grow in popularity until we can get our schools back on track. It's my hope that someday our educational system will better respond to the learning styles of individuals, reducing the necessity of teaching children at home.

Beyond the Classroom: Tips on Discipline and Organization

Children with high ability typically are independent, self-directed, willful, dominant nonconformists. These children are not passive goody-goodies. They are often difficult to be around because they want to "run the show." Yet this same quality also makes them most interesting and stimulating to be around.

—ELLEN WINNER, *Gifted Children*

Joey, eight years old, is in the principal's office once again. This time he's in trouble for hitting Eddie on the playground. As I said earlier, one of the most striking features of children who are labeled ADD is their hypersensitivity. These two got off on the wrong foot when Eddie approached and yelled, "Hey, Joey, come play baseball!" Joey is startled by the sound of Eddie's voice and is agitated by it because Joey has such an acute sense of hearing. Joey's nervous system is also set more in "alarm" mode than the rest of us. He has the same range of emotions that all children do, such as anger, sadness, jealousy, and shame, only squared or cubed. Once Joey agreed to play, he wanted to win more than anything. So when Eddie inadvertently tripped Joey as he was rounding second base, the rage Joey felt was disproportionate to the actual deed. Joey lashed out and slugged Eddie, and had to be pulled off him by four other children and an adult.

Joey is extremely right-brained and has ADD, so it's not particularly surprising that he overreacts and is always in trouble. His intentions are good, but his temper and impulsivity often get the best of him. He tends to "live in the moment." As mentioned earlier, the part of the brain responsible for impulse control is underdeveloped in the ADD child. He also tends to process randomly and nonsequentially; he's unable to anticipate the consequences his actions may have for himself and others. Since all children with ADD are visual thinkers and have the ability to hold images longer than other children, it makes sense to harness this ability and apply it to behavior problems. I'd use this approach with Joey. For one week I'd ask him to try to anticipate the consequences his actions might bring *before* acting on impulse. I might say, "You can still go ahead and hit Eddie or scream that obscenity if you want to, but take a couple of seconds to visualize the consequences. Get out of your own head and see it from another person's perspective. After all, you do that so well anyway. That's the kind of intelligence you have. Use your spatial ability to anticipate what reactions your actions will produce."

After Joey has had some time to think about it, I ask him to tell me what some of those consequences might be, such as getting punched himself, being suspended from school, and facing the wrath of his parents. Then I have him brainstorm with me on better ways to handle the problem. Joey says he might ask Eddie if he tripped him on purpose; another option is simply to walk away. This system not only conditions Joey to "count to ten" before reacting, it applies his reasoning and spatial skills to help him make better choices. Practiced for even a day, this has proven to be a very effective technique to help children with ADD cope with the kind of impulses that usually get them into trouble.

Children like Joey need a system of discipline that's firm, fair, and consistent. They need set limits as well as a clear understanding of what the consequences will be for misbehavior. Just as they respond better in school if they see the relevance of their academic work, they'll respond to limits if you explain the reasons for them. "Because I said so" doesn't cut it with these kids. If your child is disruptive at school or at home, don't just say "knock it off." Tell him *why* his misbehavior is such a problem—that it keeps him from getting his work done, disturbs his classmates, and so on. Right-brained children respond very well when you ask them such questions as "How would you feel if you were in the middle of an artwork and Ryan knocked all your paints over?" Your child is able to get out of his own head and see how another child might feel in the same situation, which can help him understand the reasons for the rules.

If your rule is one hour of television a day, explain why. You might say that kids who watch too much TV don't do as well in school, tend to be overweight, and miss out on a lot of fun. Tell him he's too smart to spend so much time in a mind-deadening activity. You might draw a graph of brain waves during reading, with a lot of peaks and valleys, and then show a flat line of a child watching TV. He still may not like your rule, but at least he'll understand that it's not arbitrary.

Zach used to throw tantrums at the grocery store, demanding that Laurie buy every sugary cereal on the shelves that he'd seen advertised on TV. Laurie didn't just say no; she used the opportunity to compare prices of the heavily advertised cereals with those she usually buys, letting Zach see for himself how much sugar and artificial ingredients were contained in the brands he was demanding. This also provided the opportunity for a discussion of how the creators of TV commercials use subtle messages to manipulate consumers into buying their products. Now Zach has fun critiquing commercials, saying, "I'll bet those kids are being paid to *look* as if they're having fun with that slime monster action figure" or "I'll bet that candy bar isn't nearly as good as they say it is. They're just trying to trick us."

If your child is routinely disruptive, try a "chip" system with him. Teresa Sims, a speech and language specialist at Marshdale Elementary School in Evergreen, Colorado, uses this method effectively with fidgety and disruptive students. Each child gets five "chips" (checkers or poker chips work fine) at the start of a small group session. Each admonition (such as "please sit down" or "no wild behavior in class") results in one chip being taken away. Once all five are gone, the child has to quit the group activity and return to regular class. You can use a version of this at home, sending your child to his room after he loses all five chips. Quietly removing a chip takes you out of the "bad guy" role, eliminates nagging and yelling, and serves as an excellent visual reminder of how your child is measuring up.

Consequences work best if they're directly related to the misdeed. For example, if a child has a habit of forgetting his lunch box, don't yell at him or "rescue" him by dashing to school with the lunch box every day. I know it's hard to do, but let him go hungry for an afternoon. It's not likely that he'll forget his lunch again.

An excellent explanation of natural and logical consequences can be found in the book *Parenting with Love and Logic* by Dr. Foster Cline and Jim Fay. They note that many of the most disrespectful and rebellious children come from loving homes, but homes with two kinds of parents: "helicopter parents" and "drill sergeant parents." The helicopter parents "think *love* means rotating their lives around their children. . . . They hover over and rescue their children whenever trouble arises. They're forever running lunches and permission slips and homework assignments to school; they're always pulling their children out of jams; not a day goes by when they're not protecting little junior from something—usually from a learning experience the child needs or deserves." Skipping these learning experiences as a child leaves the individual unequipped for the challenges of adult life. Who will bail him out when he flunks out of college, gets fired from his job, or forgets to pay his bills?

Drill sergeant parents, Cline and Fay point out, also think they're doing what's best for their children. "They feel that the more they bark and the more they control, the better their kids will be in the long run. . . . When drill sergeant parents talk to children, their words are often filled with putdowns and I-told-you-so's. These parents are into power! If children don't do what they're told, drill sergeant parents are going to—doggone it all—make them do it." But the problem with drill sergeant parents is their offspring never learn to think for themselves. "These kids are rookies in the world of decisions. They've never had to think—the drill sergeant took care of that. The kids have been ordered around all of their lives. They're as dependent on their parents when they enter the real world as the kids of helicopter parents." These are the children who may be easy to parent when they're young but give their parents the middle-finger salute when they're teenagers.

Fay tells an amusing story of how he got his kids to go to bed at a reasonable hour without the usual bedtime battles. One evening he announced that it was getting to be a hassle to nag them into going to bed, so the new rule was that the kids could stay up as late as they wanted. The only caveat was that they had to be ready to head out the door for school at 7:30 the next morning.

You can probably guess what happened. The kids had a blast staying up all hours of the night, but the next morning their faces were in their oatmeal. They fell asleep in class and on the bus, and as soon as they got home they made a beeline for their beds. Now they've learned to set reasonable bedtimes for themselves so they can be rested and ready for the school day. They learned for themselves the reasons for a consistent, sensible bedtime.

Right-brained children in particular need to see the relevance of rules, which sometimes means experiencing, or at least imagining, the results when they aren't followed. It's much better for them to experience failure when they're young than to fail as a teenager or adult when the stakes are much higher.

When your child makes a mistake, don't humiliate him in public. The results can be devastating for a sensitive, right-brained child, and your intervention will do far more harm than good. It's much better to make your points while allowing him to save face. If you're sincere about trying to help your child, do it gently and privately. Take him aside, one-on-one, tell him he made a mistake, and talk about ways you can solve the problem together. Give him the dignity to learn from his mistakes. While it's true that he's sensitive, he almost always responds to feedback that's properly given because he's driven to be the best.

Take heart that while kids like these will always be a challenge, their behavior will improve as they gain experience coping with failure. Ages four to seven are probably the worst. How you handle their scenes and outbursts helps determine how quickly this phase will pass. It also helps to recognize that your child doesn't like himself either when he's behaving this way. What he needs is space to learn how to calm himself down and deal with his feelings of disappointment. Pursuing him as he retreats into his room, yelling at him and berating him for his obnoxious performance—"What's wrong with you? None of the other kids react this way! I'm sick of this crazy behavior!"—does nothing to solve the problem. While it takes a tremendous amount of patience to make the situation better, it's very easy to make it worse.

CALVIN AND HOBBES © 1987 Watterson. Dist. by UNIVERSAL PRESS SYNDICATE.

If he's throwing tantrums at a Little League game, acknowledge his feelings. If you give him words for his painful feelings this time, you'll increase the likelihood that he'll use words to express himself more appropriately the next time. You might say, "I know it hurts to be thrown out at first [or to strike out, and so forth]. It must really make you feel bad because you love baseball and you love to win." But let him know that his behavior is unacceptable. Explain calmly that he'll need to pull himself back together so he can continue playing. Save the larger discussion about what happened for later. I've found that when I have a concern to discuss with my son, such as his poor sportsmanship or his slipping grades in school, bedtime is a good time. I get a warm, positive response when we're alone and relaxed, and I have his undivided attention.

Always remember this premise: Do not measure your child's behavior, at least initially, against that of other children. Recognize the small gains he makes for himself and praise him for those. Because he's so competitive by nature and loves to win at all costs, set up a two-tiered structure of winning for games and sporting events. Tell him, "Of course, we'll all look at who wins the Monopoly game, so that will be one level of competition. But from now on we're going to add another level: the "good sportsmanship" award. All players who can get through the game while demonstrating good sportsmanship will get a prize when the game's over." Make the prize something he really likes, such as an extra story at bedtime or a small treat.

And this is critical: When the moment of truth arrives and he's preparing to go into tantrum mode, gently remind him about the good sportsmanship award and look for some improvement in his behavior, any improvement at all. He may still get angry, but if he refrains from marching out of the room, consider how much effort that took and reward him accordingly. As he begins to experience some success with controlling his emotions and is rewarded and recognized for that Herculean effort, he'll continue to improve until his behavior is almost or even bearable.

There's no call for shouting at children, especially ADD children. Not only does it hurt their ears, it gives them the satisfaction of knowing that this time they *really* got to you. I'm not an advocate of spanking, either; in fact, I've never spanked my child. Since right-brained children don't think sequentially, they may not see the connection between the swat on the bottom and the misdeed that occurred five minutes or five hours ago. They experience the spanki as hurtful, and rather than remembering how it came about, they remember how much they hate you. Martin Hoffman, a psychology professor at New York University, says, "Spanking and physical force in general accomplish quick compliance but build up resentment, anger, fear of the parent."

A child who is spanked may repress his anger toward you, later expressing it by picking on a safe target. He may smack a playmate at school or punch his little brother. Children who are spanked engage in much more violent and antisocial behavior than children who aren't; a study of six-to-nine-year-olds from the University of New Hampshire has found the more spankings kids endure, the more they bully, lie, destroy, and disobey. Spanking gives your child the message that "might makes right," that you rule because you're bigger than he is. (And what happens when he's a teenager and he can hit you back?) It's a myth that children who aren't spanked become delinquents. In fact, research consistently supports quite the opposite: that serious delinquents have often been punished harshly and severely by their parents.

The only exception I would concede to the no-spanking rule is when a child's deliberate disobedience puts him in a *very dangerous or life-threatening situation*. If you shout at him to stop and he runs into the street after his ball anyway, a swat on the behind with a firm "no!" may be appropriate. This gets your child's attention, and because it's used so rarely, it will have a powerful and immediate impact.

When you're absolutely at wit's end, remember that if a child like yours can survive childhood, chances are he'll be very successful in his future careers and endeavors as he effectively harnesses his perfectionism and drive to be the best. He may turn out to be a very prosperous CEO, with tremendous drive and vision—even if he does have a nasty habit of throwing his club on the golf course!

■ One of the biggest complaints parents have about their ADD children is that they're forgetful, or one might say "organizationally challenged"! How many times do your verbal instructions go "in one ear and out the other" or you hear yourself saying, "How many times do I have to tell you to . . ."? Some standard techniques to help these kids get it together include buying them Day-Timers and teaching them to write everything down. Since right-brained children process better visually than auditorily, it helps to give them *visual* cues about their behavior, rather than constantly nagging them. One of the more creative techniques I've seen comes from *The "Putting on the Brakes" Activity Book for Young People with ADHD* by Patricia Quinn and Judith Stern, which suggests that visual children draw pictures of reminders instead of making lists. Or you might put a poster on the wall with magazine cutouts to remind him of his duties, such as pictures of a child brushing his teeth, watering plants, or taking out the trash. Make liberal use of sticker and star charts to reward good behavior and accomplishments.

As an alternative you can simply ask your child to visualize the things he needs to remember to do on a particular day—that is, make a mental picture of each task. For example, if he needs to remember to bring his science project to school, tell him to close his eyes, go up to his mental blackboard, and visualize himself walking out the door with his diorama in hand. If he needs to feed the neighbor's dog after school, continue the exercise by asking him to "see" himself heading next door after school and going through the motions of opening the can of dog food, and so on. Many teens and adults with ADD who have learned to access their visual memory can lie in bed each morning and visualize their entire day, remembering everything they have to do and in what order. I myself never write anything down. I'm capable of remembering meeting times, directions to clients' homes, and phone numbers. I may be right-brained and have ADD, but I rarely miss or am late for an appointment.

■ One of the simplest things you can do to help your ADD child is to take a firm stand on the amount of television he's allowed to watch. It's disturbing that most American children spend more time glued to the TV than they spend in school! Excessive television viewing can have a particularly detrimental effect on the child with ADD, who may be more prone to hyperactivity and impulsively copying some of the negative behaviors he sees on TV.

Some suggestions on taking control of television include:

Limit television viewing to one hour per day.

Get the family together on Sunday night, with the week's programming schedule in hand, and decide which programs you're going to watch for the coming week.

Explain to your child that television is a low priority in your home, behind family time, homework, exercise, and daily chores.

He shouldn't watch TV until he's fulfilled these other obligations.

Try as much as possible to watch TV with your child.

You may be shocked at what passes for children's entertainment these days. This allows you to monitor what he's watching, answer his questions, and inject your comments and values into what's happening. Turn down the sound during the commercials; ask him to summarize what has occurred thus far. This helps him turn his mental pictures into verbal descriptions.

No "channel surfing" just to see what's on.

Make use of the VCR.

This allows you to control the content of what comes into your home and to fast-forward through commercials.

Don't put a TV set near your kitchen or dining table.

Place it where it can't interfere with precious family conversation.

As tempting as it may be (and we all do it) resist the urge to use television as a baby-sitter.

If you need some uninterrupted time, take a few minutes to set your child up with a coloring book and crayons, a good book, or some tubs of Play-Doh.

Read to your child whenever possible.

The landmark 1994 Carnegie Corporation study "Starting Points" has found only half of infants and toddlers are routinely read to by their parents. This is a national disgrace.

Don't be a couch potato yourself.

If you are, take this as an opportunity to wean yourself from TV. Spend more time on sports, hobbies, or family activities. You'll not only set a good example for your child, *you* may discover there's more to life than sitcoms!

▣ Another reason that we're seeing so many hyperactive children in the classroom is that they're not getting enough exercise *outside* the classroom. Only one-third of children participate in a daily physical education class, and our kids are fatter today than ever before. Instead of swinging hockey sticks, they're playing with joysticks. Instead of working their heart and lungs in a game of "kick the can," they're working their jaws on potato chips in front of a Power Rangers program. If more and more adults are becoming "couch potatoes," our "tater tots" or "sofa spuds" aren't far behind.

There is a powerful mind-body connection. Children who get regular exercise have lower blood pressure, higher levels of HDL, or so-called good cholesterol, and a lower percentage of body fat than children who are less active. Regular exercise produces endorphins, a brain chemical associated with a sense of happiness and well-being. I myself was a child who was "saved" by athletics. A below-average student in high school, I was fortunate to take a history class from a wonderful teacher who doubled as the track coach. He urged me to go out for the team, and with his encouragement I became the fastest miler in my school. Athletics provided me with a positive outlet for my competitiveness and perfectionism. Even though I had less time to study, my self-esteem was so much better that my grades improved geometrically. The sense of pride I gained from athletics carried over into all other aspects of my high school life. I shudder to think what might have happened to me had our school's athletic programs fallen victim to budget cuts.

How ironic that many teachers punish children for being wiggly and disruptive in class by making them stay inside during recess! Every child should engage in at least a half-hour a day of continuous, vigorous exercise. This doesn't mean you have to put him on a treadmill; just allow him opportunities to Rollerblade, ride his bicycle, or play a game of chase with his friends. Never push your child; instead, let him guide you to a sport or athletic activity that has captured his interest. Children are naturally physically active. If it's a warm day, shoo your child out the door after school instead of letting him "veg out" in front of the TV. During periods of inclement weather, you have to get creative: Get a minitrampoline or take him to an indoor pool or one of those indoor play centers for kids. Or bundle him up and introduce him to winter sports like sledding, ice skating, skiing, and snowshoeing.

When it comes to physical fitness, the best thing you can do is model good behavior for your child. What better excuse do *you* need to get in shape? Make him your workout buddy. Teach him a routine that includes stretches, sit-ups, push-ups, and weights. Go on short runs with him to train for a 5-K family fun race that's coming up. Not only will your child be healthier and better able to cope with stress, but he'll be sharing a goal with you. And the time you and he spend pursuing it will be the memories of his childhood that he (and you) will cherish.

Just as exercise produces a sense of well-being in children, so does music. Children naturally love music; they're captivated by rhyme and rhythm. But now there's a new reason to expose children of all ages to music: It may help them become math wizards. A study in the journal *Neurological Research* finds exposure to music can affect a child's spatial-temporal reasoning. This spatial thinking forms the foundation for math, engineering, and chess skills. In this particular study, researchers observed how abilities of three- and four-year-olds were affected by weekly piano lessons. After six months these

"Carnegie Hall wannabes" scored 34 percent above average on this particular reasoning skill, a remarkable increase.

How does music relate to spatial skills? Gordon Shaw at the University of California at Irvine hypothesizes that when playing the piano, "you are seeing how patterns work in space and time." More research needs to be done on the long-term effects of exposing our children to music, but this early study is encouraging and certainly provides validation for what many parents have suspected all along: that music training is critical for nurturing the brains and souls of children of all ages.

Cultivate an appreciation of music in your child from an early age by playing lullaby tapes, singing with him in the car to Raffi tunes, and encouraging him to learn piano or another musical instrument. Take him regularly to the ballet, the symphony, and other local concerts and stage productions. Make music an integral part of *your* life as well. It's a great escape from the challenges of parenting!

To Drug or Not to Drug?

◧ Torsten, at the tender age of seven, is already falling behind in school. While he is fairly bright and has some reading ability, his spelling is atrocious and his math work is inconsistent. But the biggest problem with Torsten, his teachers say, is his angry behavior in the classroom. He's a virtual maelstrom in school, yelling, jumping up and down, and bullying other children.

I'm called in to help Torsten, and while I'm able to establish a good rapport with him, it's clear that his ability to stay on task can be measured in seconds. He is distracted by the smallest thing: the wind rustling a tree branch outside or a phone ringing in another room. A typical one-hour tutoring session with Torsten might consist of fifteen minutes of calming him down and getting him in the right frame of mind to work, then five or six minutes of reading, then another ten or fifteen minutes to get him back on task, five more minutes of reading, and so on. Working with Torsten is like trying to reel in a big fish: Just when I almost have him, I lose him again. At the end of the hour I leave with the feeling that I can't do much with this child. His antennae are so outrageously acute, I figure he'll need an isolation ward in order to be taught successfully. If it's this difficult for Torsten to focus one-on-one with an expert, I wonder how much harder it must be for him to learn anything in a typical classroom. His academic future seems bleak.

I don't believe in using medication as a front-line approach to ADD, but Torsten seems to be an obvious candidate for Ritalin. When I gently bring it up with his parents, they understandably balk, telling me they're trying a variety of natural remedies. But after several months, with Torsten's behavior continuing in a downward spiral, his parents finally agree to discuss Ritalin with their pediatrician.

When Torsten and I work together again, he's a different child. He can sit still and focus for most of the tutoring session—much to his and my delight. He tells me, "I hear a lot less noise now, and when you talk, I can really listen. I used to have about twenty radio stations in my head at the same time, and now I have only one. I really like the difference." Torsten's schoolwork improves dramatically, as does his approval rating from parents and teachers. He develops some friendships, does above-average work in the basic subjects, and excels in art and music. He could be a Ritalin poster child.

The use of Ritalin, known generically as methylphenidate, has almost tripled since 1990. More than 1.5 million young people ages five through eighteen now take the drug, according to the December 1996 issue of *Pediatrics*. This represents about 3 percent of school-aged children overall in the United States. I hear reports of more than 20 percent of students in some schools taking Ritalin or other stimulants for ADD; they line up in the middle of the school day at the nurse's office, where the drug is passed out like candy.

In our short-attention-span, quick-fix, want-it-*now* society, it's no wonder that Ritalin is so popular. We have pills for everything else: to make us happy, to calm our nerves, to help us sleep. It's no wonder that we look to a pill to cure ADD. Parents march into pediatricians' offices, usually at the urging of teachers, demanding medication to "fix" their kids.

Unfortunately, not all kids respond to Ritalin as Torsten does. In fact, from observing the children in my own practice, it seems to me that Ritalin is working for a shrinking percentage of children who've been diagnosed with ADD. Many other teachers, administrators, and physicians with whom I've shared this observation agree wholeheartedly. It's almost as if ADD is developing a new strain that's "drug resistant," like a mutant virus! Of course, this is not the case. My theory is simply that Ritalin doesn't work for many of these children because *they don't really have ADD*.

While I have encountered a number of children like Torsten whom I believe truly need Ritalin to help them calm down and focus, they are quite unusual. The rest of the children taking Ritalin are using a medication that is not only unnecessary but can arguably be detrimental to their physical and mental well-being. There's no doubt that Ritalin is overprescribed as a way to help students more passively tolerate dull and outdated teaching methods. As Dr. Thomas Arm strong writes in *The Myth of the ADD Child*, "That such drugs may be used primarily to help kids adjust to the boring, routine-ridden, repetition-plagued classrooms says more about the sad state of many schools than it does about the so-called deficits of these kids." So while Ritalin is an effective weapon in our arsenal for people with ADD, it's being overprescribed to children who are simply bored and uninterested in today's regimented, irrelevant classrooms.

A more malevolent problem is Ritalin's growing popularity as a street drug. In a case recently reported in the *Denver Post*, an eighth-grade boy was suspended after allegedly bringing Ritalin from home to school and selling it to three classmates, who each paid five dollars for twenty tablets. This is hardly an isolated case. An editorial in *The New York Times* observed, "Ritalin is so plentiful that in some junior high schools it's a 'gateway drug,' the first drug a child experiments with. 'I used to mix it with marijuana,' a recovering teen-age addict in Maryland said. 'It gives you a nice buzz.' "

It's faddish nowadays to challenge Ritalin and its overuse, but it's also appropriate. Parents who seek out information about the drug are likely to find contradictory research, however, and vastly differing opinions and testimonials about its benefits and side effects. Many parents tell me after doing exhaustive research on Ritalin that they're more confused than they were when they started!

One consequence of the overprescribing of Ritalin is the equally extreme backlash it has produced. To claim that no one needs or benefits from Ritalin could result in denying a valuable drug to some children who really need it. But even when Ritalin is necessary and helpful, it isn't a panacea. It isn't a substitute for taking the time to help right-brained children learn in a way that's compatible with the way they think—or for overhauling outmoded teaching methods.

If your child's teacher suggests Ritalin, don't immediately discount the suggestion. It could be that your child really needs it. But before rushing to Ritalin, I recommend you research other bases for your child's difficulties in school and try other interventions first. Medication should be used as a last resort. The following checklist may help you eliminate other reasons for your child's behavior before you consent to a Ritalin trial:

- Ask yourself whether your child's problems with attention, focusing, and hyperactivity affect him all day long or just at school. Determine when and how often he exhibits ADD-like behavior (such as on the playground) and whether his difficulties interfere with learning. If he's having problems in the classroom only, it could be an indication of faulty teaching rather than an attention disorder. Demystify the process; don't tiptoe around the issue or use the term "ADD" in hushed tones. Talk frankly with your child about what *he* thinks may be behind his difficulties in school.
- If you know your child is right-brained, talk to the teacher about his learning style and about the modifications suggested in this book.
- Work with your child individually using the methods outlined here. In many cases, the child who's suspected of having ADD is magically "cured" when he's taught in a different way.
- Have your child evaluated by a qualified pediatrician, psychologist, or psychiatrist with extensive experience in diagnosing ADD. See if there are other medical or psychological reasons for his misbehavior.

Side Effects of Ritalin

Ritalin is one of the most exhaustively researched—and relatively safest—drugs on the market, with more than four hundred scientific studies devoted to this and other stimulant medications for treating ADD. It would appear contradictory to give a stimulant to someone who is already "wired," as are children with the hyperactivity component of ADD, ADHD, but in fact stimulants have a calming and focusing effect on children with classic ADD. Many parents have known all along that giving one of these kids a dose of caffeine in the morning works just as well, and how many adults with ADD self-medicate with coffee or cola, too?

While Ritalin has a proven track record with many children, no drug is without side effects. Daniel Feiten, a Denver-area pediatrician, says the most common side effect is the moodiness and irritability experienced by a child when "coming down" off the medication, often late in the afternoon. Many children become sad and weepy or lash out at others as the effects of Ritalin wear off. It's a powerful drug with a strong rebound effect that can put children on an emotional roller coaster. Some children taking Ritalin also report loss of appetite, stomachache, weight loss, difficulty sleeping, pounding heart, and headache. In high doses, Ritalin has been known to produce manic episodes, anxiety attacks, and aggression. Many parents anguish over whether it's worth it to keep their child on Ritalin, given these obvious and troubling side effects.

It doesn't help that many pediatricians who prescribe Ritalin know very little about ADD. They hear about kids like Torsten, write a prescription for the pills, and it's adios, see you at your next annual checkup. According to Dr. George Dorry, a common mistake that physicians make in prescribing Ritalin is to assign a starting dosage and then insufficiently monitor its effects on a child. An inappropriate dosage may result in unpleasant side effects or ineffectiveness, leading doctors or parents to assume the drug doesn't work for the child when what's needed is an adjustment in the dosage. It's not enough to monitor the effects of stimulants every six months, every year, or every two years, as is often the case. We need to monitor a child's body weight with regard to Ritalin, much as we check his shoe size. For a growing child it's obvious that the same dose of Ritalin will lose its effect over time—when the child gains thirty pounds and grows four inches!

My opinion is that while the short-term effects of Ritalin have been exhaustively researched, we still don't know enough about its long-term effects. I cannot assure parents beyond a doubt that Ritalin has no significant side effects, and I believe the jury is still out. Perhaps the best way to determine if Ritalin is working for your child is to ask him. Does he feel a powerful, almost immediate effect upon taking it, which allows him to focus and finish a task that would have been impossible before? Ritalin, with the right patient and the correct dose, can work within twenty or thirty minutes and produce dramatic results. For these people, life without medication would be infinitely worse than any side effects it produces. Dr. Russell A. Barkley, professor of psychiatry and neurology at the University of Massachusetts Medical Center and well-known ADD expert, touts a combined therapy for ADD that includes Ritalin, behavior modification techniques, family therapy, and special education services, noting, "No treatment is curative, but in combination these treatments can assist ADHD children in being more productive in school, having better family relationships, reducing the teasing and rejection they receive from peers, decreasing the amount of punishment they may receive, and helping them stay in school longer than they might otherwise have done without treatment."

So while Ritalin can be a godsend for some children, for most children with ADD it's only a small piece of the puzzle—if it fits into the puzzle at all. Notwithstanding its usefulness in some cases, it's unquestionably overprescribed, abused, and used as a substitute for good teaching.

Dexedrine and Cylert

Because of variations in individual body chemistry, Ritalin doesn't work for everyone, even for children with ADD who truly need medication. Doctors usually prescribe Ritalin as the first drug of choice for children with ADD because it's been so exhaustively researched. But if, after several adjustments in dosage, Ritalin still doesn't produce the desired effect, physicians may be inclined to switch to one of two lesser-known stimulant medications: Dexedrine and Cylert.

Dexedrine is chemically very similar to Ritalin and has the advantage of being less costly. While less is known about long-term side effects of Dexedrine, it appears that they are similar to that of its chemical cousin: loss of appetite, anxiety, headache, irregular heartbeat, and trouble sleeping.

Cylert is rapidly falling into disfavor as an alternative to Ritalin for two reasons: It can slow the growth rate of children and cause liver problems. A recent study links Cylert with liver toxicity; children taking the drug are supposed to undergo liver testing every three to six months, yet many parents and doctors fail to closely monitor the drug's effects. While it may be that Cylert is the only drug that helps your child, it's important to carefully weigh the benefits versus the risks.

Clonidine

Some hypersensitive children who fail to respond to Ritalin or other stimulants may do very well with a lesser-known but highly effective drug called clonidine. This drug was originally developed to treat high blood pressure, but it has the interesting effect of being able to temper the extreme sensitivity and mood swings of many children. It works by reducing levels of a neurotransmitter in the brain known as noradrenaline. High levels of this chemical messenger are associated with aggression, overarousal, and impulsivity. Dr. Bruce Perry at Baylor College of Medicine has found that clonidine can help some children become less impulsive, anxious, and moody, while improving their attentiveness and concentration.

When prescribed appropriately, clonidine serves to lower the antennae of the hypersensitive child, helping him filter and respond to stimuli more effectively. Dr. Dorry recommends clonidine in conjunction with Ritalin in some cases. "We can now fine-tune symptom-specific medications that we're using instead of applying the generalization of 'more problem, more medicine.' " So rather than boosting Ritalin to the high levels that can increase the possibility of side effects, it can sometimes be prescribed at moderate levels to help the ADD child focus, and supplemented with clonidine to dampen excess nervous system activity. Clonidine is a logical choice for the ADD child who also has Tourette's syndrome because the drug can help reduce nervous tics rather than making them worse, as Ritalin sometimes does. Because clonidine lowers blood pressure, however, its use must be especially closely monitored by a physician.

A Drug Horror Story

Denise is an extreme example of what can happen when powerful medications are given inappropriately to children. A bright second grader with ADD, she could rarely finish anything. Yet Denise did above-average on her schoolwork even though she had trouble staying on task and daydreamed in class. Her parents, who were very authoritarian, tired of her resistance to helping out around the house, her moodiness, her defiance, and her lack of organization. Finally, they took her to a psychiatrist, who pronounced that she suffered from bipolar or manic-depressive disorder. Her mood swings were so extreme, the psychiatrist proclaimed, that she would be at high risk of suicide, drug abuse, or juvenile delinquency by the time she reached adolescence. The only answer, he said, was to put her on lithium.

Denise lasted two days on the drug, then suffered a violent and life-threatening grand mal seizure. She was immediately taken off the drug and sent to a psychologist who correctly diagnosed her as having ADD with depression, which is often misdiagnosed as bipolar disorder. As Edward Hallowell and John Ratey have observed in *Driven to Distraction*, ADD and depression often coexist. But they also point out that the person with ADD doesn't stay in a funk for long; he'd rather get up and keep pushing than wallow in despair. Remember that individuals with classic ADD have exaggerated sensory awareness; they really do pick up more and feel more than most people. It's natural for them to appear giddier when they're happy and more depressed when they're sad.

Denise's brush with bad medicine still affects her today. Seven years later, Denise has memory lapses and a tremor that she and her parents believe are the result of the seizure. I'm working regularly with Denise, and she's now getting all A's at an alternative charter school in Colorado. She's been taking Ritalin for some time now, and while it has definitely helped her school performance, it has been no "magic bullet." Ritalin hasn't changed Denise's personality; she's still moody, agitated, and mostly at war with her parents. The reality is that Denise has extreme tendencies in her emotions that are a fundamental part of who she is. They're as much a part of Denise as the color of her hair or eyes. To look for a way to alter them would be to deprive Denise of a vital part of herself. My perception is that Denise's parents, sadly, can't accept her the way she is. They want a model of compliance, a "Stepford child," if you will, and can't accept that Denise will never be a perfectly obedient child. In spite of her academic success, she will always be broken in their eyes. Because Denise is so sensitive, she knows it.

Stories like Denise's aren't that unusual; in fact, similar misdiagno-

ses occur every day. ADD is sometimes misdiagnosed as bipolar disorder, with children being given powerful drugs such as lithium or
Depakote. While other children may not have a severe seizure as
Denise did, they may suffer side effects like fatigue, loss of interest in
life, worsening depression, or zombielike behavior. Bipolar disorder
can also be just another trendy label that the medical community uses
to explain troublesome behavior in children. Just as with ADD, while
there are certainly some children who actually have the condition,
there are just as many, perhaps more, who are simply children acting
out the stresses they feel in our modern-day culture.

As you make the difficult decision about medication for your ADD
child, it's important to keep in mind what drugs are *for*. Giving your
child a pill won't (and shouldn't be used to) supply your child with a
new personality, especially before he's had a chance to really blossom
and discover who he is. Nor are drugs meant to be a substitute for
helping your child understand how his mind works and how he can
best approach learning. Under the most favorable circumstances,
drugs can help get some children in the right frame of mind for such
work.

Other Treatments for ADD

▣ There are many alternative therapies for Attention Deficit Disorder, most of which are faddish, "snake oil" remedies. These miracle cures pop up periodically, initially show great promise, and then the inevitable disappointment sets in, and we move on to the next hot cure for ADD. Naturopathic formulas for ADD, such as "Kidalin," are gaining popularity today as we experience a backlash to Ritalin. These contain herbs such as passion flower, chamomile, catnip, cinnamon bark, and clover. While some parents attest that herbal remedies for hyperactivity produce some results, there has been no major research to document their effectiveness. Remember, just because a product is billed as "natural" doesn't mean it is necessarily safe. Consult your child's physician before using any of these herbal products on a long-term basis.

Entrepreneurs are salivating over the growing interest and diagnosis of ADD and are all too eager to get a piece of this gold mine. Most of these fad treatments disappear as quickly as they arrive on the scene, but a few have at least some lasting value and merit a brief discussion here.

OCCUPATIONAL THERAPY

Occupational therapy, or OT, is a popular tool for children with delayed motor skills and sensory integration (SI) problems. Sensory integration refers to a child's ability—or in the case of many right-brained children, the lack thereof—to use and separate the senses. Children with ADD often manifest delays in fine or gross motor skills, or experience problems with sensory integration, says Dr. Feiten. Occupational therapy addresses this by having the child work with a therapist on a variety of skills such as crawling, hopping, jumping, and handwriting. The goal is to use regular exercises not only to improve motor skills and coordination but to produce some positive behavioral changes as well.

Occupational therapy can certainly have some benefits for children with ADD, creating greater mind-body awareness (kids with ADD tend to mostly "live in their heads," so any physical activity that requires focusing will be beneficial) as well as enhancing motor skills. I've seen many children attain good results with OT in the areas of balance, hopping, walking, and throwing a ball (improving hand-eye coordination). However, many parents who turn to OT as a way of improving their child's handwriting may be discouraged. As noted earlier, handwriting is generally not a strength of right-brained individuals. While it can be developed, good penmanship does not come naturally for them.

Sensory integration therapy is an offshoot of occupational therapy that works with the difficulties many ADD children have in understanding the limits of their physical selves. Sensory integration incorporates exercises such as jumping on a trampoline, catching a ball, hopping, and skipping to improve coordination, balance, and body awareness. A child might be asked to kick a ball into a soccer goal both with and without a blindfold to feel the difference. This therapy has some limited success in getting ADD children out of their heads and more into their bodies. It's one of the more promising treatments for one facet of ADD, although, again, it should not be considered a panacea.

BRAIN GYM

The Brain Gym isn't a *body* workout. It's a series of exercises designed to activate or "switch on" specific areas of the brain. Brain Gym was developed by Dr. Paul Dennison, a dyslexic who founded the Educational Kinesiology Foundation in Ventura, California. The premise of the program is sound: that many children and adults need to move to learn and that we should try other interventions before rushing to put children on Ritalin. Dennison's exercises are designed to stimulate or "wake up" thinking and reasoning centers, to help the learning disabled or ADD individual process new information.

The Brain Gym program includes a couple of dozen specific exercises. Many focus on stress reduction and relaxation. Others may work on balance, strengthening eye muscles, or sharpening hand-eye coordination. Children participating in Brain Gym or educational kinesiology programs might also be asked to write their name or draw circles with the nondominant hand. A movement called the "cross crawl" uses cross-patterning movements—having children cross the midpoint of the body with both hands—which theoretically forces the left- and right-brain to work in concert, producing a more active, whole brain. For example, the participant might march slowly in place, touching their right hand to their left knee and their left hand to their right knee.

My own experience working with people who have dabbled with the Brain Gym or educational kinesiology programs is that individuals may notice some improvement in the initial stages. For example, their handwriting may improve or they may more effectively process lecture material. But in virtually every case that I've seen, within thirty to sixty days of stopping the program, the child reverts to more or less his condition when he started.

I don't accept the premise that we can dramatically shift brain dominance after adolescence. I would concede, however, that Brain Gym and educational kinesiology may serve to allow an individual to at least *glimpse* what it would be like to make greater use of the nondominant side of the brain. These therapies should be considered windows of experience with this potential, and nothing more. Anyone looking for permanent results will most likely be disappointed.

BIOFEEDBACK

Biofeedback is a kind of "mind over body" technique that has certainly achieved some positive results in the area of relaxation and stress management. But its usefulness as a tool for managing ADD has fallen under serious question in recent years.

When you're practicing biofeedback, you're hooked up to a machine that measures physiological responses to stress, such as brain activity, blood pressure, heart rate, muscle tension, and skin temperature. Through the use of this device it's easy to monitor whether you're more or less stressed under certain conditions. You can measure how your body responds to various methods such as relaxation, visualization, or deep breathing while being coached by a trained therapist. The goal is to help you learn to recognize how your body reacts to stress and how to control it.

A recent issue of the *University of California, Berkeley, Wellness Letter* reports that even as a method to manage pain or reduce stress, the benefits of biofeedback are questionable. "Though many studies have found that biofeedback can be beneficial, just as many have not. In addition, biofeedback has often been found to offer no advantage over low-tech relaxation techniques."

Faddish in the early 1990s as a tool for managing ADD, biofeedback was used under the guise of helping the impulsive, hyperactive child experience what it's like to be calm and focused, then coach him to replicate those feelings in high-pressure situations. While this goal is admirable, the technique did not produce the promised results; many clinics that were founded to treat ADD children with biofeedback have since folded.

Dr. Dorry is skeptical about biofeedback's application in treating ADD, saying, "Biofeedback has not reached a level of scientific validity with regard to Attention Deficit Disorder sufficient for me to encourage people to use it." He notes that while biofeedback certainly has demonstrated applications for anxiety reduction, the jury is still out on whether it can help an individual with ADD. There are no large, controlled double-blind studies that prove biofeedback is beneficial for people with Attention Deficit Disorder. In fact, he says, even if we found some improvement, it would be hard to determine whether the biofeedback itself was at work or whether the child benefited simply by spending many hours one-on-one with a caring adult.

DIET AND NUTRITION

It could be said that our ADD-like culture is being fueled by an ADD diet, consisting of fast food, sugar, and caffeine. Espresso bars and coffeehouses are all the rage from coast to coast. Many teens and adults consume a six-pack or more a day of Mountain Dew or Jolt Cola. Our youth are self-medicating with caffeine, sugar, nicotine, speed, and cocaine. As the pace of our lives becomes more frenetic, we turn to stimulants to help us focus and cope with the pressures of deadlines, pagers, faxes, and ringing cell phones.

Many people with ADD whom I've tutored are addicted to fatty foods that are loaded with chemicals, dyes, preservatives, and other additives that can promote allergies and poor health. This may occur because the individual with ADD gets a quick rush of adrenaline when he eats foods to which he's slightly allergic, or foods that have a high sugar or caffeine content. He gets hooked on the "buzz" that the caffeine, sugar, or allergic reaction produces, and when faced with the letdown that invariably occurs, he craves the same foods again.

While changing your child's diet alone won't cure ADD, I believe that a healthy, additive-free diet can be beneficial. As I mentioned earlier, there's a good chance that your ADD child is more sensitive to chemicals and additives than the average child. Logically, the more right-brained the individual, the more exaggerated the sensitivities to everything in the environment, including pollutants, food coloring, caffeine, and even over-the-counter medications.

THE BUCKETS by Scott Stantis

The BUCKETS reprinted by permission of United Feature Syndicate, Inc.

It's simplistic and, by most recent accounts, inaccurate to blame sugar for hyperactivity in children. Numerous studies of late have debunked the sugar-causes-hyperactivity myth. Some recent research even suggests that glucose, or sugar, may actually *help* some children focus better and score higher on standard tests!

The Feingold diet, popular in the 1970s, probably helped many hyperactive kids because it reduces the amount of toxins they put into their ever-so-sensitive systems. This controversial diet was the brainchild of California allergist Benjamin Feingold, who told a 1973 meeting of the American Medical Association that more than half of his hyperactive patients improved on diets that eliminated artificial flavors, colors, preservatives, and salicylate-containing foods (such as apples, berries, grapes, pickles, peaches, plums, tomatoes, and all coffees and teas). I believe that Feingold had some success with his program not because additives produce ADD, but because this approach reduces the chemical stresses on the body.

Dr. William G. Crook has also done extensive research into the food-hyperactivity connection, saying that proper diet drastically reduces the need for Ritalin among his hyperactive patients. Crook not only shares Feingold's view that chemicals and toxins can affect hyperactivity, but he makes an interesting connection between recurrent ear infections in infancy and ADD. In his book *Help for the Hyperactive Child*, he cites a *Clinical Pediatrics* study that found that "69% of children being evaluated for school failure who were receiving medication for hyperactivity, gave a history of greater than 10 ear infections. . . . By comparison, only 20% of non-hyperactive children had more than 10 infections."

Crook's theory goes that when a child develops an ear infection, he's treated with broad-spectrum antibiotics such as amoxicillin. While these drugs knock out infections, they also kill friendly germs, allowing an overgrowth of common and usually benign yeasts in the intestinal tract. Dr. Crook believes this imbalance produces toxins that adversely affect the immune and nervous systems, possibly contributing to hyperactivity. (While this may be true, I would add another perspective on why recurrent ear infections may be linked to ADD: A child who has difficulty hearing will, by definition, be more visual and therefore more likely to exhibit right-brained characteristics. The child may also *appear* to have ADD because he doesn't attend or process well.)

Crook's program includes avoiding foods that promote yeast growth, particularly sugar. He also recommends nystatin or other antifungal medications, plus substances with live, active cultures that discourage yeast growth, such as yogurt. Consult your pediatrician before applying Crook's program; your doctor may first want to rule out any food-related allergies that may be causing your child's hyper-activity and irritability.

A review of other medical research on dietary changes and ADD produces conflicting results so that even the most persistent and in-formed parent is left feeling baffled. I'm somewhat of a health freak myself and have heard a great deal of anecdotal evidence in support of an additive-free diet. Many parents tell me they observe a noticeable improvement in their ADD children's behavior after eliminating satu-rated fats, food dyes, chemicals, additives, and preservatives from fam-ily meals. What do you have to lose? A natural, balanced diet won't cure ADD, but you'll probably have a healthier, less irritable child.

It's important to note that many children make gains simply because of the nurturing, individual attention they receive, regardless of the method. There is no "cure" for ADD; there is no magic bullet. The best way to manage this emerging learning style is a multifaceted approach that includes appropriate medical intervention, behavioral management, and educational therapies that capitalize on the child's many strengths.

THE COMPUTER AGE

Whenever I visit Zach, I always get a kick out of his four-year-old brother, Taylor, who is already hooked on the computer. His feet not even touching the floor, Taylor will spend long periods of time im-mersed in programs such as Reader Rabbit, Math Blaster, and Millie's Science House. I chuckle at the sight of this freckled preschooler concentrating on the computer screen, with one hand on the mouse and the other pudgy thumb in his mouth!

Just as television brought sweeping changes to our generation, com-puters are revolutionizing the world in which our children are being born. Computers are omnipresent. Children who don't have one at home will most likely find one or more in their classroom. An article in *Parade* magazine pronounces that "computers are fast becoming the fourth 'R' in American education." Fancy computer camps are replac-ing traditional camps and their fishing, bunk beds, and "Kumbaya." In many parts of the United States, computer consultants and tutors are working with children as young as two.

Many of my right-brained students are glued to the computer when they're not in school. It's not a huge leap to suggest that many of them even *think* like their computers, tapping out E-mail messages to their friends and spending time in chat rooms on the Internet. The student becomes so engrossed with the computer that he loses all concept of space and time; four hours may seem like forty minutes. Yet, ironically, these are the same students who are often accused of having no attention span in school.

Microsoft chairman Bill Gates, who, I suspect, is *extremely* right-brained, is often compared to a computer. In a recent *Time* magazine cover story, Gates's work ethic was described as follows: "He works on two computers, one with four frames that sequence data streaming in from the Internet, the other handling the hundreds of E-mail messages and memos that extend his mind into a network. He can be so rigorous as he processes data that one can imagine his mind may indeed be digital: no sloppy emotions or analog fuzziness, just trillions of binary impulses coolly converting input into correct answers." Gates is perceived by some as actually exhibiting autistic traits. Well-known autistic Temple Grandin discusses Gates in her book *Thinking in Pictures:* "Gates rocks during business meetings and on airplanes; autistic children and adults rock when they are nervous. Other autistic traits he exhibits are lack of eye contact and poor social skills. . . . As a child, Gates had remarkable savant skills. He could recite long passages from the Bible without making a single mistake. His voice lacks tone, and he looks young and boyish for his age."

As with television or sheep cloning, the technology of computers is far ahead of our ability to comprehend its impact. The computer world is fluctuating and changing on an almost daily basis; not a day goes by that we don't hear of a new technological development or a new application for the Internet. The research organization Public Agenda says eight in ten Americans consider computer skills "absolutely essential." Just as we're retooling our society, we need to retool our schools to prepare children for the growing role that computers will play in our lives. Not an easy task, considering that many schools don't even have enough money to buy books.

Right now our schools, with their emphasis on phonics, handwriting, and sequential, auditory processing, are preparing children for a world that will no longer exist in five or ten years. We're ignoring the trend toward more computerization and less work by hand and are continuing to place heavy emphasis on penmanship, punctuation, and computational math. Many teachers are only vaguely computer literate and shy away from computers because they don't understand them. Teachers can be viewed as the last sentinels protecting a system that has become increasingly irrelevant to children over the last two decades and that will become even more irrelevant in the new millennium.

The same right-brained children who are being labeled and shamed in our schools are the very individuals who have the skills necessary to lead us into the twenty-first century. These children process visually and randomly, and think holistically. They are intuitive problem solvers who get the big picture. They thrive on visual imagery and stimulation; these "attention deficit" kids can spend hours with computer and CD-ROM programs that mirror their thought processes. It's no wonder they are attracted to computers. *The use of computers is congruent with the way right-brained children think.*

While our schools are gradually recognizing the potential for computers and are budgeting for them, schools once again, in typical left-brained fashion, are compartmentalizing their application. Students go from history class to math class to computer lab without an understanding of how computers should be integrated into *all* subject areas. Our schools are still clinging to traditions and a left-brained vision of the way the world ought to be; in the meantime, we're quickly falling behind and losing our opportunities to get our schools on the information superhighway. This is a tragedy. Teachers are busily preparing students for the world they hope will be there when these children graduate. Sadly, this is the *teachers'* world, not the real world. A growing number of employers comment that today's high school and college graduates don't have the necessary skills to complete even the most entry-level tasks. Many companies are in the position of providing the most basic training for new employees to make up for skills that weren't addressed or mastered in school. Even my high school students seem to understand that many of the skills being taught in their schools are irrelevant. They constantly pose such questions as "What am I learning this for? I'll never use it."

While putting a computer in every classroom isn't *the* answer to our educational crisis, there is evidence that computers can make a real difference, particularly for children who are considered at risk. Microsoft and Compaq donated software and computers for five hundred students at the Maxwell Middle School in Tucson, Arizona, an economically depressed area that was plagued by gang violence. Children were allowed to take laptops home; four highly trained teachers used computers to teach not just computer lab but *every subject*. The results are impressive: In just one year, absenteeism dropped and standardized test scores rose 11 to 25 percent. Microsoft's Pete Higgins says, "We were hoping just to familiarize kids with computers. But the kids actually became more engaged in school. It's pretty inspiring." Higgins agrees that we're selling our children short if we limit the use of computers to just one lab a day or a week: "It . . . raises the question of what's better for kids—spending an hour in a computer lab or carrying a computer around all the time like a pencil."

California and Missouri seem to be leading the way when it comes to kids and computers. California organized two "Net Days" in 1996, wiring K–12 schools to the Internet. This "high-tech barnraising" involved more than fifty thousand volunteers who installed more than 6 million feet of cable in classrooms. Even with all this effort, California has only one Internet-connected computer for every seventy-three students.

As we look to the next century, schools have to factor in the impact of not only computers in general but voice-activated computers. Will they render handwriting and keyboarding skills obsolete? The voice-activated computer may be to expression what the calculator is to computational math: Children will still need to master these basic skills to survive in the world, but with the aid of technology, the importance of handwriting, keyboarding, spelling, and performing simple calculations will be dramatically reduced. Just as the computer is taking the place of dictionaries and encyclopedias, it will soon replace the thesaurus and the study of grammar and punctuation.

Gates, in his 1994 videotaped address "Information at Your Fingertips: 2005," envisions a brave new world as we enter the twenty-first century. He notes that as prices come down, computers will be available to a broader market of Americans. By the year 2005, Gates sees this technology changing our lives in dramatic ways. For example, instead of using credit cards, we may be carrying a "wallet PC" that transfers money from our accounts to vendors, reminds us of appointments, and even stores images of our children! We'll have computers in our cars that can quickly access city maps, give us video conference calling ability, and put us on the Internet. Gates predicts we'll no longer be confined to cable and television programming schedules but will have the ability to receive programming on demand. In Gates's words, "You're no longer tied down to the particular schedule where that show comes out on. It's not just movies, it's also any type of show, educational video, anything you want to do. You're in control."

This technology has tremendous applications for our classrooms as well. Gates foresees a day when students will do their grade school reports entirely on video, do research on the computer, generate a report on a word processor or dictate it into a voice-activated PC, and even use a computer to design graphics to accompany the presentation. Gates correctly notes that this more visual and stimulating approach to learning is "making it compelling in a way that will allow them [teachers] to compete with the production values of TV that kids are exposed to so much of the time." Computer graphics are already so innovative and interesting that any child who has access to them would find classroom lectures boring by comparison. I foresee a day, perhaps ten or twenty years from now, when the learning environment will center around computers of a much more advanced generation than we have now. The role of teachers will change dramatically: Educators will serve as "network guides," directing their pupils to exercises and information on the computer. How long will it take our schools to keep up with this technology and the students who have already adapted to it?

The software being developed today reflects the right-brained, spatial characteristics of its designers. These are aggressive, forward-thinking individuals who either work for themselves or for innovative companies, and they are living proof that the workforce of the future will require almost none of the skills being focused on in today's classrooms. While we drag our feet, debating issues such as school prayer and sex education, we're losing thousands of students who are cynical and fed up with the educational system and its petty debates.

Unless we reach a consensus on where our schools need to go and how to get there, this cynicism will only escalate as technology increases at a geometric pace and schools stay essentially the same.

The future is here. We can either stick our heads in the sand, or get out on the cutting edge, with innovative ideas on how to better integrate computers into our classrooms. For the sake of our children, I hope we choose the latter.

▣ Hardly a day goes by that we don't pick up the newspaper or catch the evening news and find a story about the sorry state of our schools. Whether it is rising dropout rates, lower literacy rates, declining test scores, or higher incidences of ADD, one thing is clear: Our left-brained schools are failing to reach a majority of these children. Educators still teach to the left-of-center on my left-right brain continuum, yet our culture is producing a generation of children who are more right-brained and visual than ever. This gulf is widening and will continue to do so until we understand what's really behind the so-called crisis in education.

As we find growing numbers of these right-brained children in a left-brained world, we face a tremendous challenge. Our schools must not only be retooled so that they identify and understand these children, but educators must teach from a new paradigm that recognizes and harnesses their many strengths. After all, it won't be long before the right-brained, "attention deficit disordered" student is in the majority and the so-called normal student is viewed as learning disabled.

As we enter the new millennium, we must erase the commonly held misconception that these students are somehow broken and appreciate that their learning style is more in sync with the increasingly visual nature of our society. We can cling to a simpler time, before the term "Attention Deficit Disorder" was even invented. We can continue to break these children of their learning style, desperately trying to prepare them for a world that no longer exists. But the result will invariably be more shaming—more children who see themselves as being fundamentally flawed. In extreme cases, they lead lives of desperation. They drop out, give birth out of wedlock, become substance abusers, join gangs, commit suicide, or end up in prison. In less extreme cases, they simply lack the confidence and esteem to believe in themselves, pursuing less-than-satisfying relationships and careers. They never glimpse their potential. Either way, it's not only the individual but our society that suffers when we fail to cultivate our most precious natural resource.

All too often I'm reminded of this tragedy when I meet the parents of children who have classic ADD. In many cases, when a child is identified as having Attention Deficit Disorder, an entire family is diagnosed; the condition can be traced back through generations of "social misfits." The effect of this can be profound and life-changing; for many parents, the recognition that they, too, have ADD can have the effect of an emotional A-bomb. At last, there's an explanation for everything. No longer does the individual feel that he or she was simply a failure. Finally, there's a name for the condition that has plagued them their entire life.

I had the occasion to meet such an adult when I performed a routine screening of an eleven-year-old girl who was suspected of having ADD. An intelligent child, Sharon was described by her teachers as "a daydreamer who never really applied herself." I determined after talking with her parents and having a session with her that Sharon was extremely right-brained and had the classic signs of ADD. I knew I could help her, and I relished the challenge.

After that first meeting, Sharon left with her mother. Her father quietly approached me, his face muscles working as he struggled for the right words. A self-employed mechanic, he was thin with callused hands and gray hair. He told me he was forty-three years old, but he looked sixty; his pockmarked face and sad eyes reflected a hard life. He thought I might better understand Sharon if he shared his story with me; he related it to me while brushing back tears.

Darrell spoke of his childhood, telling me school had been torture for him. He never recovered from the shame of flunking second grade and was always considered an underachiever. He struggled with reading, had terrible penmanship, and was embarrassed about his inability to take timed tests. He considered himself lucky to get a C. His parents were constantly telling him how ashamed they were of him. Darrell barely graduated from high school and signed up for the army; college was out of the question. Upon discharge from the military, he married. With five children to support, Darrell did the only thing he could: He tried to make ends meet by rebuilding engines, but his family was relying on food stamps to stay afloat.

Darrell wept bitterly as he related story after story of his failed school career and his ruined life. The realization that his daughter had ADD was a revelation about himself. Now, Darrell said, he understood everything. As he picked up his shabby jacket and shuffled toward the door, he turned around and said, "By the way, Jeff, I always thought I was smart, so a couple years ago I took the Mensa test, just for kicks. You know what? I passed." I watched him go, my heart heavy with the reminder that ADD has been ruining lives for generations.

People with ADD are almost universally bright, creative, and intuitive in ways that left-brained, sequential people cannot even fathom. All that's needed for them to reach their potential is a classroom environment that meets them halfway. I felt Darrell's loss and pain acutely that day, and I also glimpsed what the toll must be if we measure it in hundreds of thousands. I can only hope that the future of Darrell's children and grandchildren is a brighter one.

Dorry, George. "The Perplexed Perfectionist." In *ADD and Adolescence: Strategies for Success from CH.A.D.D.* Plantation, Fla.: Children and Adults with Attention Deficit Disorders, 1996.

*Elkind, David. *The Hurried Child: Growing Up Too Fast Too Soon.* Reading, Mass.: Addison-Wesley, 1989.

Fowler, Rick, and Jerilyn Fowler. *"Honey, Are You Listening?" How Attention Deficit Disorder Could Be Affecting Your Marriage.* Nashville: Thomas Nelson, 1995.

*Gardner, Howard. *Frames of Mind: The Theory of Multiple Intelligences.* New York: Basic, 1993.

————. *Multiple Intelligences: The Theory in Practice.* New York: Basic, 1993.

Gehret, Jeanne. *Eagle Eyes: A Child's View of Attention Deficit Disorder.* Fairport, N.Y.: Verbal Images, 1991.

*Goleman, Daniel. *Emotional Intelligence.* New York: Bantam, 1995.

*Grandin, Temple. *Thinking in Pictures: And Other Reports from My Life with Autism.* New York: Vintage, 1996.

*Hallowell, Edward M., M.D., and John J. Ratey, M.D. *Driven to Distraction: Recognizing and Coping with Attention Deficit Disorder from Childhood through Adulthood.* New York: Touchstone, 1995.

*————. *Answers to Distraction.* New York: Bantam, 1996.

*Hartmann, Thom. *Attention Deficit Disorder: A Different Perception.* Lancaster, Pa.: Underwood-Miller, 1993.

————. *ADD Success Stories: A Guide to Fulfillment for Families with Attention Deficit Disorder: Maps, Guidebooks, and Travelogues for Hunters in This Farmer's World.* Grass Valley, Calif.: Underwood, 1995.

————. *Beyond ADD: Hunting for Reasons in the Past and the Present.* Grass Valley, Calif.: Underwood, 1996.

*Healy, Jane, M.D. *Endangered Minds: Why Our Children Don't Think.* New York: Touchstone, 1991.

Himmelfarb, Gertrude. "A Neo-Luddite Reflects on the Internet." *The Chronicle of Higher Education,* November 1, 1996.

Isaacson, Walter. "In Search of the Real Bill Gates." *Time,* January 13, 1997.

Johnson, Jean, et al. "Getting By: What American Teenagers Really Think About Their Schools." New York: Public Agenda, 1997.

*Kotulak, Ronald. *Inside the Brain: Revolutionary Discoveries of How the Mind Works.* Kansas City, Mo.: Andrews & McMeel, 1997.

Levine, Louis S. "The American Teacher: A Tentative Psychological Description." Available from the ERIC Document Reproduction Service (EDRS), Springfield, Va.

Bibliography

*Amen, Daniel G. *Windows into the ADD Mind: Understanding and Treating Attention Deficit Disorders in the Everyday Lives of Children, Adolescents and Adults.* Fairfield, Calif.: Mindworks, 1997.

*Armstrong, Thomas. *The Myth of the ADD Child: 50 Ways to Improve Your Child's Behavior and Attention Span Without Drugs, Labels or Coercion.* New York: Plume, 1997.

Bloom, Benjamin. *Developing Talent in Young People.* New York: Ballantine, 1985.

*Brooks, Andrée Aelion. *Children of Fast-Track Parents: Raising Self-Sufficient Children in an Achievement-Oriented World.* New York: Penguin, 1990.

Carnegie Task Force on Meeting the Needs of Young Children. "Starting Points: Meeting the Needs of Our Youngest Children." New York: Carnegie Corporation, 1994.

Castellanos, F. Xavier, et al. "Quantitative Brain Magnetic Resonance Imaging in Attention-Deficit Hyperactivity Disorder." *Archives of General Psychiatry*, vol. 53, July 1996.

Chubb, John E., and Terry M. Moe. *Politics, Markets, and America's Schools.* Washington, D.C.: Brookings Institution, 1990.

*Cline, Foster, and Jim Fay. *Parenting with Love and Logic: Teaching Children Responsibility.* Colorado Springs, Colo.: Navpress, 1990.

Cohen, Matthew D. "The Limits of Discipline Under IDEA and Section 504." In *ADD and Adolescence: Strategies for Success from CH.A.D.D.* Plantation, Fla.: Children and Adults with Attention Deficit Disorders, 1996.

Crook, William G. *Help for the Hyperactive Child: A Good-Sense Guide for Parents of Children with Hyperactivity, Attention Deficits, and Other Behavior and Learning Problems.* Jackson, Tenn.: Professional Books, 1991.

*Davis, Ronald D., and Eldon M. Braun. *The Gift of Dyslexia: Why Some of the Smartest People Can't Read and How They Can Learn.* New York: Perigee, 1997.

*Dixon, John Philo. *The Spatial Child.* Springfield, Ill.: Charles C. Thomas, 1983.

*Books of special interest to parents

Lou, Hans, et al. "Striatal Dysfunction in Attention Deficit and Hyperkinetic Disorder." *Archives of Neurology*, vol. 46, January 1989.

————. "Focal Cerebral Dysfunction in Developmental Learning Disabilities." *The Lancet*, January 6, 1990.

Merrow, John. "Reading, Writing and Ritalin." *The New York Times*, October 21, 1995.

Nash, J. Madeleine. "Fertile Minds." *Time*, February 3, 1997.

Parker, Harvey C. "Medical Management of Children with Attention Deficit Disorders: Commonly Asked Questions," *CHADDER*, Fall/Winter 1991.

Quinn, Patricia O., and Judith M. Stern. *The "Putting on the Brakes" Activity Book for Young People with ADHD*. New York: Magination, 1988.

Ratey, John, M.D., and Catherine Johnson, Ph.D. *Shadow Syndromes*. New York: Pantheon, 1997.

Saunders, Antoinette, and Bonnie Remsburg. *The Stress-Proof Child: A Loving Parent's Guide*. New York: Holt, Rinehart and Winston, 1985.

Saunders, Jacqulyn, and Pamela Espeland. *Bringing Out the Best: A Resource Guide for Parents of Young Gifted Children*. Minneapolis: Free Spirit, 1986.

Schwartz, Evan I. "The Changing Minds of Children." *Omni*, January 1995.

Shaywitz, Sally E. "Dyslexia." *Scientific American*, November 1996.

Silver, Larry B. *Dr. Larry Silver's Advice to Parents on Attention-Deficit Hyperactivity Disorder*. Washington, D.C.: American Psychiatric Press, 1993.

Spears, Dana Scott, and Ron L. Braund. *Strong-Willed Child or Dreamer?* Nashville: Thomas Nelson, 1996.

Toffler, Alvin. *Future Shock*. New York: Bantam, 1991.

Vail, Priscilla. *The World of the Gifted Child*. New York: Penguin, 1980.

————. *Smart Kids with School Problems: Things to Know and Ways to Help*. New York: New American Library, 1989.

Vitale, Barbara Meister. *Unicorns Are Real: A Right-Brained Approach to Learning*. New York: Warner, 1994.

*West, Thomas G. *In the Mind's Eye: Visual Thinkers, Gifted People with Learning Difficulties, Computer Images, and the Ironies of Creativity*. Buffalo, N.Y.: Prometheus, 1991.

Winik, Lyric Wallwork. "Do Computers Help Children Learn?" *Parade*, February 2, 1997.

*Winner, Ellen. *Gifted Children: Myths and Realities*. New York: Basic, 1996.

Index